W9-AVB-524

 **The California State University**

Expository Reading and Writing Course

Second Edition

STUDENT READER

Developed by the CSU Expository Reading and Writing Course Advisory Committee

The contents of the Expository Reading and Writing Course were developed under an Investing in Innovation Development Grant from the Department of Education awarded to the Fresno County Office of Education. However, these contents do not necessarily represent the policy of the Department of Education, and you should not assume endorsement by the Federal Government. Funding was also provided by The California State University and these foundation partners: The Rosalinde and Arthur Gilbert Foundation, The William and Flora Hewlett Foundation, Walter S. Johnson Foundation, California Community Foundation, and James Irvine Foundation.

CSU The California State University

The *Expository Reading and Writing Course: Student Reader* (2nd Ed.) was developed by the California State University (CSU) Expository Reading and Writing Course Advisory Committee, chaired by John R. Edlund of California State Polytechnic University, Pomona. It was printed by Commerce Printing; the cover and interior design were created by the staff of Commerce Printing. It was published by the California State University Press, The California State University, Office of the Chancellor, 401 Golden Shore, Long Beach, CA 90801-4210. It was distributed under the provisions of the Library Distribution Act and *Government Code* Section 11096.

ISBN 978-0-9818314-6-6

Copies of this document are available for purchase by high schools that have adopted the CSU Expository Reading and Writing Course. Other course material can be obtained only by participating in professional learning programs sponsored by the California State University and/ or the California County Superintendents Educational Services Association. Please see the following link for more information: http://www.calstate.edu/eap/englishcourse.

Contents

MODULE 8: Juvenile Justice

MODULE 9: Language, Gender, and Culture

MODULE 10: 1984

MODULE 12: Bullying: A Research Project

Additional Readings:

Credits

Introduction

The reading selections in this collection form the basis of the CSU Expository Reading and Writing Course (ERWC). The course is designed to foster critical thinking through a rhetorical approach to reading and writing. In the ERWC, students are asked to analyze arguments and evidence, think about who the writer is and what his or her purposes and intentions are, and look for rhetorical strategies that are designed to elicit an emotional response from the reader. To this end, readings were chosen that engage student interest and provide a foundation for principled debate and argument. The course designers were careful to select issues in which legitimate arguments could be made from several different perspectives or viewpoints, so that students would have to think critically about the issues and come to their own well-reasoned conclusions.

The selections here include editorials, feature articles, op-ed pieces, and even academic journal articles. All are part of the public process of a society engaging with important issues and problems, a process we want our students to be fully capable of joining and influencing. Critical reading and thinking are also an essential part of the university experience, and we hope these selections will help prepare students to be successful in higher education. Successful students will learn to take part in civic and academic conversations of all types, as they learn how to form and contribute their own ideas and insights on a specific topic.

Finally, one of the core principles of the ERWC is that critical reading and writing are essentially two sides of the same coin. Critical reading is not simply reading to understand the focal text or texts of the module and memorizing some facts; it involves thinking beyond the focal texts to the conversations behind and around the issues of the text. Critical writing means that the student joins those conversations by presenting and responding to the ideas of the text at hand, synthesizing other texts, and generating new ones.

We hope that students and teachers enjoy working with these texts and joining these conversations. We also would like to thank the authors of these articles for allowing us to use these materials for this important educational purpose.

Note: All reading selections are reprinted with permission. The primary reading selections for Modules 6, 10, and 11 are not included in this document. Schools adopting the Semester One and Two of the CSU Expository Reading and Writing Course need to purchase the books for those modules: *Into the Wild, 1984,* and/or *Brave New World.* In addition, no readings are included for Module 7; students do Web-based research in that module and identify their own readings.

What's Next? Thinking About Life After High School

Want to Get Into College? Learn to Fail

Commentary

By Angel B. Pérez
Education Week, February 1, 2012

1   I ask every student I interview for admission to my institution, Pitzer College, the same question, "What do you look forward to the most in college?" I was stunned and delighted recently when a student sat across from me at a Starbucks in New York City and replied, "I look forward to the possibility of failure." Of course, this is not how most students respond to the question when sitting before the person who can make decisions about their academic futures, but this young man took a risk.

2   "You see, my parents have never let me fail," he said. "When I want to take a chance at something, they remind me it's not a safe route to take. Taking a more rigorous course or trying an activity I may not succeed in, they tell me, will ruin my chances at college admission. Even the sacrifice of staying up late to do something unrelated to school, they see as a risk to my academic work and college success."

3   I wish I could tell you this is an uncommon story, but kids all over the world admit they are under tremendous pressure to be perfect. When I was traveling in China last fall and asked a student what she did for fun, she replied: "I thought I wasn't supposed to tell you that? I wouldn't want you to think I am not serious about my work!"

4   Students are usually in shock when I chuckle and tell them I never expect perfection. In fact, I prefer they not project it in their college applications. Of course, this goes against everything they've been told and makes young people uncomfortable. How could a dean of admission at one of America's most selective institutions not want the best and the brightest? The reality is, perfection doesn't exist, and we don't expect to see it in a college application. In fact, admission officers tend to be skeptical of students who present themselves as individuals without flaws.

5   These days, finding imperfections in a college application is like looking for a needle in a haystack. Students try their best to hide factors they perceive to be negative and only tell us things they believe we will find impressive. This is supported by a secondary school culture where teachers are under pressure to give students nothing less than an A, and counselors are told not to report disciplinary infractions to colleges. Education agents in other countries are known to falsify student transcripts, assuming that an outstanding GPA is the ticket to admission.

6   Colleges respond to culture shifts, and admission officers are digging deeper to find out who students really are outside of their trophies, medals, and test scores. We get the most excited when we read an application that seems real. It's so rare to hear stories of defeat and triumph that when we do, we cheer. If their perspectives are of lessons learned or challenges overcome, these applicants tend to jump to the top of the heap at highly selective colleges. We believe an error in high school should not define the rest of your life, but how you respond could shape you forever.

7   I've spent enough time in high schools to know teenagers will never be perfect. They do silly things, mess up, fall down, and lack confidence. The ability to bounce back is a fundamental life skill students have to learn on their own. The lessons of failure can't be taught in a classroom; they are experienced and reflected upon. During my weekend of interviews, another student told me, "I'm ashamed to admit I failed precalculus, but I decided to take it again and got a B-plus. I'm now taking calculus, and even though I don't love it, I'm glad I pushed through!" I asked him what he learned from the experience. "I learned to let go of shame," he said. "I realized that I can't let a grade define my success. I also learned that if you want anything bad enough, you can achieve it."

8   I smiled as I wrote his words down on the application-review form. This kid will thrive on my campus. Not only will the faculty love him, but he has the coping skills he needs to adjust to the rigors of life in a residential college setting. Failure is about growth, learning, overcoming, and moving on. Let's allow young people to fail. Not only will they learn something, it might even get them into college.

Angel B. Pérez is the Vice President and Dean of Admission and Financial Aid at Pitzer College, in Claremont, Calif. He teaches in the College-Counseling Certification Program of the University of California, Los Angeles.

Hidden Intellectualism
An excerpt from *They Say/I Say:*
The Moves that Matter in Academic Writing

By Gerald Graff

1   Everyone knows some young person who is impressively "street smart" but does poorly in school. What a waste, we think, that one who is so intelligent about so many things in life seems unable to apply that intelligence to academic work. What doesn't occur to us, though, is that schools and colleges might be at fault for missing the opportunity to tap into such street smarts and channel them into good academic work.

2   Nor do we consider one of the major reasons why schools and colleges overlook the intellectual potential of street smarts: the fact that we associate those street smarts with anti-intellectual concerns. We associate the educated life, the life of the mind, too narrowly and exclusively with subjects and texts that we consider inherently weighty and academic. We assume that it's possible to wax intellectual about Plato, Shakespeare, the French Revolution, and nuclear fission, but not about cars, dating, fashion, sports, TV, or video games.

3   The trouble with this assumption is that no necessary connection has ever been established between any text or subject and the educational depth and weight of the discussion it can generate. Real intellectuals turn any subject, however lightweight it may seem, into grist for their mill through the thoughtful questions they bring to it, whereas a dullard will find a way to drain the interest out of the richest subject. That's why a George Orwell writing on the cultural meanings of penny postcards is infinitely more substantial than the cogitations of many professors on Shakespeare or globalization (104-16).

4   Students do need to read models of intellectually challenging writing—and Orwell is a great one—if they are to become intellectuals themselves. But they would be more prone to take on intellectual identities if we encouraged them to do so at first on subjects that interest them rather than ones that interest us.

5   I offer my own adolescent experience as a case in point. Until I entered college, I hated books and cared only for sports. The only reading I cared to do or could do was sports magazines, on which I became hooked; becoming a regular reader of *Sport* magazine in the late forties, *Sports Illustrated* when it began publishing in 1954, and the annual magazine guides to professional baseball, football, and basketball. I also loved the sports novels for boys of John R. Tunis and Clair Bee and autobiographies of sports stars like Joe DiMaggio's *Lucky to Be a Yankee* and Bob Feller's *Strikeout Story*. In short, I was your typical teenage anti-intellectual—or so I believed for a long time. I have recently come to think, however, that my preference for sports over schoolwork was not anti-intellectualism so much as intellectualism by other means.

6   In the Chicago neighborhood I grew up in, which had become a melting pot after World War II, our block was solidly middle class, but just a block away—doubtless concentrated there the real estate companies—were African Americans, Native Americans, and "hillbilly" whites who had recently fled postwar joblessness in the South and Appalachia. Negotiating this class boundary was a tricky matter. On the one hand, it was necessary to maintain the boundary between "clean cut" boys like me and working class "hoods," as we called them, which meant that it was good to be openly smart in a bookish sort of way. On the other hand, I was desperate for the approval of the hoods, whom I encountered daily on the playing field and in the neighborhood, and for this purpose it was not at all good to be book smart. The hoods would turn on you if they sensed you were putting on airs over them: "Who you lookin' at, smart ass?" as a leather jacketed youth once said to me as he relieved me of my pocket change along with my self-respect.

7   I grew up torn then, between the need to prove I was smart and the fear of a beating if I proved it too well; between the need not to jeopardize my respectable future and the need to impress the hoods. As I lived it, the conflict came down to a choice between being physically tough and being verbal. For a boy in my neighborhood and elementary school, only being "tough" earned you complete legitimacy. I still recall endless, complicated debates in his period with my closest pals over who was "the toughest guy in the school." If you were less than negligible as a fighter, as I was, you settled for the next best thing, which was to be inarticulate, carefully hiding telltale marks of literacy like correct grammar and pronunciation.

8   In one way, then, it would be hard to imagine an adolescence more thoroughly anti-intellectual than mine. Yet in retrospect, I see that it's more complicated, that I and the 1950s themselves were not simply hostile toward intellectualism, but divided and ambivalent. When Marilyn Monroe married the playwright Arthur Miller in 1956 after divorcing the retired baseball star Joe DiMaggio, the symbolic triumph of geek over jock suggested the way the wind was blowing. Even Elvis, according to his biographer Peter Guralnick, turns out to have supported Adlai over Ike in the presidential election of 1956. "I don't dig the intellectual bit," he told reporters. "But I'm telling you, man, he knows the most" (327).

9   Though I too thought I did not "dig the intellectual bit," I see now that I was unwittingly in training for it. The germs had actually been planted in the seemingly philistine debates about which boys were the toughest. I see now that in the interminable analysis of sports teams, movies, and toughness that my friends and I engaged in—a type of analysis, needless to say, that the real toughs would never have stooped to—I was already betraying an allegiance to the egghead world. I was practicing being an intellectual before I knew that was what I wanted to be.

10   It was in these discussions with friends about toughness and sports, I think, and in my reading of sports books and magazines, that I began to learn the rudiments of the intellectual life: how to make an argument, weigh different kinds of evidence, move between particulars and generalizations, summarize the views of others, and enter a conversation about ideas. It was in reading and arguing about sports and toughness that I experienced what it felt like to propose a generalization, restate and respond to a counterargument, and perform other intellectualizing operations, including composing the kind of sentences I am writing now.

11   Only much later did it dawn on me that the sports world was more compelling than school because it was *more intellectual than school,* not less. Sports after all was full of challenging arguments, debates, problems for analysis, and intricate statistics that you could care about, as school conspicuously was not. I believe that street smarts beat out book smarts in our culture not because street smarts are nonintellectual, as we generally suppose, but because they satisfy an intellectual thirst more thoroughly than school culture, which seems pale and unreal.

12   They also satisfy the thirst for community. When you entered sports debates, you became part of a community that was not limited to your family and friends, but was national and public. Whereas schoolwork isolated you from others, the pennant race or Ted Williams's .400 batting average was something you could talk about with people you had never met. Sports introduced you not only to a culture steeped in argument, but to a public argument culture that transcended the personal. I can't blame my schools for failing to make intellectual culture resemble the Super Bowl, but I do fault them for failing to learn anything from the sports and entertainment worlds about how to organize and represent intellectual culture, how to exploit its game-like element and turn it into arresting public spectacle that might have competed more successfully for my youthful attention.

13   For here is another thing that never dawned on me and is still kept hidden from students, with tragic results: that the real intellectual world, the one that existed in the big world beyond school, is organized very much like the world of team sports, with rival texts, rival interpretations and evaluations of texts, rival theories of why they should be read and taught, and elaborate team competitions in which "fans" of writers, intellectual systems, methodologies, and -isms contend against each other.

14   To be sure, school contained plenty of competition, which became more invidious as one moved up the ladder (and has become even more so today with the advent of high stakes testing). In this competition, points were scored not by making arguments, but by a show of information or vast reading, by grade grubbing, or other forms of one-upmanship. School competition, in short, reproduced the less attractive features of sports culture without those that create close bonds and community.

15   And in distancing themselves from anything as enjoyable and absorbing as sports, my schools missed the opportunity to capitalize on an element of drama and conflict that the intellectual world shares with sports. Consequently, I failed to see the parallels between the sports and academic worlds that could have helped me cross more readily from one argument culture to the other.

16   Sports is only one of the domains whose potential for literacy training (and not only for males) is seriously underestimated by educators, who see sports as competing with academic development rather than a route to it. But if this argument suggests why it is a good idea to assign readings and topics that are close to students' existing interests, it also suggests the limits of this tactic. For students who get excited about the chance to write about their passion for cars will often write as poorly and unreflectively on that topic as on Shakespeare or Plato. Here is the flip side of what I pointed out before: that there's no necessary relation between the degree of interest a student shows in a text or subject and the quality of thought or expression such a student manifests in writing or talking about it. The challenge, as college professor Ned Laffhas put it, "is not simply to exploit students' nonacademic interests, but to get them to see those interests through academic eyes."

17   To say that students need to see their interests "through academic eyes" is to say that street smarts are not enough. Making students' nonacademic interests an object of academic study is useful, then, for getting students' attention and overcoming their boredom and alienation, but this tactic won't in itself necessarily move them closer to an academically rigorous treatment of those interests. On the other hand, inviting students to write about cars, sports, or clothing fashions does not have to be a pedagogical cop-out as long as students are required to see these interests "through academic eyes," that is, to think and write about cars, sports, and fashions in a reflective, analytical way, one that sees them as microcosms of what is going on in the wider culture.

18   If I am right, then schools and colleges are missing an opportunity when they do not encourage students to take their nonacademic interests as objects of academic study. It is self defeating to decline to introduce any text or subject that figures to engage students who will otherwise tune out academic work entirely. If a student cannot get interested in Mill's *On Liberty* but will read *Sports Illustrated* or *Vogue* or the hip-hop magazine *Source* with absorption, this is a strong argument for assigning the magazines over the classic. It's a good bet that if students get hooked on reading and writing by doing term papers on *Source,* they will eventually get to *On Liberty*. But even if they don't, the magazine reading will make them more literate and reflective than they would be otherwise. So it makes pedagogical sense to develop classroom units on sports, cars, fashions, rap music, and other such topics. Give me the student anytime who writes a sharply argued, sociologically acute analysis of an issue in *Source* over the student who writes a lifeless explication of *Hamlet* or Socrates' *Apology*.

Gerald Graff, one of the co authors of this book, is a professor of English and education at the University of Illinois at Chicago. He is a past President of the Modern Language Association, a professional association of scholars and teachers of English and other languages. This essay is adapted from his 2003 book *Clueless in Academe: How Schooling Obscures the Life of the Mind.*

Works Cited

Cramer, Richard Ben. *Joe DiMaggio: The Hero's Life.* New York: Simon and Schuster, 2000. Print.

DiMaggio, Joe. *Lucky to Be a Yankee.* New York: Bantam Books, 1949. Print.

Feller, Bob. *Strikeout Story.* New York: Bantam Books, 1948. Print.

Guralnick, Peter. *Last Train to Memphis: The Rise of Elvis Presley.* Boston: Little, Brown and Co., 1994. Print.

Orwell, George. *A Collection of Essays.* New York: Harcourt, Inc., 1953. Print.

10 Rules for Going To College When Nobody Really Expected You To

By Joe Rodriguez
MercuryNews.com, June 4, 2012

1   A vital revolution in American education has launched a slew of academic programs and charter schools that pluck bright minority, poor and blue-collar students from the educational abyss and turn them into college-bound scholars. Teachers are inspiring them to dream while showing them how to study, do research, write term papers, think critically and effectively cram for finals.

2   In many ways, the kids have learned the hard parts of surviving college.

3   But when the mere act of attending college is totally unexpected, there are unforeseen obstacles—including family and friends—that tend to blow nontraditional students off their paths like land mines.

4   Recently I spoke to a high school graduating class at Menlo-Atherton Computer Academy, a program in Silicon Valley that captures bright students who would have fallen through the cracks in the school system. Of the 41 students, 37 are slated for school next fall. And because they are excellent students, they imagine college being a piece of cake.

5   As someone who was lucky to attend college, I know there are difficult challenges unique to that particular group, one that is expanding here and all over the country.

6   I grew up in East Los Angeles and attended the famous Garfield High of the 1988 film "Stand and Deliver." I was gone by the time Jaime Escalante, an unorthodox math teacher, had the nerve to successfully teach advanced placement calculus to underachieving Mexican-American kids.

7   As a book-loving barrio kid, I went off to college having no idea it would take me eight years to muddle through because I did not know then what I know now.

8   That's why my graduation speech at Menlo was dubbed "Top 10 Rules for the Guess Who's Going to College?" Like a certain late-night TV host, let's start this adaptation of my talk at the end and work our way to the top.

9   Rule No. 10: Be a total student. Even if you live at home, work full-time and attend school part-time, you must feel and think like a full-time student. Studying is the highest priority. Hang out more on campus. Join student clubs. Get involved. Hang out less or not at all with old friends who aren't doing anything. Just say no to those who would interfere with your studies, even if they don't mean to get in the way.

10   No. 9: Resist the temptation to buy expensive stuff. Do you really need a late-model car or those shiny, spinning, chrome rims to make it look cooler? I've been there, done that. I bought a motorcycle when I should have selected an electric typewriter. A nice set of wheels may carry you many miles, but a good education will carry you for life.

11   No. 8: Handle the family crises that pressure students like you to leave school. Somebody dear to you will likely become deathly ill. It takes only one medical catastrophe or foreclosure or something as terrible to make you feel guilty about attending college. Some issues might set your siblings against you for not doing your share to help. Always remember: The best thing you can do for your family is to be the one who got a college education.

12   No. 7: Your parents will love this one: Don't worry too much about the high cost of college tuition. In most cases, only the wealthy pay the full bill. Go to the best school for you—no matter what. Some wise financial digging—at almost any school—will unearth a reasonable combination of grants, loans and work-study.

13   No. 6: Study harder in college. Put in more time, effort and energy than you did in high school. College professors rule on campus. And often, they're egomaniacal and nasty compared with the kindly, nurturing teachers you've had until now—so don't take it personally. And trust your fellow pupils, but be cautious. College breeds dangerous depths of competition.

14   No. 5: You will become lonely or homesick and it will upset you very much. Many minority and blue-collar students feel terrible isolation at big, public campuses and also at small, elite colleges. Don't question whether you belong there—you do. And don't "run" home. Call home, seek out students with similar interests and backgrounds and discuss your mutual anxieties. Soon the worst will pass.

15   No. 4: Get to know students of different racial, ethnic or social backgrounds. College is a prime gateway to our ever-shrinking, globalizing, melting-pot world. Learn another language. Success comes to those who branch out, not to those to shrink back to the only corner they ever knew.

16   No. 3: Ignore career confusion. Stay in school even if your dream job seems to become a delusion. Taking a break to rethink your future is only for rich kids. For you, that idea is Armageddon—the first step to dropping out. It's OK to change your major, just remain intent on graduating as soon as you can. You will pick up missing pieces on the job or in graduate school.

17   No. 2: You are much more than a future employee, so don't think like one. College isn't a four-year application for a specific job. Study what you love. Campuses are delightful villages of practical and heart's delight learning. Embrace and expand there, even if the job market says you're an idiot. I have two nieces who graduated with liberal studies degrees. Guess what? They both got plum jobs with a multinational insurance company before graduation day. Take that, business majors!

18   No. 1: Remember where you came from and who helped you get this far. Your family and community installed good things in your head, heart and soul. That foundation is what will support you as you figure out this world, improve upon it and attempt to correct the injustices you, your family and your community have endured. Jump off that foundation and you plop down in quicksand and so do all the people who helped you ascend. There is no worse sinking feeling than that.

19   Thank you and good luck.

Not Going to College is a Viable Option

By Lawrence B. Schlack
education.com, 2012

1   Any retired superintendent who's running around the country telling high school seniors not to go to college had darn well better explain himself or herself. OK, here goes.

2   I've seen too many high school graduates who have gone off to college in September but are back home with mom and dad in December. And I've seen those who have made it through the first year but transferred back home to a community college for the second. And there are plenty of those who have stuck it out for a year or two, changing majors, dropping classes, starting over, racking up debt and finally dropping out—with debt but no degree.

3   The go-to-college tsunami has given us colleges full of young people who really don't know why they are there or where they are going. They've been told college is their only option and they are using the experience as a very expensive and often futile form of career exploration.

4   Status, economics and competition are three powerful forces behind the pressure to attend college that exists today. It's become a status issue. Going to college is first class. Not going to college is second class. High school seniors who can't declare they are college bound are made to feel like failures.

5   It's an economic issue. Students are told they will land better jobs and earn more money with a college degree. And it's an international competition issue. There's widespread belief the United States is somehow running behind other nations in producing a competitive workforce and more college degrees will make us more competitive.

Honorable Alternatives

6   College, however, is not always the logical next step for high school graduates. There are plenty of honorable and viable choices for the year after high school. The decision not to go to college should not necessarily be viewed in negative terms.

7   Europeans use the term "Gap Year." It's the year after secondary education in which the graduate takes time off for travel, work or public service before making a decision whether to go on to higher education.

8   Many could profit by simply going to work in a field they want to explore. Here's an example. A sign on the door at my local gas station reads "Assistant Manager Wanted." I ask the manager whether he'd hire an 18-year-old right out of high school. Sure would, he says. Qualifications are honesty in handling money, good customer relations and dependability. Couldn't this be a good career beginning for someone wanting to own or manage a business? Instead of paying tuition you earn money while learning business skills.

9   Other honorable non-college choices right out of high school include military service, cultural immersion while working in an overseas country, doing mission work in Central or South America, becoming a nanny, a hospital aide, or teaching English overseas.

Important Questions

10   Here are some questions we should ask members of the class of 2007. The answers would help them chart a productive post-graduate path.

11   "Senior, can you list your strengths, talents, aptitudes, abilities? Can you name four or five careers you can realistically aspire to? Can you describe where you want to go and what you want to do in life? Do you really need college to get where you want to go?"

12   For those who answer, "Yes, I know my strengths and I have a pretty good idea where I want to go in life and I do need college to get there," college is the right choice. If the answer is, "I'm not really sure what my strengths are or where I want to go in life," then deferring college is the better choice.

13   High school doesn't always prepare students to answer these important questions. Too many young people graduate without a realistic picture of their own talents and aptitudes and too many don't have any clear idea of where these strengths might take them in the work world. Better preparation with these questions could result in fewer misguided students going on to college.

Narrow Perspectives

14   School leaders—particularly in suburban communities where the go-to-college push is most apparent—should be out in front on this issue. These are the districts that take pride in saying things like "90 percent of our senior class went on to college last year." They should stand up and be clear that college is not the only path to success in life.

15   Best current estimates are that not more than 20 percent of careers in the work world of tomorrow will require a four-year degree. A Penn State professor, Kenneth Gray, goes further, quoting U.S. Bureau of Labor Statistics predictions that as few as 12 percent of all jobs will require a B.A. Most of the work world will require a high school diploma and perhaps an additional year or two of training. And that work world will include high-flying non-college graduates such as Dell Computer founder Michael Dell, TV talk show host Larry King and Wendy's Restaurants founder Dave Thomas.

16   Last fall an 8th-grade student in my hometown was quoted in our local newspaper saying, "College is like your life. If you don't go to college ... you can't live a successful life."

17   Too many students believe this. School leaders can get out in front and help them see there are many paths to a successful life and college is only one of them.

Lawrence Schlack, a former superintendent, is a consultant at Kalamazoo Regional Educational Service Agency, 1819 E. Milham Road. Kalamazoo, MI 49002. E-mail: lawr@ net-link.net

Why Go to College?

How 2 Choose, University of North Texas
March 23, 2010

Consider these statistics:

1   • The average four-year college education at a public university in Texas (in-state tuition and fees) costs about $19,434 — less than the average price of a new car.

2   • The annual income for a person with a bachelor's degree is nearly twice that of someone with only a high school diploma.

3   You'll get more mileage out of a college education than you will from a car, and a four-year education will likely enable you to buy a car or two and many other things in your lifetime. In making the decision of whether — and where — to attend college, you and your parents should consider those four years as a lifetime investment, not just as annual expenses for job training.

Factoid

4   A college education can challenge you to explore and broaden your interests, attain your goals and meet some of the best friends you'll ever have.

Starting a new chapter

5   Many high school students look forward to putting high school behind them and moving on with their lives. At college, you'll explore and broaden your interests, pursue your goals, meet lifelong friends and define yourself in ways you can only imagine now. This website will guide you through the sometimes confusing process of selecting a college so that you can concentrate on starting a new chapter of your life.

The big payback

6   The competitive advantage is yours if you choose to graduate from college. Experts who have researched the performance and job success of college graduates have concluded that, nationwide, college graduates with a bachelor's degree earn 74 percent more per year than those who only complete high school. In fact, those whose education stops with a high school diploma may see their real wages decline over time.

The big picture

7   Right now, it's probably tough to imagine where you'll be in a year or two, much less 10, 20, 30 or 40 years down the road. Where do you expect to be, and what do you want out of life? By attending college immediately after high school, you get a head start on answering those important questions.

8   But you don't have to sign a four-year contract, and you don't even have to decide immediately on a major area of study. College is a time to test yourself and to see what you can achieve. Academic advisors and professors are accessible on campus, and tutoring and other forms of academic support are available. At most universities, a counseling staff is available to help see you through tough times.

9   You'll be able to pursue your own interests through extracurricular activities and perhaps discover a career direction you've never considered or a talent that's been waiting to blossom. College gives you the chance to say "yes" to you.

Which college is best?

10   Two key words are missing in that question. It should read, "Which college is best for you?" Your choices depend on your interests, career goals and academic record. Talk to your high school counselor about your options and attend College Night at school. Most Texas high school seniors are allowed a certain number of days to visit college campuses.

11   You may discover that you prefer the intimacy of a smaller campus or the setting of a community or church affiliated college. On the other hand, you may be ready for the swirling activity and myriad opportunities of a large university. The only way to find out is to visit. You'll get the most value out of your four-year investment by being open to many possibilities now, while you're still in high school.

Great expectations

12   As you outline your future, spend time considering what you want to do with your life. As with any major purchase, you'll want to be a wise consumer: look at the choices, compare prices, think about what's important to you and go for the best quality your money can buy. College doesn't guarantee happiness and success, but it does help you make the best of your own life.

What, no money?

13   Financial aid is available to everyone with a desire for a college education. Scholarships, loans, grants and prepaid tuition programs are out there, and this website will help you find them. On-campus jobs are also available, with flexible schedules that allow you to attend classes.

14   Whether you attend a public or private institution, you can expect to receive financial aid information from your high school counselor and college representatives. Incidentally, earning a degree from an Ivy League school or an expensive private college is no guarantee that you'll land the best job and have the highest earning potential. In fact, the effect on future earnings may only be marginal.

Are you better off going to college?

15   A high school graduate is confronted with the choice of accepting a job or entering a four-year college program. Is the student better off going to college? Because college graduates can expect to earn a salary almost double that of high school graduates, the student is much better off going to college. The difference in salary earned compounds over a lifetime.

U.S. Mean Annual Earnings by Education	
Education	Annual Income
No High School	$28,881
High School	$37,303
Some College	$42,868
Bachelor's Degree	$66,445

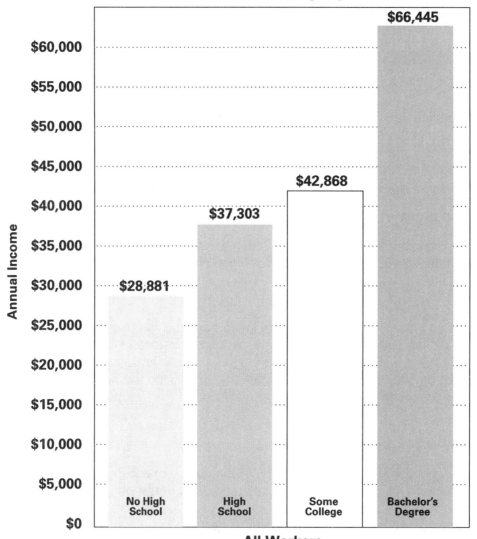

U.S. Mean Annual Earnings by Education

All Workers

Source: U.S. Census Bureau, Current Population Survey

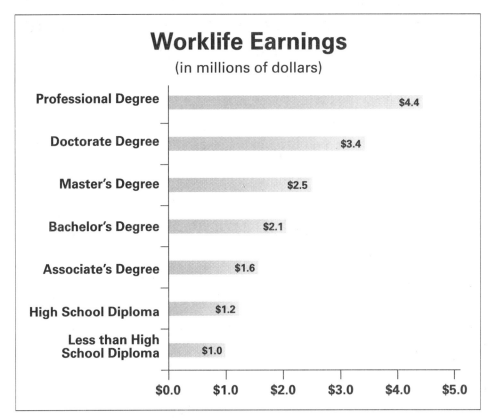

Worklife Earnings
(in millions of dollars)

Education	Earnings
Professional Degree	$4.4
Doctorate Degree	$3.4
Master's Degree	$2.5
Bachelor's Degree	$2.1
Associate's Degree	$1.6
High School Diploma	$1.2
Less than High School Diploma	$1.0

(Earnings for full-time, year-round workers by educational
attainment for worklife of approximately 40 years.
Source: U.S. Census Bureau)

Worklife Earnings	
Education	**Earnings (in millions of dollars)**
Professional Degree	$4.4
Doctorate	$3.4
Master's Degree	$2.5
Bachelor's Degree	$2.1
Associate Degree	$1.6
High School Diploma	$1.2
Less than High School Diploma	$1.0

Earnings for full-time, year-round workers by educational attainment
for work life of approximately 40 years. Source: U.S. Census Bureau.

The 10 Most Common Excuses for NOT Going to College *and Why They're All Wrong!*

Author unknown
www.everycircle.com/articles/tenexcuses.htm

1   *So you think that college isn't for you?* Well, you're wrong! You don't have to be "lucky" or have lots of money to go to college. You don't have to have straight "A's" in high school or know already what you want to do with the rest of your life. You do have to really want to go to college—and be ready to work hard once you get there. Unfortunately, too many students make up excuses for why they can't go to college. If you're one of those students, here's a list of the 10 most common excuses—and why they're all wrong. Please share this with others.

2   **EXCUSE #1:** Nobody in my family has ever gone to college before. Why not be the first? It's true that being the first to do anything can be difficult and maybe even a little frightening, but being the first in your family to receive a college education should give you a sense of pride. Not going to college is the kind of family "tradition" you should break.

3   **EXCUSE #2:** My grades are not good enough for college. How do you know they're not unless you apply? Even if you haven't obtained all good grades in school, you can still be admitted to a good college that will be right for you. Colleges look at more than just grades and test scores. They look at such things as letters from teachers and other adults; extracurricular activities; jobs you might have had; special talents in art, music, and sports; and interviews. When deciding who gets in, colleges examine the whole person, not just one small part.

4   **EXCUSE #3:** I can't afford it. There's a lot of financial aid available to help you pay for college. This year alone there are about $26 BILLION waiting for students who need money for college. If you apply for aid, and you demonstrate that you need it, your chances are as good as anybody else's that you will receive help. There's money available from the federal government, from your state, from the colleges you apply to, and from thousands of grant, scholarship, and work-study programs. But you won't see any of it if you don't check it out.

5   **EXCUSE #4:** I don't know how to apply to college, or where I want to go. You're not alone. You can start by looking at college catalogs in your high school or local library, and you can talk to your high school counselor, favorite teacher, or someone you know who's gone to college. There's a lot of good advice available, but you have to ask for it. With more than 3,000 colleges to choose from, there's bound to be one that's right for you.

6   **EXCUSE #5:** I think college may be too difficult for me. Not likely, if you're willing to work hard. Thousands of students graduate from college every year, and chances are many of them were afraid college would be too difficult for them—but they made it in spite of their fears. College is a big change from high school. The competition will be greater and the homework assignments will be longer and tougher. And it isn't always easy to adjust to strange surrounding and make new friends. But once you get involved with your work, you'll find that many of your classmates feel as you do. Who doesn't worry sometimes that they might not make it? And even if you find that you're not doing well in certain subjects, you can still do something about it. Tutoring is available from professors or fellow students, and counseling for personal problems is available on campus too.

7   **EXCUSE #6:** I'm not sure that I'll "fit in" in college. Just about any college you might attend will have students from all kinds of backgrounds, so you are sure to find other people whom you can relate to. If you're a minority student, for example, find about student clubs sponsored by African Americans, Hispanics/Latinos, Native Americans, Asians, or other groups. Such clubs can help give you a sense of community away from home. Regardless of your ethnic background, you should remember that one of the good things about college is getting to know all kinds of people. It will be interesting to learn about different life-styles and cultures, and it will help prepare you for the world you will face after graduation.

8   **EXCUSE #7:** I don't even know what I want to major in or do with my life. The great majority of college freshmen don't have a clue about these things either. Giving you choices is what college is all about. You can take courses in different fields and see what you like and what you're good at. You may be surprised to find a subject or a career field that you never would have thought of before. The biggest mistake you can make is to think that any decision you make is cast in concrete and that you can never change your major—or your life.

9   **EXCUSE #8**: There's no way I can go to college full-time. So go part-time. Most colleges offer programs you can attend in the evening or on weekends. Some colleges even give classes where you work or in neighborhood churches and community centers. You can also study many subjects through correspondence courses in home-study programs, and a number of states have external degree programs that let you work for a degree without—believe it or not—any classroom attendance! Ask your counselor about these possibilities.

10   **EXCUSE #9:** I'm too old to go to college. Nonsense! You're never too old to learn. Even if you've been out of high school for a while, you can still go to college. Almost half of all full-time and part-time students in the country are adults older than 25 years of age. If they can do it, so can you!

11   **EXCUSE #10:** I just want to get a good job and make lots of money. College will help you with that and more. Studies have shown that a college graduate will earn several hundred thousand dollars more during the course of his or her working life than someone who has only a high school diploma. Of course, money isn't everything, but most challenging and interesting jobs with good futures require a college education. A college degree will also give you a greater variety of job choices. There's something else that college will give you: a sense of personal satisfaction, confidence, and self-respect. These are not easy to measure, but they are very important in helping you become the kind of person you want to be. There are probably many other reasons you can think of for not going to college. But why sit around making up excuses when you can use that time and energy to do something that will benefit you the rest of your life? Decide now that you want to go to college and then start working at it. This is the bottom line: If you are willing to give it a shot, college can be for you too.

FAQ (Frequently Asked Questions) Guide for College or Work

By Rick Hansen

Things to Do When Planning for College

This can be an overwhelming and complicated process. There is no best way to go about this other than to be as thorough as you can be and to collect as much information as you can. Consult "Web Site Resources" to help you identify sources for research.

Deciding where to begin your research depends on how well formed your plans are. If you already know where you are going to college, then you might want to begin the application process for that institution. If you are not sure where you want to go to college, you may want to start with looking at college cultures, the kind of programs or majors they offer, and how easy it is to get in.

If you think you want to go to college, but are unsure of why or what you would do, you may want to start looking at the relation between your career plans and the programs colleges offer in your area of interest.

In short, there is no single best way to begin, but once you begin, make sure you keep careful records. It is important to keep a folder for each school you are considering.

Here is a brief list of what you should record:

1. The address of Web sites you visit and information about what you found there

2. Any information about deadlines, requirements, and passwords you need to develop in order to continue to explore a particular college (the CSU system requires you to establish a user name and password.)

3. Any information about tests you need to take or records you need to have access to

4. Information about financial aid, how to apply, and who to contact

5. Any contact information, Web addresses, and phone numbers

6. A calendar that shows who you contacted and when

7. A space for writing notes, planning, and doing more research about going to college

Things to Consider When Building Your FAQ

- The Application
  - Deadlines
  - Admission requirements
  - Grades and tests
  - Addresses
  - Contacts
  - Majors and impacted majors

- Financial Aid
  - Requirements for Cal Grant
  - Requirements for Federal Grants (FAFSA)
  - Deadlines
  - Filing options
  - Recent announcements

- Your college major
  - What can you do with the major?
  - Which colleges offer it?
  - What kind of knowledge is associated with your major?
  - What sort of things do majors read and study?
  - What kind of groups or communities are formed around the major?

- The kind of college you want to attend
  - What are the costs of attending?
  - Who is accepted?
  - What is the graduation rate?
  - Who goes to the college?
  - What kind of support is offered there?
  - What is life around the college like?

Remember that your task here is to find answers to questions that you have about attending college. The questions provided above are not comprehensive. While you are researching, you should pay attention to questions that surface as you gather more information about applying for and attending college. Finally, remember to keep records; you will need to use the information you have gathered about college not just to fill out an application, but to use in your personal statement letter.

Things to Do When Planning for a Career:

Planning for a career or any job opportunity takes patience and a little imagination if you are going to explore possibilities and perhaps expand your sense of what is possible for you as a high school graduate hoping to enter the work force. One way to begin this process is by taking a look at John Holland's "Theory of Career Choice." Reading this document will help you make some larger decisions about your areas of interest and how your interests may be matched with some types of jobs, sometimes called "job families." You will find the Web address for this document in "Web Site Resources" in the section, Web Suggestions for Career-Bound Students.

Once you have considered areas of interest for yourself, it will be a good idea to start looking at specific kinds of work. Both the *Oklahoma Career Planner* and the *Oklahoma Career Information System* will provide you with access to links that provide a wealth of information about jobs.

The *California Careers* Web site will also provide you with information. If you work through its multiple Web sites, you should be able to find an abundance of information about jobs, job availability, job requirements, and life on the job you are interested in. Web addresses for these sites are also listed in "Web Site Resources."

Here is a brief list of things you need for your search:

- **A folder for keeping records:**

  - Taking in so much information calls for some organization on your part. You should have a folder to keep all information in, a place to take notes on what you discover, and a place to keep records of Web addresses, resources, and other information that may help you plan for work.

- **A plan**

  - Simply looking around isn't going to be very helpful if you plan to make your research effective. Here are a few suggestions about things to look for when considering the kind of career you want.

    - What kind of activity does this job require?
    - What are the common tasks?
    - What are the working conditions?
    - What skills or abilities do I need to have?
    - What do I need to know in order to do this job?
    - What kind of preparation do I need for this line of work?
    - How do people get hired?
    - What can I expect to get paid for this work?
    - What are the chances for advancement?
    - What is the outlook for this kind of work in the future?
    - What programs help prepare for this kind of work?
    - Are there any resources that can help me learn more about this line of work?

Keeping a record of what you learn about different jobs will help you make an informed decision about the line of work you want to pursue and, perhaps, will help you make a decision to continue your learning either in college or some other setting. Remember that you are doing this research not only to learn about potential careers, but also to prepare yourself for writing a letter of introduction to a future employer. What does this information help you understand about the way you need to represent yourself?

Web Site Resources

By Rick Hansen

Web Suggestions for College-Bound Students

General

- The college checklist for academic and financial preparation
  - http://studentaid.ed.gov/prepare-for-college/checklists

Financial Aid Information

- College financial aid terms: US News and World Report> The Scholarship Coach
  - http://www.usnews.com/education/blogs/the-scholarship-coach/2012/07/19/12-college-financial-aid-terms-defined

- Cal Grants
  - http://www.calgrants.org

- Federal Grants (FAFSA)
  - http://www.fafsa.ed.gov

Applying to California colleges:

- CaliforniaColleges.edu—information on all California colleges
  - http://californiacolleges.edu

- University of California
  - http://www.universityofcalifornia.edu/admissions

- California State University
  - http://www.csumentor.edu
  - http://www.csusuccess.org

- California Community Colleges
  - http://www.cccapply.org

Choosing a College and Information about College Life

- The Choice, NY Times, Education- student and professional blogs
  - http://thechoice.blogs.nytimes.com

- US News and World Report-advice of all kinds
  - http://www.usnews.com/education

- College Insight—good site for thinking about costs
  - http://college-insight.org/#spotlight/go

- College Board-facts about schools
  - http://www.collegeboard.org/

- Unigo—information from students about college life
  - http://www.unigo.com/

Advice about Choosing a Major

- College Majors 101
  - http://www.collegemajors101.com

Web Suggestions for Career-Bound Students

The Career Key—Holland's Interest Chart.

- Good source for linking your interests to particular fields of work
  - http://www.careerkey.org/asp/your_personality/hollands_theory_of_career_choice.html

Oklahoma Career Planner

- Does not provide local information, but a very good resource for looking at careers by industry, occupation, or military.
- Best link indexes occupations and provides information about work conditions, physical demands, wages, opportunities and much more.
  - http://www.okcareerplanner.com/index.php?id=3

Occupations Index in the Oklahoma Career Information System

- This is a good site to check into the requirements for many different jobs.
  - Go to: http://okcistest.intocareers.org/index_cluster.aspx?FileID=Occ
    - Then choose a cluster
    - Choose a specific occupation
    - Read overview and then in the left hand column
    - Select any of the other links for more information

California Careers Info

- This is the home page for three excellent Web sites that provide everything a you will need to consider your future work plans.
  - http://www.californiacareers.info/

Career Zone:

- This site provides information on a wide range of job families (types) and specific careers within different job families. A great place to start thinking about the relation between your interests and job possibilities.
  - http://www.cacareerzone.org/
    1. Go to the site and register, it's free. Remember to write down your user name and password.

2. Once inside, click on any of the links to

    a. Assess yourself.

    b. Explore job families.

    c. Get a reality check about your plans.

3. Inside "Assess yourself" you will find all kinds of information about jobs.

    a. Click on your areas of interest.

    b. Click on "View Results."

    c. On the next page you can reset any dollar amounts, or job families you are interested in.

    d. Then open the list on "in job family" and select a family that interests you.

    e. Select a line of work and open the page.

    f. There you will find information about the job, names for the job, what they do, things you need to know to do the job, wages, work prospects in California and much more.

    g. Explore as many areas of interest as you can and take notes on information you may use in your letter of introduction to the community (Portfolio, remember?).

Explore Job Families:

- This is the second link on the Career Zone home page.
  - http://www.cacareerzone.org/clusters
- This page allows you to explore job families. Job families are clusters or groups of jobs that seem to relate to common interests or shared work. Best here to

  1. Select a "family" (Health Care Practitioner and Technical Occupations);

  2. Skim through the jobs and examine their qualities (occupational therapist, emergency medical technician, and so on); and

  3. Once inside a job, take notes on its requirements and opportunities. Do your best to see if the job description matches your own sense of what you want to do with your life after high school.

Get a Reality Check:

- This link allows you to figure out how much money you will need to live the way you may be imagining yourself to live in the near—or distant—future.
  - http://www.californiarealitycheck.com/
- Simply work through the 1, 2, 3 directions to get a final summary and "reality check" for your plans.
- Don't forget, once you have filled out all the information about how you want to live, check out the kind of occupations that seem to match your lifestyle choices.

California Jobs and Career Information

- This site lists jobs and their salaries. It also provides links to Career Schools in California. In those links you can find information about any kind of tech or vocational school.
  - http://www.seniorjobbank.org/database/California/California.html

The Rhetoric of the Op-Ed Page: Ethos, Logos, and Pathos

Three Ways to Persuade

By John R. Edlund

1   Over 2,000 years ago the Greek philosopher Aristotle argued that there were three basic ways to persuade an audience of your position: *ethos, logos,* and *pathos.*

Ethos: The Writer's Character or Image

2   The Greek word *ethos* is related to our word *ethics* or *ethical,* but a more accurate modern translation might be "image." Aristotle uses *ethos* to refer to the speaker's character as it appears to the audience. Aristotle says that if we believe that a speaker has good sense, good moral character, and goodwill, we are inclined to believe what that speaker says. Today we might add that a speaker should also appear to have the appropriate expertise or authority to speak knowledgeably about the subject matter. *Ethos* is often the first thing we notice, so it creates the first impression that influences how we perceive the rest. *Ethos* is an important factor in advertising, both for commercial products and in politics. For example, when an actor in a pain reliever commercial puts on a doctor's white coat, the advertisers are hoping that wearing this coat will give the actor the authority to talk persuasively about medicines. Of course, in this particular instance the actor's *ethos* is a deceptive illusion, but the character, background, and authority of the speaker or writer can be a legitimate factor in determining whether we find him or her credible.

3   A writer's *ethos* is created largely by word choice and style. Student writers often have a problem with *ethos* because they are asked to write research papers, reports, and other types of texts as if they have authority to speak persuasively, when in fact they are newcomers to the subject matter and the discourse community. Sometimes students try to create an academic image for themselves by using a thesaurus to find difficult and unusual words to sprinkle throughout their texts. Unfortunately, this sort of effort usually fails, because it is difficult to use a word correctly that you have not heard or read in context many times.

4   Sometimes a writer or speaker will use what is called an *ad hominem* argument, an argument "against the man." In this strategy, the writer attacks the character or personality of the speaker instead of attacking the substance of his or her position. This kind of argument is usually considered to be a logical fallacy, but it can be very effective and is quite common in politics. This type of argument undermines a speaker or writer's *ethos.* When you are writing a paper, consider the following questions.

Questions for Discussion:
1. What kind of image do you want to project to your audience?
2. What can you do to help project this image?
3. What words or ideas do you want to avoid in order not to harm your image?
4. What effect do misspelled words and grammatical errors have on your image?

Logos: Logical Arguments

5   In our society, logic and rationality are highly valued and this type of persuasive strategy is usually privileged over appeals to the character of the speaker or to the emotions of the audience. However, formal logic and scientific reasoning are usually not appropriate for general audiences, so we must rely on a more *rhetorical* type of reasoning.

6   For Aristotle, formal arguments are based on what he calls syllogisms. This is reasoning that takes the form:
    All men are mortal.
    Socrates is a man.
    Therefore, Socrates is mortal.

7   However, Aristotle notes that in ordinary speaking and writing we often use what he calls a rhetorical syllogism or an *enthymeme.* This is an argument in which some of the premises or assertions remain unstated or are simply assumed. For example, no one in ordinary life would think that Socrates could be immortal. We would simply *assume* that Socrates could be killed or that he would die of natural causes after a normal lifespan. As a result, we can logically say the following: Socrates is a man; therefore, Socrates is mortal. Not all assumptions are as obvious as this one, however.

8   For example, when the bubonic plague swept through Europe and parts of Asia in the 14th century, killing as much as three quarters of the population in less than 20 years, it was not known how the disease was spread. At one point, people thought that the plague was spread by cats. If one *assumes* that cats spread the disease, the obvious solution to the problem is to eliminate the cats, and so people began killing cats on sight. However, we now know that the plague is spread by fleas which live on rats. Because cats kill rats, killing off the cat population led to an increase in the rat population, a corresponding increase in plague carrying fleas, and thus an increase in cases of plague in humans. Killing off the cats was a logical solution to the problem of plague, but it was based on a faulty assumption.

9   Rhetorical arguments are often based on probabilities rather than certain truth. The people of medieval Europe really had no way to determine what the real cause of the plague was, but they felt that they had to do something about it, and the cat hypothesis seemed probable to them. Unfortunately, this is true of many of the problems we face even today. We cannot know with absolute certainty what the real solution is, yet we must act anyway.

10   Persuasion, to a large extent, involves convincing people to accept our assumptions as probably true and to take appropriate action. Similarly, exposing questionable assumptions in someone else's argument is an effective means for preparing the audience to accept your own contrary position.

Questions for Discussion:
1. Imagine some arguments that start from faulty assumptions, such as "If pigs could fly," or "If money grew on trees." What would be some of the logical consequences?
2. Do you think that logical arguments are a better support for a position than arguments that are based on authority or character? In other words, would you support a policy just because a celebrity or an important expert supported it?
3. Can you think of a time when you successfully used a logical argument to persuade someone of something? What was it?

Pathos: The Emotions of the Audience

11 Most of us think that we make our decisions based on rational thought. However, Aristotle points out that emotions such as anger, pity, fear, and their opposites, powerfully influence our rational judgments. Due to this fact, much of our political discourse and much of the advertising we experience is directed toward moving our emotions.

12 Anger is a very powerful motivating force. Aristotle says that if we want to make an audience angry we need to know three things: 1) the state of mind of angry people, 2) who the people are that this audience usually gets angry at, and 3) on what grounds this audience gets angry at those people. While the actual causes of a war may be economic or political, and thus related to *logos,* the mobilization of a people or a nation to war inevitably consists of appeals to *pathos.* Leaders mobilize their followers to go to war by reminding them of their historical grievances against other groups or nations, blaming other groups for economic difficulties, and focusing on perceived insults, crimes, and atrocities committed against their own citizens by others. In the twentieth century, such appeals to *pathos* inspired the Holocaust in Germany, genocide in Rwanda, and ethnic cleansing in the former Yugoslavia. Individuals were inspired through *pathos* to attack, rape, or kill neighbors who had lived near them all their lives, simply because of their ethnicity or religion.

13 Many political decisions have an emotional motivation. For example, when a gunman with an assault rifle shot up a schoolyard full of children, people were suddenly interested in banning such weapons. In this case, several emotions are involved, but perhaps the strongest one is pity for the small children and their families. The logical arguments for banning or not banning assault rifles had not changed at all, but people were emotionally engaged with the issue after this event and wanted to *do* something.

14 Of course, not all appeals to *pathos* result in violence or political action. Advertisements for consumer goods often aim at making us insecure about our attractiveness or social acceptability and then offer a remedy for this feeling in the form of a product. This is a common strategy for selling mouthwash, toothpaste, chewing gum, clothing, and even automobiles.

15 Appeals to the emotions and passions are often very effective and are very common in our society. Such appeals are not always false or illegitimate. It is natural to feel strong emotions about tragedies, victories, and other powerful events as well as about one's own image and identity. You may find it effective to use *pathos* in your own writing.

Questions for Discussion:

1. Can you think of an advertisement for a product or a political campaign that uses your emotions to persuade you to believe something? Describe it, and analyze how it works.

2. When do you think it is unfair or deceptive to try to use emotions to persuade people?

3. Have you ever made a decision based on your feelings that you regretted later?

4. Did emotions ever serve you well in making a decision?

A Change of Heart about Animals
They are more like us than we imagined, scientists are finding.

By Jeremy Rifkin
Los Angeles Times, September 1, 2003

1   Though much of big science has centered on breakthroughs in biotechnology, nanotechnology and more esoteric questions like the age of our universe, a quieter story has been unfolding behind the scenes in laboratories around the world—one whose effect on human perception and our understanding of life is likely to be profound.

2   What these researchers are finding is that many of our fellow creatures are more like us than we had ever imagined. They feel pain, suffer and experience stress, affection, excitement and even love—and these findings are changing how we view animals.

3   Strangely enough, some of the research sponsors are fast food purveyors, such as McDonald's, Burger King and KFC. Pressured by animal rights activists and by growing public support for the humane treatment of animals, these companies have financed research into, among other things, the emotional, mental and behavioral states of our fellow creatures.

4   Studies on pigs' social behavior funded by McDonald's at Purdue University, for example, have found that they crave affection and are easily depressed if isolated or denied playtime with each other. The lack of mental and physical stimuli can result in deterioration of health.

5   The European Union has taken such studies to heart and outlawed the use of isolating pig stalls by 2012. In Germany, the government is encouraging pig farmers to give each pig 20 seconds of human contact each day and to provide them with toys to prevent them from fighting.

6   Other funding sources have fueled the growing field of study into animal emotions and cognitive abilities.

7   Researchers were stunned recently by findings (published in the journal Science) on the conceptual abilities of New Caledonian crows. In controlled experiments, scientists at Oxford University reported that two birds named Betty and Abel were given a choice between using two tools, one a straight wire, the other a hooked wire, to snag a piece of meat from inside a tube. Both chose the hooked wire. Abel, the more dominant male, then stole Betty's hook, leaving her with only a straight wire. Betty then used her beak to wedge the straight wire in a crack and bent it with her beak to produce a hook. She then snagged the food from inside the tube. Researchers repeated the experiment and she fashioned a hook out of the wire nine out of 10 times.

8   Equally impressive is Koko, the 300-pound gorilla at the Gorilla Foundation in Northern California, who was taught sign language and has mastered more than 1,000 signs and understands several thousand English words. On human IQ tests, she scores between 70 and 95.

9   Tool-making and the development of sophisticated language skills are just two of the many attributes we thought were exclusive to our species. Self-awareness is another.

10   Some philosophers and animal behaviorists have long argued that other animals are not capable of self-awareness because they lack a sense of individualism. Not so, according to new studies. At the Washington National Zoo, orangutans given mirrors explore parts of their bodies they can't otherwise see, showing a sense of self. An orangutan named Chantek who lives at the Atlanta Zoo used a mirror to groom his teeth and adjust his sunglasses.

11   Of course, when it comes to the ultimate test of what distinguishes humans from the other creatures, scientists have long believed that mourning for the dead represents the real divide. It's commonly believed that other animals have no sense of their mortality and are unable to comprehend the concept of their own death. Not necessarily so. Animals, it appears, experience grief. Elephants will often stand next to their dead kin for days, occasionally touching their bodies with their trunks.

12   We also know that animals play, especially when young. Recent studies in the brain chemistry of rats show that when they play, their brains release large amounts of dopamine, a neurochemical associated with pleasure and excitement in human beings.

13   Noting the striking similarities in brain anatomy and chemistry of humans and other animals, Stephen M. Siviy, a behavioral scientist at Gettysburg College in Pennsylvania, asks a question increasingly on the minds of other researchers. "If you believe in evolution by natural selection, how can you believe that feelings suddenly appeared, out of the blue, with human beings?"

14   Until very recently, scientists were still advancing the idea that most creatures behaved by sheer instinct and that what appeared to be learned behavior was merely genetically wired activity. Now we know that geese have to teach their goslings their migration routes. In fact, we are finding that learning is passed on from parent to offspring far more often than not and that most animals engage in all kinds of learned experience brought on by continued experimentation.

15   So what does all of this portend for the way we treat our fellow creatures? And for the thousands of animals subjected each year to painful laboratory experiments? Or the millions of domestic animals raised under the most inhumane conditions and destined for slaughter and human consumption? Should we discourage the sale and purchase of fur coats? What about fox hunting in the English countryside, bull fighting in Spain? Should wild lions be caged in zoos?

16   Such questions are being raised. Harvard and 25 other U.S. law schools have introduced law courses on animal rights, and an increasing number of animal rights lawsuits are being filed. Germany recently became the first nation to guarantee animal rights in its constitution.

17   The human journey is, at its core, about the extension of empathy to broader and more inclusive domains. At first, the empathy extended only to kin and tribe. Eventually it was extended to people of like-minded values. In the 19th century, the first animal humane societies were established. The current studies open up a new phase, allowing us to expand and deepen our empathy to include the broader community of creatures with whom we share the Earth.

Jeremy Rifkin, author of *The Biotech Century*, is the president of the Foundation on Economic Trends in Washington, D.C.

Letters to the editor in response to "A Change of Heart about Animals"

1   Re "A Change of Heart About Animals," Commentary, Sept. 1: Jeremy Rifkin argues that science has shown that the differences between animals and humans are less than we think and that we should extend more "empathy" to animals. I disagree. In nature, animals naturally kill and eat each other. If the hawk does not care about the feelings of the rabbit that it eats, why should humans be any different? Is Rifkin saying that nature is wrong?

2   Rifkin goes so far as to say that pigs need social contact and should be provided with toys. There are many real human children in the world who do not have these things. Are animals more important than human children? Should our society spend scarce resources on toys for pigs?

3   Anyone who has owned a pet knows that animals can feel pain, happiness, anger, and other simple emotions. Most people have heard a parrot or a mynah bird talk, but this is just imitation and mimicry. We don't need science to tell us that animals can do these things. However, does a parrot understand what it is saying? Can an animal write a poem, or even a grocery list?

4   Rifkin is simply an animal rights activist hiding behind a handful of scientific studies. He wants to ignore human suffering and focus on animal discomfort. He wants animals to have more rights than humans. Let's not be fooled.

Bob Stevens

1   Much thanks to Jeremy Rifkin for showing us that science supports what we pet owners and animal rights activists have known in our hearts all along: animals have feelings and abilities not very different from humans. I found the stories about Koko the gorilla who is fluent in sign language, and Betty and Abel, the tool-making crows, intriguing and heart-warming. When will more people begin to realize that we share this world with many creatures deserving of our care and respect?

2   However, Rifkin should take his argument farther. Animals have a right to live without being confined, exploited, tormented or eaten. That means no animal experimentation, no fur or leather clothing, and a vegan or vegetarian lifestyle. Meat eating and animal abuse lead to spiritual disturbance and physical disease. Let's free ourselves from the evils of the past and live in harmony with our fellow creatures!

Lois Frazier

Hooked on a Myth

Do fish feel pain? A biologist says we shouldn't be so quick to believe they don't.

By Victoria Braithwaite
Los Angeles Times, October 8, 2006

1   Every year, sportsmen around the world drag millions of fish to shore on barbed hooks. It's something people have always done, and with little enough conscience. Fish are ... well, fish. They're not dogs, who yelp when you accidentally step on their feet. Fish don't cry out or look sad or respond in a particularly recognizable way. So we feel free to treat them in a way that we would not treat mammals or even birds.

2   But is there really any biological justification for exempting fish from the standards nowadays accorded to so-called higher animals? Do we really know whether fish feel pain or whether they suffer—or whether, in fact, our gut sense that they are dumb, unfeeling animals is accurate?

3   Determining whether any type of animal really suffers is difficult. A good starting place might be to consider how people feel pain. When a sharp object pierces the human body, specialized nerve endings called nociceptors alert us to the damage. Incredibly, no one ever seems to have asked before whether fish have nociceptors around their mouths. My colleagues and I in Edinburgh, Scotland, recently looked in trout and found that they do. If you look at thin sections of the trigeminal nerve, the main nerve for the face for all vertebrates, fish have the same two types of nociceptors that we do—A-delta and C fibers. So they do have the necessary sensory wiring to detect pain.

4   And the wiring works. We stimulated the nociceptors by injecting diluted vinegar or bee venom just under the skin of the trout. If you've ever felt the nip of vinegar on an open cut or the sting of a bee, you will recognize these feelings as painful. Well, fish find these naturally irritating chemicals unpleasant too. Their gills beat faster, and they rub the affected area on the walls of their tank, lose interest in food and have problems making decisions.

5   When I have a headache, I reach for the aspirin. What happens if we give the fish painkillers after injecting the noxious substances? Remarkably, they begin to behave normally again. So their adverse behavior is induced by the experience of pain.

6   But just because fish are affected by pain, does that mean they actually "feel" it? To answer that, we need to probe deeper into their brains (and our own) to understand what it means to feel pain.

7   To determine what fish go through mentally when they experience painful stimuli, we also need to determine whether they have a capacity to feel emotion and to suffer.

8   This is a much harder problem. It goes to the very heart of one of the biggest unresolved issues in biology: Do nonhuman animals have emotions and feelings? Are nonhuman animals conscious?

9   Scientists and philosophers have long debated consciousness and what it is and whether it is exclusively human. There are multiple definitions and, frankly, we haven't really come to grips with what it means to be conscious ourselves. Are we conscious because we are capable of attributing mental states to others, or perhaps because we have a qualitative awareness of feelings, whether positive or negative? And if we can't define our own consciousness, can we expect to detect it in fish?

10   Perhaps not, but we can look for behaviors and abilities that we believe contribute to human consciousness—for example, complex cognitive abilities and specialized brain regions that process emotion and memory.

11   It turns out that the stereotype of fish as slow, dim-witted creatures is wrong; many fish are remarkably clever. For example, they can learn geometrical relationships and landmarks—and then use these to generate a mental map to plan escape routes if a predator shows up.

12   And their brains are not as different from ours as we once thought. Although less anatomically complex than our own brain, the function of two of their forebrain areas is very similar to the mammalian amygdala and hippocampus—areas associated with emotion, learning and memory. If these regions are damaged in fish, their learning and emotional capacities are impaired; they can no longer find their way through mazes, and they lose their sense of fear.

13   None of this tells us that fish are "conscious," but it does demonstrate them to be cognitively competent: They are more than simple automata.

14   So do we have to change the way we treat fish? Some still argue that fish brains are so less well developed than those of birds and mammals that it isn't possible for fish to suffer. In my view, that case is not proven.

15   Moreover, we actually have as much evidence that fish can suffer as we do that chickens can. I think, therefore, that we should adopt a precautionary ethical approach and assume that in the absence of evidence to the contrary, fish suffer.

16   Of course, this doesn't mean that we necessarily must change our behavior. One could reasonably adopt a utilitarian cost-benefit approach and argue that the benefits of sportfishing, both financial and recreational, may outweigh the ethical costs of the likely suffering of fish.

17   But I do find it curious that it has taken us so long even to bother to ask whether fish feel pain. Perhaps no one really wanted to know. Perhaps it opens a can of worms—so to speak—and begs the question of where do we draw the line. Crustacean welfare? Slug welfare? And if not fish, why birds? Is there a biological basis for drawing a line?

Victoria Braithwaite, a behavioral biologist at Edinburgh University, is on sabbatical at the Institute for Advanced Study in Berlin.

Of Primates and Personhood: Will According Rights and "Dignity" to Nonhuman Organisms Halt Research?

By Ed Yong
SEEDMAGAZINE.COM, December 12, 2008

1   Two major legal developments in the past few months are deepening a schism between leading primatologists, biologists, and ethicists around the world. A pending Spanish law that would grant unprecedented protections to great apes, and a recent extension to a Swiss law that protects the "dignity" of organisms, are the latest fronts in a battle to redefine the meaning of human rights, and indeed whether such rights are the exclusive domain of humans.

2   At the forefront of the battle is the Great Ape Project (GAP). Established in 1993, it demands a basic set of moral and legal rights for chimpanzees, gorillas, bonobos, and orangutans. This June, GAP persuaded the Spanish Parliament's environmental committee to approve a resolution supporting those goals.

3   Other countries, including the United Kingdom and New Zealand, have taken steps to protect great apes from experimentation, but this is the first time that actual rights would be extended to apes. The resolution establishes a set of laws based on GAP's principles, which Spain promises to implement by the end of the year. Those laws would ban the use of apes in experiments or entertainment or commercial ventures, and they would set higher standards for their conditions in captivity. The message is clear: These animals are not property. "It's a historic breakthrough in reducing the barrier between humans and nonhuman animals," says Peter Singer, an Australian philosopher and the head of GAP.

4   Not everyone is comfortable with GAP's rights-based approach, however. Primatologist Frans de Waal of Emory University says, "I do think we have special obligations to the great apes as our closest relatives, but if we give rights to apes, what would be the compelling reason not to give rights to monkeys, dogs, rats, and so on?"

5   GAP's goals are, for now, focused on apes, but Singer agrees that there is no clear place to draw the line. "Speaking personally, I feel we should extend rights to a wide range of nonhuman animals," he says. "All creatures that can feel pain should have a basic moral status."

6   That list would include other mammals, including the bulls regularly killed in Spanish stadiums. This iconic sport, along with Spain's lack of any ape research of its own, makes it an odd location from which to launch an opening salvo. Nevertheless, it's where GAP's efforts first gained traction, and it will be the origin of future efforts.

7   Such moves are already under way. "The Green Party in Germany is preparing two bills supporting the Great Ape Project," says GAP's Pedro Pozas. In Austria this August, GAP member David Diaz visited Hiasl, a former research chimpanzee who has become an ape-rights icon as his sanctuary faces bankruptcy and he faces homelessness. Hiasl's fate hangs on being legally declared a person, an effort in line with GAP's greater mission. The matter is now being debated in the Strasbourg Court of Human Rights.

8   In the US, there is greater resistance to the idea of ape rights, though Congress has begun to make inroads. In April, three representatives, including former animal researcher Roscoe Bartlett, introduced a bill called the Great Ape Protection Act. It calls for scientists to cease invasive research on great apes and "rigorously apply existing alternatives" but stops short of extending rights to the animals themselves. Weaker than its Spanish counterpart, the bill would nevertheless have an impact in a country that performs more ape research than any other.

9   In the EU, renowned chimpanzee researcher Jane Goodall has called for a gradual end to all biomedical animal experimentation. However, the paragon of the animal rights movement is the unaligned nation in the EU's midst. Switzerland's strict constitutional laws on animal experiments are based on a slippery concept; since 1992, they have demanded that researchers respect the "dignity of creation." They protect animals from "unjustified interventions on their appearance, from humiliation and being disproportionately instrumentalized." As of September 1, these laws even require that animal owners keep social species, such as dogs, goldfish, and guinea pigs, in groups of two or more.

10   At its most extreme, the Swiss concept of dignity could soon be applied to plants. A discussion paper by the Federal Ethics Committee on Non-Human Biotechnology defines the "decapitation of wild flowers at the roadside without rational reason" as "morally impermissible." While this clause is generally viewed as being rhetorical, more worrisome is the Committee's preliminary stance on the genetic engineering of plants: only permissible if their "reproductive ability and adaptive ability are ensured."

11   Kevan Martin, of Zurich's Federal Institute of Technology, is one researcher whose work has already been affected by this dignity-based approach. He uses live macaques to understand how the brain changes during learning, and his experiments have been approved by ethical reviews many times over. But in 2006 the Swiss Health Department refused to renew Martin's license after a local advisory committee protested that his work had no immediate clinical relevance. "The result is that basic science on primates is effectively not possible," says Martin. "This research is not a luxury. The failure of gene therapy and AIDS vaccines is due to pressure to produce 'cures' before understanding the underlying biological mechanisms, which cannot be accessed by experiments with humans."

12   In the US, Edwin McConkey, a biologist on the team that initially proposed the Chimpanzee Genome Project, agrees that apes should be treated with more respect. He acknowledges, however, that there is at least one area in which applying human standards to apes would hinder important experimentation. "To understand the genetic basis for human uniqueness, it is necessary to compare both gene structure and gene expression in humans and apes," says McConkey. "This means obtaining early embryos from apes by surgical termination of pregnancy."

13   One kind of primate experiment seems to be safe in this debate. "I would strongly argue for continued noninvasive studies," says de Waal, "ones we wouldn't mind applying to human volunteers." Far from harming apes, such research could even enrich their lives—the chimpanzees that de Waal works with are so enamored of computers that they will actually line up for cognitive tests. Once their work is done, many can now be relocated to places like ChimpHaven, an outdoor facility that acts as a retirement home.

14   De Waal sits on that facility's board of directors. The care it extends to chimps is typical of the approach he favors. "What if we drop all this talk of rights and instead advocate a sense of obligation?" he asks. "In the same way that we teach children to respect a tree by mentioning its age, we should use the new insights into animals' mental life to foster in humans an ethic of caring in which our interests are not the only ones in the balance."

Racial Profiling

Jim Crow Policing

By Bob Herbert
New York Times, February 2, 2010

1   The New York City Police Department needs to be restrained. The nonstop humiliation of young black and Hispanic New Yorkers, including children, by police officers who feel no obligation to treat them fairly or with any respect at all is an abomination. That many of the officers engaged in the mistreatment are black or Latino themselves is shameful.

2   Statistics will be out shortly about the total number of people who were stopped and frisked by the police in 2009. We already have the data for the first three-quarters of the year, and they are staggering. During that period, more than 450,000 people were stopped by the cops, an increase of 13 percent over the same period in 2008.

3   An overwhelming 84 percent of the stops in the first three-quarters of 2009 were of black or Hispanic New Yorkers. It is incredible how few of the stops yielded any law enforcement benefit. Contraband, which usually means drugs, was found in only 1.6 percent of the stops of black New Yorkers. For Hispanics, it was just 1.5 percent. For whites, who are stopped far less frequently, contraband was found 2.2 percent of the time.

4   The percentages of stops that yielded weapons were even smaller. Weapons were found on just 1.1 percent of the blacks stopped, 1.4 percent of the Hispanics, and 1.7 percent of the whites. Only about 6 percent of stops result in an arrest for any reason.

5   Rather than a legitimate crime-fighting tool, these stops are a despicable, racially oriented tool of harassment. And the police are using it at the increasingly enthusiastic direction of Mayor Michael Bloomberg and Police Commissioner Ray Kelly.

6   There were more than a half-million stops in New York City in 2008, and when the final tally is in, we'll find that the number only increased in 2009.

7   Not everyone who is stopped is frisked. When broken down by ethnic group, the percentages do not at first seem so wildly disproportionate. Some 59.4 percent of all Hispanics who were stopped were also frisked, as were 56.6 percent of blacks, and 46 percent of whites. But keep in mind, whites composed fewer than 16 percent of the people stopped in the first place.

8   These encounters with the police are degrading and often frightening, and the real number of people harassed is undoubtedly higher than the numbers reported by the police. Often the cops will stop, frisk and sometimes taunt people who are at their mercy, and then move on—without finding anything, making an arrest, or recording the encounter as they are supposed to.

9   Even the official reasons given by the police for the stops are laughably bogus. People are stopped for allegedly making "furtive movements," for wearing clothes "commonly used in a crime," and, of course, for the "suspicious bulge." My wallet, my notebook and my cellphone would all apply.

10   The police say they also stop people for wearing "inappropriate attire for the season." I saw a guy on the Upper West Side wearing shorts and sandals a couple weeks ago. That was certainly unusual attire for the middle of January, but it didn't cross my mind that he should be accosted by the police.

11   The Center for Constitutional Rights has filed a class-action lawsuit against the city and the Police Department over the stops. Several plaintiffs detailed how their ordinary daily lives were interrupted by cops bent on harassment for no good reason. Lalit Carson was stopped while on a lunch break from his job as a teaching assistant at a charter school in the Bronx. Deon Dennis was stopped and searched while standing outside the apartment building in which he lives in Harlem. The police arrested him, allegedly because of an outstanding warrant. He was held for several hours then released. There was no outstanding warrant.

12   There are endless instances of this kind of madness. People going about their daily business, bothering no one, are menaced out of the blue by the police, forced to spread themselves face down in the street, or plaster themselves against a wall, or bend over the hood of a car, to be searched. People who object to the harassment are often threatened with arrest for disorderly conduct.

13   The Police Department insists that these stops of innocent people—which are unconstitutional, by the way—help fight crime. And they insist that the policy is not racist.

14   Paul Browne, the chief spokesman for Commissioner Kelly, described the stops as "life-saving." And he has said repeatedly that the racial makeup of the people stopped and frisked is proportionally similar to the racial makeup of people committing crimes.

15   That is an amazingly specious argument. The fact that a certain percentage of criminals may be black or Hispanic is no reason for the police to harass individuals from those groups when there is no indication whatsoever that they have done anything wrong.

16   It's time to put an end to Jim Crow policing in New York City.

The Value of Life

Hamlet's Soliloquy

(from Shakespeare's *Hamlet, Prince of Denmark,* Act III, Scene i)

HAMLET:

To be, or not to be—that is the question:

Whether 'tis* nobler in the mind to suffer   *it is

The slings and arrows of outrageous fortune

Or to take arms against a sea of troubles

And by opposing end them. To die, to sleep—   5

No more—and by a sleep to say we end

The heartache, and the thousand natural shocks

That flesh is heir to. 'Tis a consummation*   *resolution

Devoutly to be wished. To die, to sleep—

To sleep—perchance to dream: ay, there's the rub,*   *problem   10

For in that sleep of death what dreams may come

When we have shuffled off this mortal coil,*   *life

Must give us pause. There's the respect

That makes calamity* of so long life.   *tragedy

For who would bear the whips and scorns of time,   15

Th' oppressor's wrong, the proud man's contumely,*   *contempt

The pangs of despised love, the law's delay,

The insolence of office, and the spurns

That patient merit of th' unworthy takes,

When he himself might his quietus* make   *death   20

With a bare bodkin*? Who would fardels† bear,   *dagger
†*burdens*

To grunt and sweat under a weary life,

But that the dread of something after death,

The undiscovered country, from whose bourn*   **border

No traveler returns, puzzles the will,   25

And makes us rather bear those ills we have

Than fly to others that we know not of?

Thus conscience does make cowards of us all,

And thus the native hue* of resolution   *natural color

Is sicklied o'er with the pale cast of thought,   30

And enterprise of great pitch and moment

With this regard their currents turn awry

And lose the name of action.

Roger Ebert: The Essential Man [Excerpts]

By Chris Jones
Esquire, February 16, 2010

1   **For the 281st time** in the last ten months Roger Ebert is sitting down to watch a movie in the Lake Street Screening Room, on the sixteenth floor of what used to pass for a skyscraper in the Loop. Ebert's been coming to it for nearly thirty years, along with the rest of Chicago's increasingly venerable collection of movie critics. More than a dozen of them are here this afternoon, sitting together in the dark. Some of them look as though they plan on camping out, with their coats, blankets, lunches, and laptops spread out on the seats around them.

2   The critics might watch three or four movies in a single day, and they have rules and rituals along with their lunches to make it through. The small, fabric-walled room has forty-nine purple seats in it; Ebert always occupies the aisle seat in the last row, closest to the door. His wife, Chaz, in her capacity as vice-president of the Ebert Company, sits two seats over, closer to the middle, next to a little table. She's sitting there now, drinking from a tall paper cup. Michael Phillips, Ebert's bearded, bespectacled replacement on *At the Movies,* is on the other side of the room, one row down. Steve Prokopy, the guy who writes under the name Capone for Ain't It Cool News, leans against the far wall. Jonathan Rosenbaum and Peter Sobczynski, dressed in black, are down front.

3   "Too close for me," Ebert writes in his small spiral notebook.

4   Today, Ebert's decided he has the time and energy to watch only one film, Pedro Almodóvar's new Spanish-language movie, *Broken Embraces.* It stars Penélope Cruz. Steve Kraus, the house projectionist, is busy pulling seven reels out of a cardboard box and threading them through twin Simplex projectors.

5   Unlike the others, Ebert, sixty-seven, hasn't brought much survival gear with him: a small bottle of Evian moisturizing spray with a pink cap; some Kleenex; his spiral notebook and a blue fine-tip pen. He's wearing jeans that are falling off him at the waist, a pair of New Balance sneakers, and a blue cardigan zipped up over the bandages around his neck. His seat is worn soft and reclines a little, which he likes. He likes, too, for the seat in front of him to remain empty, so that he can prop his left foot onto its armrest; otherwise his back and shoulders can't take the strain of a feature-length sitting anymore.

6   The lights go down. Kraus starts the movie. Subtitles run along the bottom of the screen. The movie is about a film director, Harry Caine, who has lost his sight. Caine reads and makes love by touch, and he writes and edits his films by sound. "Films have to be finished, even if you do it blindly," someone in the movie says. It's a quirky, complex, beautiful little film, and Ebert loves it. He radiates kid joy. Throughout the screening, he takes excited notes—references to other movies, snatches of dialogue, meditations on Almodóvar's symbolism and his use of the color red. Ebert scribbles constantly, his pen digging into page after page, and then he tears the pages out of his notebook and drops them to the floor around him. Maybe twenty or thirty times, the sound of paper being torn from a spiral rises from the aisle seat in the last row.

7   The lights come back on. Ebert stays in his chair, savoring, surrounded by his notes. It looks as though he's sitting on top of a cloud of paper. He watches the credits, lifts himself up, and kicks his notes into a small pile with his feet. He slowly bends down to pick them up and walks with Chaz back out to the elevators. They hold hands, but they don't say anything to each other. They spend a lot of time like that.

8   **Roger Ebert can't remember** the last thing he ate. He can't remember the last thing he drank, either, or the last thing he said. Of course, those things existed; those lasts happened. They just didn't happen with enough warning for him to have bothered committing them to memory—it wasn't as though he sat down, knowingly, to his last supper or last cup of coffee or to whisper a last word into Chaz's ear. The doctors told him they were going to give him back his ability to eat, drink, and talk. But the doctors were wrong, weren't they? On some morning or afternoon or evening, sometime in 2006, Ebert took his last bite and sip, and he spoke his last word.

9   Ebert's lasts almost certainly took place in a hospital. That much he can guess. His last food was probably nothing special, except that it was: hot soup in a brown plastic bowl; maybe some oatmeal; perhaps a saltine or some canned peaches. His last drink? Water, most likely, but maybe juice, again slurped out of plastic with the tinfoil lid peeled back. The last thing he said? Ebert thinks about it for a few moments, and then his eyes go wide behind his glasses, and he looks out into space in case the answer is floating in the air somewhere. It isn't. He looks surprised that he can't remember. He knows the last words Studs Terkel's wife, Ida, muttered when she was wheeled into the operating room ("Louis, what have you gotten me into now?"), but Ebert doesn't know what his own last words were. He thinks he probably said goodbye to Chaz before one of his own trips into the operating room, perhaps when he had parts of his salivary glands taken out—but that can't be right. He was back on TV after that operation. Whenever it was, the moment wasn't cinematic. His last words weren't recorded. There was just his voice, and then there wasn't.

10   Now his hands do the talking. They are delicate, long-fingered, wrapped in skin as thin and translucent as silk. He wears his wedding ring on the middle finger of his left hand; he's lost so much weight since he and Chaz were married in 1992 that it won't stay where it belongs, especially now that his hands are so busy. There is almost always a pen in one and a spiral notebook or a pad of Post-it notes in the other—unless he's at home, in which case his fingers are feverishly banging the keys of his MacBook Pro.

11   He's also developed a kind of rudimentary sign language. If he passes a written note to someone and then opens and closes his fingers like a bird's beak, that means he would like them to read the note aloud for the other people in the room. If he touches his hand to his blue cardigan over his heart, that means he's either talking about something of great importance to him or he wants to make it clear that he's telling the truth. If he needs to get someone's attention and they're looking away from him or sitting with him in the dark, he'll clack on a hard surface with his nails, like he's tapping out Morse code. Sometimes—when he's outside wearing gloves, for instance—he'll be forced to draw letters with his finger on his palm. That's his last resort.

...

12   **Seven years ago,** he recovered quickly from the surgery to cut out his
cancerous thyroid and was soon back writing reviews for the *Chicago Sun-Times* and appearing with Richard Roeper on *At the Movies*. A year later, in
2003, he returned to work after his salivary glands were partially removed,
too, although that and a series of aggressive radiation treatments opened the
first cracks in his voice. In 2006, the cancer surfaced yet again, this time in
his jaw. A section of his lower jaw was removed; Ebert listened to Leonard
Cohen. Two weeks later, he was in his hospital room packing his bags, the
doctors and nurses paying one last visit, listening to a few last songs. That's
when his carotid artery, invisibly damaged by the earlier radiation and the
most recent jaw surgery, burst. Blood began pouring out of Ebert's mouth
and formed a great pool on the polished floor. The doctors and nurses leapt
up to stop the bleeding and barely saved his life. Had he made it out of his
hospital room and been on his way home—had his artery waited just a few
more songs to burst—Ebert would have bled to death on Lake Shore Drive.
Instead, following more surgery to stop a relentless bloodletting, he was left
without much of his mandible, his chin hanging loosely like a drawn curtain,
and behind his chin there was a hole the size of a plum. He also underwent a
tracheostomy, because there was still a risk that he could drown in his own
blood. When Ebert woke up and looked in the mirror in his hospital room, he
could see through his open mouth and the hole clear to the bandages that
had been wrapped around his neck to protect his exposed windpipe and his
new breathing tube. He could no longer eat or drink, and he had lost his voice
entirely. That was more than three years ago.

13   Ebert spent more than half of a thirty-month stretch in hospitals. His breathing
tube has been removed, but the hole in his throat remains open. He eats
through a G-tube—he's fed with a liquid paste, suspended in a bag from an
IV pole, through a tube in his stomach. He usually eats in what used to be
the library, on the brownstone's second floor. (It has five stories, including a
gym on the top floor and a theater—with a neon marquee—in the basement.)
A single bed with white sheets has been set up among the books, down a
hallway filled with Ebert's collection of Edward Lear watercolors. He shuffles
across the wooden floor between the library and his living room, where he
spends most of his time in a big black leather recliner, tipped back with his
feet up and his laptop on a wooden tray. There is a record player within reach.
The walls are white, to show off the art, which includes massive abstracts,
movie posters *(Casablanca, The Stranger)*, and aboriginal burial poles. Directly
in front of his chair is a black-and-white photograph of the Steak 'n Shake in
Champaign-Urbana, Illinois, one of his hometown hangouts.

14   He believes he's had three more surgeries since the removal of his lower
jaw; Chaz remembers four. Each time, however many times, surgeons carved
bone and tissue and skin from his back, arm, and legs and transplanted them
in an attempt to reconstruct his jaw and throat. Each time, he had one or two
weeks of hope and relief when he could eat a little and drink a little and talk
a little. Once, the surgery looked nearly perfect. ("Like a movie star," Chaz
remembers.) But each time, the reconstructive work fell apart and had to be
stripped out, the hole opened up again. It was as though the cancer were
continuing to eat away at him, even those parts of him that had been spared.

His right shoulder is visibly smaller than his left shoulder; his legs have been weakened and riddled with scars. After each attempt at reconstruction, he went to rehabilitation and physical therapy to fix the increasing damage done. (During one of those rehabilitation sessions, he fell and broke his hip.) He still can't sit upright for long or climb stairs. He's still figuring out how to use his legs.

…

15 **There are places where Ebert** exists as the Ebert he remembers. In 2008, when he was in the middle of his worst battles and wouldn't be able to make the trip to Champaign-Urbana for Ebertfest—really, his annual spring festival of films he just plain likes—he began writing an online journal. Reading it from its beginning is like watching an Aztec pyramid being built. At first, it's just a vessel for him to apologize to his fans for not being downstate. The original entries are short updates about his life and health and a few of his heart's wishes. Postcards and pebbles. They're followed by a smattering of Welcomes to Cyberspace. But slowly the journal picks up steam, as Ebert's strength and confidence and audience grow. *You are the readers I have dreamed of,* he writes. He is emboldened. He begins to write about more than movies; in fact, it sometimes seems as though he'd rather write about anything other than movies. The existence of an afterlife, the beauty of a full bookshelf, his liberalism and atheism and alcoholism, the health-care debate, Darwin, memories of departed friends and fights won and lost—more than five hundred thousand words of inner monologue have poured out of him, five hundred thousand words that probably wouldn't exist had he kept his other voice. Now some of his entries have thousands of comments, each of which he vets personally and to which he will often respond. It has become his life's work, building and maintaining this massive monument to written debate—argument is encouraged, so long as it's civil—and he spends several hours each night reclined in his chair, tending to his online oasis by lamplight. Out there, his voice is still his voice—not a reasonable facsimile of it, but his.

16 "It is saving me," he says through his speakers.

17 He calls up a journal entry to elaborate, because it's more efficient and time is precious:

18 *When I am writing my problems become invisible and I am the same person I always was. All is well. I am as I should be.*

19 He is a wonderful writer, and today he is producing the best work of his life. In 1975 he became the first film critic to win the Pulitzer prize, but his TV fame saw most of his fans, at least those outside Chicago, forget that he was a writer if they ever did know. (His Pulitzer still hangs in a frame in his book-lined office down the hall, behind a glass door that has THE EBERT COMPANY, LTD.: FINE FILM CRITICISM SINCE 1967 written on it in gold leaf.) Even for Ebert, a prolific author—he wrote long features on Paul Newman, Groucho Marx, and Hugh Hefner's daughter, among others, for this magazine in the late 1960s and early '70s and published dozens of books in addition to his reviews for the *Sun-Times*—the written word was eclipsed by the spoken word. He spent an entire day each week arguing with Gene Siskel and then Richard Roeper, and he became a regular on talk shows, and he shouted to crowds from red carpets. He lived his life through microphones.

20   But now everything he says must be written, either first on his laptop and funneled through speakers or, as he usually prefers, on some kind of paper. His new life is lived through Times New Roman and chicken scratch. So many words, so much writing—it's like a kind of explosion is taking place on the second floor of his brownstone. It's not the food or the drink he worries about anymore—*I went thru a period when I obsessed about root beer + Steak + Shake malts,* he writes on a blue Post-it note—but how many more words he can get out in the time he has left. In this living room, lined with thousands more books, words are the single most valuable thing in the world. They are gold bricks. Here idle chatter doesn't exist; that would be like lighting cigars with hundred-dollar bills. Here there are only sentences and paragraphs divided by section breaks. Every word has meaning.

21   Even the simplest expressions take on higher power here. Now his thumbs have become more than a trademark; they're an essential means for Ebert to communicate. He falls into a coughing fit, but he gives his thumbs-up, meaning he's okay. Thumbs-down would have meant he needed someone to call his full- time nurse, Millie, a spectral presence in the house.

22   Millie has premonitions. She sees ghosts. Sometimes she wakes in the night screaming—so vivid are her dreams.

23   Ebert's dreams are happier. *Never yet a dream where I can't talk,* he writes on another Post-it note, peeling it off the top of the blue stack. *Sometimes I discover—oh, I see! I CAN talk! I just forget to do it.*

24   In his dreams, his voice has never left. In his dreams, he can get out everything he didn't get out during his waking hours: the thoughts that get trapped in paperless corners, the jokes he wanted to tell, the nuanced stories he can't quite relate. In his dreams, he yells and chatters and whispers and exclaims. In his dreams, he's never had cancer. In his dreams, he is whole.

25   *These things come to us, they don't come from us,* he writes about his cancer, about sickness, on another Post-it note. *Dreams come from us.*

26   We have a habit of turning sentimental about celebrities who are struck down—Muhammad Ali, Christopher Reeve—transforming them into mystics; still, it's almost impossible to sit beside Roger Ebert, lifting blue Post-it notes from his silk fingertips, and not feel as though he's become something more than he was. He has those hands. And his wide and expressive eyes, despite everything, are almost always smiling.

27   *There is no need to pity me,* he writes on a scrap of paper one afternoon after someone parting looks at him a little sadly. *Look how happy I am.*

28   In fact, because he's missing sections of his jaw, and because he's lost some of the engineering behind his face, Ebert can't really do anything but smile. It really does take more muscles to frown, and he doesn't have those muscles anymore. His eyes will water and his face will go red—but if he opens his mouth, his bottom lip will sink most deeply in the middle, pulled down by the weight of his empty chin, and the corners of his upper lip will stay raised, frozen in place. Even when he's really angry, his open smile mutes it: The top

half of his face won't match the bottom half, but his smile is what most people will see first, and by instinct they will smile back. The only way Ebert can show someone he's mad is by writing in all caps on a Post-it note or turning up the volume on his speakers. Anger isn't as easy for him as it used to be. Now his anger rarely lasts long enough for him to write it down....

29 **His doctors would like to try** one more operation, would like one more chance to reclaim what cancer took from him, to restore his voice. Chaz would like him to try once more, too. But Ebert has refused. Even if the cancer comes back, he will probably decline significant intervention. The last surgery was his worst, and it did him more harm than good. Asked about the possibility of more surgery, he shakes his head and types before pressing the button.

30 "Over and out," the voice says.

31 Ebert is dying in increments, and he is aware of it.

32 *I know it is coming, and I do not fear it, because I believe there is nothing on the other side of death to fear, he writes in a journal entry titled "Go Gently into That Good Night." I hope to be spared as much pain as possible on the approach path. I was perfectly content before I was born, and I think of death as the same state. What I am grateful for is the gift of intelligence, and for life, love, wonder, and laughter. You can't say it wasn't interesting. My lifetime's memories are what I have brought home from the trip. I will require them for eternity no more than that little souvenir of the Eiffel Tower I brought home from Paris.*

33 There has been no death-row conversion. He has not found God. He has been beaten in some ways. But his other senses have picked up since he lost his sense of taste. He has tuned better into life. Some things aren't as important as they once were; some things are more important than ever. He has built for himself a new kind of universe. Roger Ebert is no mystic, but he knows things we don't know.

34 *I believe that if, at the end of it all, according to our abilities, we have done something to make others a little happier, and something to make ourselves a little happier, that is about the best we can do. To make others less happy is a crime. To make ourselves unhappy is where all crime starts. We must try to contribute joy to the world. That is true no matter what our problems, our health, our circumstances. We must try. I didn't always know this, and am happy I lived long enough to find it out.*

35 Ebert takes joy from the world in nearly all the ways he once did. He has had to find a new way to laugh—by closing his eyes and slapping both hands on his knees—but he still laughs. He and Chaz continue to travel. (They spent Thanksgiving in Barbados.) And he still finds joy in books, and in art, and in movies—a greater joy than he ever has. He gives more movies more stars.

36   But now it's getting late, which means he has his own work to do. Chaz heads off to bed. Millie, for the moment, hasn't been seized by night terrors, and the brownstone is quiet and nearly dark. Just the lamp is lit beside his chair. He leans back. He streams *Radio Caroline*—the formerly pirate radio station—and he begins to write. Everything fades out but the words. They appear quickly. Perfect sentences, artful sentences, illuminating sentences come out of him at a ridiculous, enviable pace, his fingers sometimes struggling to keep up.

37   Earlier today, his publisher sent him two copies of his newest book, the silver-jacketed *Great Movies III,* wrapped in plastic. Ebert turned them over in his hands, smiling with satisfaction—he wrote most of it in hospital beds—before he put them on a shelf in his office, by the desk he can no longer sit behind. They filled the last hole on the third shelf of his own published work; later this year, another book—*The Pot and How to Use It,* a collection of Ebert's rice-cooker recipes—will occupy the first space on a fourth shelf. Ebert's readers have asked him to write his autobiography next, but he looks up from his laptop and shrugs at the thought. He's already written a lot about himself on his journal, about his little childhood home in Champaign-Urbana and the days he spent on TV and in hospitals, and he would rather not say the same thing twice.

38   Besides, he has a review to finish. He returns his attention to his laptop, its glow making white squares in his glasses. Music plays. Words come.

39   *Pedro Almodóvar loves the movies with lust and abandon and the skill of an experienced lover. "Broken Embraces" is a voluptuary of a film, drunk on primary colors, caressing Penélope Cruz, using the devices of a Hitchcock to distract us with surfaces while the sinister uncoils beneath. As it ravished me, I longed for a freeze-frame to allow me to savor a shot.*

40   Ebert gives it four stars.

Read more: Roger Ebert Cancer Battle - Roger Ebert Interview - Esquire
http://www.esquire.com/features/roger-ebert-0310#ixzz2CW0YOtky

What Is a Life Worth?
To compensate families of the victims of Sept. 11, the government has invented a way to measure blood and loss in cash. A look at the wrenching calculus.

By Amanda Ripley

With reporting by Nadia Mustafa and Julie Rawe/New York and Karen Tumulty/Washington

Time, February 11, 2002

1   A train barreled over Joseph Hewins' body on a wintry evening in 1845 in the Massachusetts Berkshires. Hewins had spent the workday shoveling snow off the tracks, only to be killed on his trip back to town when a switchman got distracted. Hewins left behind a wife and three children, who were poor even before his death. His widow sued but lost at every level. Had the train merely chopped off Hewins' leg, the railroad would have paid. But in the perverse logic of that time, when a man died, he took his legal claims with him. And so the thinking went for most of the century, until something unheard of began to happen. The courts started to put a dollar value on a life—after death.

2   The concept of assigning a price tag to a life has always made people intensely squeamish. After all, isn't it degrading to presume that money can make a family whole again? And what of the disparities? Is a poor man's life worth less than a rich man's? Over the past 100 years, U.S. courts have crafted their answers to these questions. Forensic economists testify on the value of a life every day. They can even tell you the average valuation of an injured knee (about $200,000). But until now, the public at large has not had to reckon with the process and its imperfections. Until the terrorist attacks of Sept. 11 created a small city's worth of grieving families and the government established an unprecedented fund to compensate them, the mathematics of loss was a little-known science. Now the process is on garish display, and it is tempting to avert the eyes.

3   On the morning of Jan. 18 [2002], about 70 family members file into the rows of crimson seats at the Norwalk, Conn., city hall auditorium. They listen quietly to special master Kenneth Feinberg, whom the government has entrusted with dispersing its money to those most affected by the Sept. 11 tragedy. His first job is to persuade them to join the federal Victim Compensation Fund, the country's largest experiment in paying mass victims and their families without placing blame. The effort is being closely watched for the precedents it will set.

4   Much has been made of the enormous charity funds raised after the attacks. Donations to those groups do funnel thousands of dollars to the victims' families—in particular, the families of firefighters and police officers. But overall, the nearly $2 billion in charity money is chump change compared with the cash that will flow out of government coffers. There is no limit to the federal fund, but the tab is likely to be triple the size of the charity pot. And while charity funds are doled out to a vast pool of people, including businesses hurt by the attacks, the government money will go exclusively to the injured and to families of the deceased.

5   Feinberg, in a black-and-white polka dot tie, speaks in short, punchy sentences and a loud voice. He has already given the speech 32 times up and down the East Coast. The main thrust: The government, for the first time ever, has agreed to write large checks to victims' families without any litigation. The checks will arrive within four months after a claim is filed—no legal fees, no agonizing 10- year lawsuit. But every award will be based on a cold calculus, much the way courts handle wrongful-death claims.

6   That means different sums for different families. In a TIME/CNN poll taken last month, 86 percent said all families should receive the same amount. But that's not how it's going to work.

7   The calculus has several steps, Feinberg explains. First, the government will estimate how much a victim would have earned over his or her lifetime had the planes never crashed. That means a broker's family will qualify for a vastly higher award than a window washer's family. To estimate this amount, each family was handed an easy-to-read chart on the way into the meeting: Find your loved one's age and income and follow your finger to the magic number. Note that the lifetime earnings have been boosted by a flat $250,000 for "pain and suffering"—noneconomic losses, they are called. Tack on an extra $50,000 in pain and suffering for a spouse and for each child. The charts, while functional, are brutal, crystallizing how readily the legal system commodifies life.

8   Then—and this is crucial—don't get too excited. That first number may be quite high—in the millions for many. But you must, according to the rules of the fund, subtract all the money you are getting from other sources except charities. A court settlement would not be diminished this way, but this is not a court, Feinberg repeatedly points out. Deduct life insurance, pension, Social Security death benefits, and workers' compensation. Now you have the total award the government is offering you for your loss.

9   The deductions have the effect of equalizing the differences in the awards. Critics have called this Feinberg's "Robin Hood strategy." For many people in the room, the number is now at or close to zero. Feinberg says he will make sure no one gets zero. "Leave it to me," he says. But nowhere will that be written into the rules when they are finalized in mid-February. Likewise, many fiancés and gay partners will be at the mercy of Feinberg's discretion in seeking awards. Before finding out exactly what they will get—and the rules are complex—families will have to agree never to sue anyone for the attacks. "Normally, that would be a difficult call," says Feinberg. "Not here. The right to sue in this case is simply not a reasonable alternative."

10   That's because Congress has capped the liability of the airlines, the airport owners, the aircraft manufacturers, the towers' landlord, and the city of New York. In the name of the economy, the government severely restricted the victims' rights to sue—whether they join the fund or not. It is this lack of a viable option, even if they would not take it, that galls many families.

11   Congress created the fund as a safety net for the victims' families, to ensure that they maintain something resembling their current standard of living—whether they get assistance from private insurance or government money. The families see it as so much more. For the traumatized, the charts are like a Rorschach test. Some view the money as a halfhearted apology for the breakdown in security and intelligence that made the attacks possible. Others can't help seeing the award as a callous measure of their loved one's value. Many regard it as a substitute for the millions they think they may have got in court, had the liability not been capped. When the total comes out to be underwhelming, these families take it personally. There's a fundamental clash between the way they interpret the purpose of the fund and the way the government sees it.

12   After Feinberg speaks, he stands back and braces himself for an artillery of angry rhetorical questions. Gerry Sweeney, whose brother died in Tower 2, Floor 105, points at Feinberg and explains why $250,000 is not enough for pain and suffering in the case of her now fatherless nephew. "Have you ever seen a twelve-year-old have a nervous breakdown?" she asks. Another woman concocts an analogy to illustrate for Feinberg what it was like to talk to loved ones as they came to accept their imminent, violent deaths and to watch the towers collapse on live TV. "If your wife was brutally raped and murdered and you had to watch and listen to it happen, what would you think the right amount would be?" Finally, Maureen Halvorson, who lost her husband and her brother, speaks up from the front row in a quiet, bewildered voice. "I just can't accept the fact that the Federal Government is saying my husband and my brother are worth nothing." Feinberg is silent.

13   The more than 3,000 victims of the Sept. 11 attacks are frozen in snapshots, wide-smiling men and women in crisp suits and uniforms who liked to build birdhouses on weekends and play practical jokes. In the literature of grief, they have become hardworking innocents, heroes, and saints. But those they left behind are decidedly human. Some compete with others for most bereaved status; others demand an apology even when no one is listening. Some are popping pills, and others cannot leave the house. Most days, they are inconsolable. And as the rest of the country begins to ease back into normalcy, these families stand, indignant, in the way.

14   Already, some Americans have lost patience with them. "My tax money should not be given to someone with a $750,000 mortgage to pay who needs a set of fresh, matching towels in her bathroom every season," one person wrote anonymously to the Department of Justice's Web page on victim compensation. "I'm shocked and appalled and very disappointed," wrote a Florida resident, "that some individuals are living in such a rare and well- gilded ivory tower that they feel $250,000 is not sufficient compensation. Most of us, the working people of America, make $20,000 to $40,000 per year. Where do these wealthy, spoiled, greedy folks in New York get off, pretending that what happened to them was so uniquely horrible? I'm over it. Yeah, it was unique. Yeah, it was horrible. Yeah, I sent money to help. And after reading about them suing for more money, I begin to regret it."

15   It's true that some families' behavior has been less than dignified. The divorced parents of a woman killed in the Pentagon, who are eligible for money because their daughter left no dependents, have filed competing claims. Lawyers are now involved. Says her father: "I guarantee she loved her daddy as much as she loved her mom. I feel that I'm entitled to something."

16   And it's also a fact that these families will get more money from charities and the government combined than anyone has so far received after the Oklahoma City bombing or the 1998 bombing of the Nairobi embassy. For that matter, if these victims had been killed in a drive-by shooting, they probably would not have received more than a few thousand dollars from state victim-compensation funds.

17   That fact is not lost on the public, particularly people whose relatives have died in everyday tragedies. At the Wichita Eagle in Kansas, editorial-page director Phil Brownlee has received calls and letters from locals disgusted by the families' complaints, and he agrees. "It's just frustrating that the goodwill demonstrated by the government seems to be deteriorating," he says. "Now you've got families who are upset with what most Americans deem to be generous contributions. It's the loss of the spirit of Sept. 11, the souring of that sense of solidarity."

18   But it may not be fair to compare Sept. 11 with a street crime or even Oklahoma City. After all, these recent attacks involved an orchestrated, simultaneous security breach on four airplanes, carried out by 19 men who had been living and training on our soil. A better comparison might be past international terrorist attacks and plane crashes. Those that have been resolved—and that's a major distinction—do show higher payouts than the average amount likely to come out of the Sept. 11 federal fund.

19   In 25 major aviation accidents between 1970 and 1984, the average compensation for victims who went to trial was $1 million in current dollars, according to a Rand Corp. analysis. Average compensation for cases settled without a lawsuit was $415,000. The biggest aviation payout in history followed the crash of Pan Am Flight 103 over Lockerbie, Scotland, in 1988. Settlements ranged all over the spectrum, with a couple dozen exceeding $10 million, according to Manhattan attorney Lee Kreindler, who acted as lead counsel. Dividing the total $500 million payout over the 270 victims yields an average award of $1.85 million. However, the families had to hand about a third of their awards to their lawyers, and they waited seven to eight years to see any money. And the families of the six people killed in the 1993 World Trade Center bombing are still waiting for their day in civil court.

20   In the end, most families will probably choose the fund over litigation. The Lockerbie millions are simply not a realistic possibility. It is always extremely difficult to sue the government. And the liability for the Sept. 11 attacks was capped by Congress at about $1.5 billion per plane. So while the families of those killed in the Pennsylvania and Pentagon crashes may have enough to go around, there are far too many victims in New York. "The court model works perfectly when you don't have $50 billion in damages or 3,000 deaths," says Leo Boyle, a Boston lawyer and president of the Association of Trial Lawyers of America, which supports the fund option and has lined up more than 2,000 attorneys to offer free help navigating its rules. Even without the caps, Boyle insists, victims could not have extracted more money by putting United and American Airlines through bankruptcy. So far, only a handful of suits have been filed.

21   In any event, there was no talking Congress out of the liability caps when it drafted the airline-bailout package 10 days after the attacks. The airlines could not fly without insurance, and their coverage was far short of what it would take to pay the damages. Federal Reserve Chairman Alan Greenspan privately told congressional leaders that getting the planes up again was the single biggest "multiplier" that could revive the economy on every level. So the Democrats, who usually balk at limiting the ability to sue, accepted the idea of an airline bailout—as long as it came with a mechanism to compensate victims. Oklahoma Senator Don Nickles, the No. 2 Republican in the Senate and a longtime proponent of tort reform, pushed hard to limit how much the victims' families could claim, but he did not prevail.

22   But once the interim rules were drawn up by Feinberg's office—in conjunction with the Department of Justice and the Office of Management and Budget—there were some surprises. In particular, the figures for pain and suffering astonished some who had backed the fund. "The numbers are low by any measure," says Boyle. Feinberg says he chose the $250,000 figure because that's how much beneficiaries receive from the Federal Government when firefighters and police die on the job. The additional $50,000 for the spouse and each child is, he admits, "just some rough approximation of what I thought was fair." He calls the fund "rough justice."

23   The American Tort Reform Association, backed mostly by Republicans, has been lobbying since 1986 to limit noneconomic damages in some suits to $250,000. John Ashcroft, head of the Justice Department, pushed for such a cap on punitive damages when he was a senator. But Feinberg, a Democrat, insists he was not pressured by the administration to keep the numbers low.

24   No matter how many times tearful widows accuse him of protecting the airlines, Feinberg does not blush. A lawyer with decades of experience in the messy art of compromise (Feinberg was special master for the $180 million distributed to veterans exposed to Agent Orange), he is accustomed to rage. "On Tuesday I get whacked for this or that in New Jersey. The next day it's New York. It goes with the job." But he rejects the theory that greed is a factor. "People have had a loved one wrenched from them suddenly, without warning, and we are only five months beyond that disaster. It was nearly yesterday. And they are desperately seeking, from what I've seen, to place as much of a value on that lost loved one as they can. So here is where they seek to amplify the value of that memory. They do it by saying we want more, as a validation of the loss. That's not greed. That's human nature."

25   Susan and Harvey Blomberg of Fairfield County, Conn., have been to three
      meetings on the victim-compensation fund, even though, as parents of a victim
      who has left a wife and kids behind, they are not in line for compensation. The
      rules give preference to the victim's spouse and children. But the Blombergs
      come to these meetings to be part of something, to be counted. And they
      linger after everyone else has left. "My daughter-in-law was upset when we
      went to the meetings," Susan says. "She said, 'It's not really about you. It's
      about the widows and children.' And I said, 'I want more information.' You
      can't compare grief, because nobody can get inside you. But I feel like an
      orphan. When they did this formula, why didn't they consider the parents? My
      daughter-in-law was married for five years. We had Jonathan for 33 years."

26   "It's a horrible thing that this is where our energies need to be pulled,"
      says Cheri Sparacio, 37, the widow of Thomas Sparacio, a currency trader at
      Euro Brokers who died in Tower 2. In their modest house in Staten Island,
      littered with the toys of her twin two-year-olds, she explains why she sees
      the estimated $138,000 she would get from the fund as a cheap bribe. "The
      government is not taking any responsibility for what it's done. This was just
      one screw-up after another." She is also worried about her financial stability;
      in less than a month, she will have their third child. Thomas was the primary
      wage earner, although Cheri worked as a part-time school psychologist until
      Sept. 11. She doesn't see how she can go back to work with an infant and two
      toddlers unless she hires full-time help. "Please, come step into my shoes for
      a minute," she says, her eyes flat and unblinking. "I am not looking to go to
      Tahiti."

27   But uptown in the apartment where Samuel Fields once lived, the fund acts
      like a quiet equalizer, a way for the government to guarantee that victims with
      less insurance emerge with basic support. Fields was a security guard for
      six years in Tower 1. He made $22,000 a year and lived with his family in a
      housing project in Harlem. On Sept. 11, he helped people evacuate the building
      and then went back inside to help some more. Fields never came home. Next
      month his widow Angela will give birth to their fifth child. Because Fields made
      a small salary, his family's preliminary award is less than Sparacio's. But his
      family's deductions are also smaller. In the end, Angela's estimated $444,010
      award will probably be three times the size of Cheri's.

28   In valuing different lives differently—the first part of the equation—the fund
      follows common legal practice. Courts always grant money on the basis of a
      person's earning power in life. That's because the courts are not attempting to
      replace "souls," says Philip Bobbitt, a law professor at the University of Texas
      who has written about the allocation of scarce resources in times of tragedy.
      "We're not trying to make you psychologically whole. Where we can calculate
      the loss is in economic loss." The Feinberg plan differs from legal norms in
      deducting the value of life insurance and pensions. Also, it allows no flexibility
      in determining noneconomic damages. In court, pain and suffering would be
      weighed individually.

29   Money aside, a lawsuit can be an investigative device like no other, forcing answers about what led to a death. Some Sept. 11 families say they might file suit for that reason alone, even if they never get a dime. And for other families, there is enormous value in no lawsuits at all. David Gordenstein lost his wife, Lisa Fenn Gordenstein, on American Flight 11. "Am I sad? I've had my heart torn out," he says. But he would rather devote his life to raising his two young daughters than pursuing a lawsuit. He will probably file a claim with the federal fund, which he acknowledges is not perfect. "I am proud of what my country tried to do. I think the intention is noble."

30   The night before Lisa died, she slipped a clipping under the door of David's home office, something she often did. It was a saying from theologian Charles Swindoll that read, "Attitude, to me, is more important than facts. It is more important than the past, than education, than money, than circumstances, than failures, than successes, than what other people think or say or do...It will make or break a company, a church, a home." David read it at her memorial. And while he jokes that it's kind of clichéd—"typical Lisa"—he says he thinks its message might help carry his family through this.

Human Life Value Calculator

Life Insurance

| Life Insurance | Health Insurance | Disability Insurance | Long-Term Care Insurance | Small Business Planning | Find an Agent |

Who needs it?
What are the different types?
How much do I need?
  Human life value calculator
  Insurance needs calculator
What to know when buying?
Where do I buy it?
Life events
Printable consumer guide
Glossary
realLIFEstories

HOW MUCH DO I NEED?
Human life value calculator

The human life value calculator has been designed to help you assess your financial value to those you love by estimating the future financial contributions you will make to your family ... or, more starkly, the financial loss that your family would incur if you were to die today. For the purposes of this calculator, a human life only has economic value in its relation to other lives, specifically a spouse or dependent children. Therefore, if you have neither, the calculator will not generate a result.

Please note, this calculator will provide only a rough sense of your human life value, which can be a factor in determining the amount of insurance you should have in your financial portfolio. Typically, the amount of life insurance someone needs is less than his or her human life value due to the availability of other sources of income (e.g., existing life insurance coverage, Social Security benefits, etc.). For an analysis of your life insurance needs, please visit the Life Insurance Needs Calculator or contact a professional agent or advisor in your area.

This calculator projects typical lifetime income for someone with the characteristics you provide in the input section, less taxes and expenditures devoted to your own consumption, plus any fringe benefits your family receives from your employer, such as health insurance, and the services you provide around the house. The resulting estimate is an approximate measure of your net financial contribution to your family - your human life value.

This human life value calculator should not be viewed as a comprehensive assessment. For example, you will notice that it does not account for the specific occupation and education of you or your spouse. Also, to simplify your responses, only general information is sought regarding your non-wage income, which impacts both your consumption and your income taxes. Furthermore, the dollar value of your fringe benefits is assumed to be equal to the average for someone of your income and family situation. Nevertheless, we believe that, given the limited information the calculator is using, it is the best estimate available. Click here for more information on the assumptions used to generate these estimates.

Enter only numbers or letters, no commas or dollar signs.

1. Your age at nearest birthday:
20

2. Sex:
Female ▾

3. Your planned retirement age (e.g., 65):
65

4. Major occupation category: 6 ▾
  1. Executive, Administrative, and Managerial
    -(e.g., Chief Executives, Managers, Accountants, Marketers, Buyers)
  2. Professional Specialty
    -(e.g., Engineers, Scientists, Teachers, Lawyers, Doctors, Nurses, Artists)
  3. Technicians, Computer Programmers, and Related Support
    -(e.g., Electrical, Mechanical and Health Technicians)

4. Sales
   -(e.g., Real Estate, Insurance, Retail and Personal Services)

5. Administrative Support, Including Clerical Support

6. Service and Public Safety
   -(e.g., Food, Health and Cleaning Services, Police, Firefighters, and Security)

7. Farming, Forestry, Fishing

8. Craft, Repair, Skilled Laborers
   -(e.g., Mechanics, Construction Workers, Textile and Food Production, Inspectors)

9. Operators, Fabricators, Laborers
   -(e.g., Machine Operators, Motor Vehicle Operators, Assembler, Rail Transportaion)

5. Your annual wage earnings before taxes:

18000

6. Does your employer provide fringe benefits?

Yes ▾

7. Do you have a spouse?

No ▾

If yes, then:
Age of spouse:

Is spouse employed?

No ▾

Spouse's planned retirement age (e.g., 65):

Spouse's annual wage earnings before taxes:

8. Annual non-wage earnings (e.g. investment or rental income)

0

9. Ages of children under 23:

2 ▾   -- ▾   -- ▾   -- ▾   -- ▾
-- ▾   -- ▾   -- ▾   -- ▾   -- ▾

Analysis | Clear Form

Return to calculator input

Back to Top

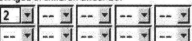
LIFE AND HEALTH INSURANCE FOUNDATION FOR EDUCATION   2175 K STREET, NW, SUITE 250   WASHINGTON, DC 20037-1809   202-464-5000

Your estimated human life value - the value today of your future contributions to your household - **$661,219** or about **37** times your current annual income. If you were to die today, this amount is roughly what your family would need to maintain the same standard of living they will enjoy over the course of your anticipated working life. The graphs below provide a step-by-step overview of how your approximate human life value has been estimated.

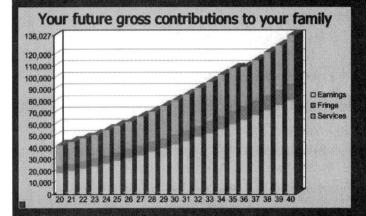

Your future gross contributions to your family

Services	$ 379,412
Fringe	114,762
Earnings	547,498
Total:	$ 1,041,672

This graph shows projections of your annual earnings, fringe benefits and household services for each future year. These projections were based on the information you provided, along with data from the U.S. Census, the professional economics literature, the U.S. Chamber of Commerce and various research universities.

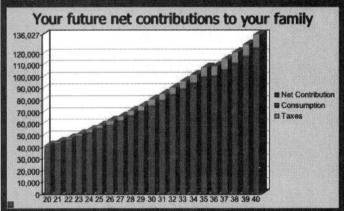

Your future net contributions to your family

Services	$ 379,412
Fringe	114,762
Earnings	547,498
Total:	$ 1,041,672
Taxes	- 63,233
Consumption	- 317,220
Net Contribution	$ 661,219

This graph shows projections of your consumption and income taxes. They were derived using information from the United States Bureau of Labor Statistics and the Internal Revenue Service. When your consumption and taxes are subtracted from the sum total of your earnings, fringe benefits and services, the result is the net financial contribution you are likely to make to your family in each and every year. This net contribution is also shown in the graph.

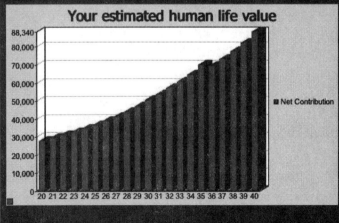

Your estimated human life value

Present Value of Your Human Life Value = $661,219

This final graph isolates the net contributions illustrated in the graph above. They comprise your human life value. The dollar value listed above is the amount of money that would need to be invested today - in a risk-free investment - to replace this human life value in the event of your death. Said another way, it is the amount necessary today to provide the same standard of living to your family that you would have provided had you lived.

Modify Input

What Is the Value of a Human Life?

By Kenneth Feinberg

May 25, 2008

Washington attorney Kenneth Feinberg specializes in alternative dispute resolution. He managed the compensation funds for the Sept. 11, 2001, attacks and Virginia Tech shootings, and he has worked with victims of human radiation experiments and Holocaust slave labor.

1   What is an individual life worth? Do our lives have equal value? Struggling with these questions led me to my belief.

2   After Sept. 11, I confronted the challenge of placing a value on human life by calculating different amounts of compensation for each and every victim. The law required that I give more money to the stockbroker, the bond trader and the banker than to the waiter, the policeman, the fireman and the soldier at the Pentagon. This is what happens every day in courtrooms throughout our nation. Our system of justice has always been based upon this idea—that compensation for death should be directly related to the financial circumstances of each victim.

3   But as I met with the 9/11 families and wrestled with issues surrounding the valuation of lives lost, I began to question this basic premise of our legal system. Trained in the law, I had always accepted that no two lives were worth the same in financial terms. But now I found the law in conflict with my growing belief in the equality of all life. "Mr. Feinberg, my husband was a fireman and died a hero at the World Trade Center. Why are you giving me less money than the banker who represented Enron? Why are you demeaning the memory of my husband?"

4   My response was defensive and unconvincing. At first I gave the standard legal argument—that I was not evaluating the intrinsic moral worth of any individual. I was basing my decision on the law, just as juries did every day. But this explanation fell on deaf ears. Grieving families couldn't hear it. And I didn't believe it myself.

5   I was engaged in a personal struggle. I felt it would make more sense for Congress to provide the same amount of public compensation to each and every victim—to declare, in effect, that all lives are equal. But in this case, the law prevailed.

6   Last year, however, in the wake of the Virginia Tech shootings and the deaths of 32 victims, I was again asked to design and administer a compensation system, this one privately funded. And I realized that Feinberg the citizen should trump Feinberg the lawyer. My legal training would no longer stand in the way. This time all victims—students and faculty alike—would receive the same compensation.

7   In the case of Sept. 11, if there is a next time, and Congress again decides to award public compensation, I hope the law will declare that all life should be treated the same. Courtrooms, judges, lawyers and juries are not the answer when it comes to public compensation. I have resolved my personal conflict and have learned a valuable lesson at the same time. I believe that public compensation should avoid financial distinctions which only fuel the hurt and grief of the survivors. I believe all lives should be treated the same.

Independently produced for *Weekend Edition Sunday* by Jay Allison and Dan Gediman with John Gregory and Viki Merrick.

'You've got to find what you love,' Jobs says

This is a prepared text of the Commencement address delivered by Steve Jobs, CEO of Apple Computer and of Pixar Animation Studios, on June 12, 2005.

Stanford Report, June 14, 2005

1   I am honored to be with you today at your commencement from one of the finest universities in the world. I never graduated from college. Truth be told, this is the closest I've ever gotten to a college graduation. Today I want to tell you three stories from my life. That's it. No big deal. Just three stories.

2   The first story is about connecting the dots.

3   I dropped out of Reed College after the first 6 months, but then stayed around as a drop-in for another 18 months or so before I really quit. So why did I drop out?

4   It started before I was born. My biological mother was a young, unwed college graduate student, and she decided to put me up for adoption. She felt very strongly that I should be adopted by college graduates, so everything was all set for me to be adopted at birth by a lawyer and his wife. Except that when I popped out they decided at the last minute that they really wanted a girl. So my parents, who were on a waiting list, got a call in the middle of the night asking: "We have an unexpected baby boy; do you want him?" They said: "Of course." My biological mother later found out that my mother had never graduated from college and that my father had never graduated from high school. She refused to sign the final adoption papers. She only relented a few months later when my parents promised that I would someday go to college.

5   And 17 years later I did go to college. But I naively chose a college that was almost as expensive as Stanford, and all of my working-class parents' savings were being spent on my college tuition. After six months, I couldn't see the value in it. I had no idea what I wanted to do with my life and no idea how college was going to help me figure it out. And here I was spending all of the money my parents had saved their entire life. So I decided to drop out and trust that it would all work out OK. It was pretty scary at the time, but looking back it was one of the best decisions I ever made. The minute I dropped out I could stop taking the required classes that didn't interest me, and begin dropping in on the ones that looked interesting.

6   It wasn't all romantic. I didn't have a dorm room, so I slept on the floor in friends' rooms, I returned coke bottles for the 5¢ deposits to buy food with, and I would walk the 7 miles across town every Sunday night to get one good meal a week at the Hare Krishna temple. I loved it. And much of what I stumbled into by following my curiosity and intuition turned out to be priceless later on. Let me give you one example:

7   Reed College at that time offered perhaps the best calligraphy instruction in the country. Throughout the campus every poster, every label on every drawer, was beautifully hand calligraphed. Because I had dropped out and didn't have to take the normal classes, I decided to take a calligraphy class to learn how to do this. I learned about serif and san serif typefaces, about varying the amount of space between different letter combinations, about what makes great typography great. It was beautiful, historical, artistically subtle in a way that science can't capture, and I found it fascinating.

8   None of this had even a hope of any practical application in my life. But ten years later, when we were designing the first Macintosh computer, it all came back to me. And we designed it all into the Mac. It was the first computer with beautiful typography. If I had never dropped in on that single course in college, the Mac would have never had multiple typefaces or proportionally spaced fonts. And since Windows just copied the Mac, it's likely that no personal computer would have them. If I had never dropped out, I would have never dropped in on this calligraphy class, and personal computers might not have the wonderful typography that they do. Of course it was impossible to connect the dots looking forward when I was in college. But it was very, very clear looking backwards ten years later.

9   Again, you can't connect the dots looking forward; you can only connect them looking backwards. So you have to trust that the dots will somehow connect in your future. You have to trust in something—your gut, destiny, life, karma, whatever. This approach has never let me down, and it has made all the difference in my life.

10   My second story is about love and loss.

11   I was lucky—I found what I loved to do early in life. Woz and I started Apple in my parents garage when I was 20. We worked hard, and in 10 years Apple had grown from just the two of us in a garage into a $2 billion company with over 4000 employees. We had just released our finest creation—the Macintosh—a year earlier, and I had just turned 30. And then I got fired. How can you get fired from a company you started? Well, as Apple grew we hired someone who I thought was very talented to run the company with me, and for the first year or so things went well. But then our visions of the future began to diverge and eventually we had a falling out. When we did, our Board of Directors sided with him. So at 30 I was out. And very publicly out. What had been the focus of my entire adult life was gone, and it was devastating.

12   I really didn't know what to do for a few months. I felt that I had let the previous generation of entrepreneurs down - that I had dropped the baton as it was being passed to me. I met with David Packard and Bob Noyce and tried to apologize for screwing up so badly. I was a very public failure, and I even thought about running away from the valley. But something slowly began to dawn on me—I still loved what I did. The turn of events at Apple had not changed that one bit. I had been rejected, but I was still in love. And so I decided to start over.

13   I didn't see it then, but it turned out that getting fired from Apple was the best thing that could have ever happened to me. The heaviness of being successful was replaced by the lightness of being a beginner again, less sure about everything. It freed me to enter one of the most creative periods of my life.

14   During the next five years, I started a company named NeXT, another company named Pixar, and fell in love with an amazing woman who would become my wife. Pixar went on to create the worlds first computer animated feature film, Toy Story, and is now the most successful animation studio in the world. In a remarkable turn of events, Apple bought NeXT, I returned to Apple, and the technology we developed at NeXT is at the heart of Apple's current renaissance. And Laurene and I have a wonderful family together.

15   I'm pretty sure none of this would have happened if I hadn't been fired from Apple. It was awful tasting medicine, but I guess the patient needed it. Sometimes life hits you in the head with a brick. Don't lose faith. I'm convinced that the only thing that kept me going was that I loved what I did. You've got to find what you love. And that is as true for your work as it is for your lovers. Your work is going to fill a large part of your life, and the only way to be truly satisfied is to do what you believe is great work. And the only way to do great work is to love what you do. If you haven't found it yet, keep looking. Don't settle. As with all matters of the heart, you'll know when you find it. And, like any great relationship, it just gets better and better as the years roll on. So keep looking until you find it. Don't settle.

16   My third story is about death.

17   When I was 17, I read a quote that went something like: "If you live each day as if it was your last, someday you'll most certainly be right." It made an impression on me, and since then, for the past 33 years, I have looked in the mirror every morning and asked myself: "If today were the last day of my life, would I want to do what I am about to do today?" And whenever the answer has been "No" for too many days in a row, I know I need to change something.

18   Remembering that I'll be dead soon is the most important tool I've ever encountered to help me make the big choices in life. Because almost everything—all external expectations, all pride, all fear of embarrassment or failure—these things just fall away in the face of death, leaving only what is truly important. Remembering that you are going to die is the best way I know to avoid the trap of thinking you have something to lose. You are already naked. There is no reason not to follow your heart.

19   About a year ago I was diagnosed with cancer. I had a scan at 7:30 in the morning, and it clearly showed a tumor on my pancreas. I didn't even know what a pancreas was. The doctors told me this was almost certainly a type of cancer that is incurable, and that I should expect to live no longer than three to six months. My doctor advised me to go home and get my affairs in order, which is doctor's code for prepare to die. It means to try to tell your kids everything you thought you'd have the next 10 years to tell them in just a few months. It means to make sure everything is buttoned up so that it will be as easy as possible for your family. It means to say your goodbyes.

20   I lived with that diagnosis all day. Later that evening I had a biopsy, where they stuck an endoscope down my throat, through my stomach and into my intestines, put a needle into my pancreas and got a few cells from the tumor. I was sedated, but my wife, who was there, told me that when they viewed the cells under a microscope the doctors started crying because it turned out to be a very rare form of pancreatic cancer that is curable with surgery. I had the surgery and I'm fine now.

21   This was the closest I've been to facing death, and I hope it's the closest I get for a few more decades. Having lived through it, I can now say this to you with a bit more certainty than when death was a useful but purely intellectual concept:

22   No one wants to die. Even people who want to go to heaven don't want to die to get there. And yet death is the destination we all share. No one has ever escaped it. And that is as it should be, because Death is very likely the single best invention of Life. It is Life's change agent. It clears out the old to make way for the new. Right now the new is you, but someday not too long from now, you will gradually become the old and be cleared away. Sorry to be so dramatic, but it is quite true.

23   Your time is limited, so don't waste it living someone else's life. Don't be trapped by dogma—which is living with the results of other people's thinking. Don't let the noise of others' opinions drown out your own inner voice. And most important, have the courage to follow your heart and intuition. They somehow already know what you truly want to become. Everything else is secondary.

24   When I was young, there was an amazing publication called *The Whole Earth Catalog,* which was one of the bibles of my generation. It was created by a fellow named Stewart Brand not far from here in Menlo Park, and he brought it to life with his poetic touch. This was in the late 1960's, before personal computers and desktop publishing, so it was all made with typewriters, scissors, and polaroid cameras. It was sort of like Google in paperback form, 35 years before Google came along: it was idealistic, and overflowing with neat tools and great notions.

25   Stewart and his team put out several issues of *The Whole Earth Catalog,* and then when it had run its course, they put out a final issue. It was the mid-1970s, and I was your age. On the back cover of their final issue was a photograph of an early morning country road, the kind you might find yourself hitchhiking on if you were so adventurous. Beneath it were the words: "Stay Hungry. Stay Foolish." It was their farewell message as they signed off. Stay Hungry. Stay Foolish. And I have always wished that for myself. And now, as you graduate to begin anew, I wish that for you.

26   Stay Hungry. Stay Foolish.

27   Thank you all very much.

Good Food/Bad Food

Bad Food? Tax It, and Subsidize Vegetables

By Mark Bittman
New York Times, July 23, 2011

1   What will it take to get Americans to change our eating habits? The need
     is indisputable, since heart disease, diabetes and cancer are all in large part
     caused by the Standard American Diet. (Yes, it's SAD.)

2   Though experts increasingly recommend a diet high in plants and low in
     animal products and processed foods, ours is quite the opposite, and there's
     little disagreement that changing it could improve our health and save tens of
     millions of lives.

3   And—not inconsequential during the current struggle over deficits and
     spending—a sane diet could save tens if not hundreds of billions of dollars in
     health care costs.

4   Yet the food industry appears incapable of marketing healthier foods. And
     whether its leaders are confused or just stalling doesn't matter, because the
     fixes are not really their problem. Their mission is not public health but profit,
     so they'll continue to sell the health-damaging food that's most profitable, until
     the market or another force skews things otherwise. That "other force" should
     be the federal government, fulfilling its role as an agent of the public good and
     establishing a bold national fix.

5   Rather than subsidizing the production of unhealthful foods, we should turn the
     tables and tax things like soda, French fries, doughnuts and hyperprocessed
     snacks. The resulting income should be earmarked for a program that
     encourages a sound diet for Americans by making healthy food more
     affordable and widely available.

6   The average American consumes 44.7 gallons of soft drinks annually. (Although
     that includes diet sodas, it does not include noncarbonated sweetened
     beverages, which add up to at least 17 gallons a person per year.) Sweetened
     drinks could be taxed at 2 cents per ounce, so a six-pack of Pepsi would cost
     $1.44 more than it does now. An equivalent tax on fries might be 50 cents per
     serving; a quarter extra for a doughnut. (We have experts who can figure out
     how "bad" a food should be to qualify, and what the rate should be; right now
     they're busy calculating ethanol subsidies. Diet sodas would not be taxed.)

7   Simply put: taxes would reduce consumption of unhealthful foods and
     generate billions of dollars annually. That money could be used to subsidize the
     purchase of staple foods like seasonal greens, vegetables, whole grains, dried
     legumes and fruit.

8   We could sell those staples cheap—let's say for 50 cents a pound—and
     almost everywhere: drugstores, street corners, convenience stores, bodegas,
     supermarkets, liquor stores, even schools, libraries and other community
     centers.

9   This program would, of course, upset the processed food industry. Oh well. It would also bug those who might resent paying more for soda and chips and argue that their right to eat whatever they wanted was being breached. But public health is the role of the government, and our diet is right up there with any other public responsibility you can name, from water treatment to mass transit.

10   Some advocates for the poor say taxes like these are unfair because low-income people pay a higher percentage of their income for food and would find it more difficult to buy soda or junk. But since poor people suffer disproportionately from the cost of high-quality, fresh foods, subsidizing those foods would be particularly beneficial to them.

11   Right now it's harder for many people to buy fruit than Froot Loops; chips and Coke are a common breakfast. And since the rate of diabetes continues to soar—one-third of all Americans either have diabetes or are pre-diabetic, most with Type 2 diabetes, the kind associated with bad eating habits—and because our health care bills are on the verge of becoming truly insurmountable, this is urgent for economic sanity as well as national health.

Justifying a Tax

12   At least 30 cities and states have considered taxes on soda or all sugar-sweetened beverages, and they're a logical target: of the 278 additional calories Americans on average consumed per day between 1977 and 2001, more than 40 percent came from soda, "fruit" drinks, mixes like Kool-Aid and Crystal Light, and beverages like Red Bull, Gatorade and dubious offerings like Vitamin Water, which contains half as much sugar as Coke.

13   Some states already have taxes on soda—mostly low, ineffective sales taxes paid at the register. The current talk is of excise taxes, levied before purchase.

14   "Excise taxes have the benefit of being incorporated into the shelf price, and that's where consumers make their purchasing decisions," says Lisa Powell, a senior research scientist at the Institute for Health Research and Policy at the University of Illinois at Chicago. "And, as per-unit taxes, they avoid volume discounts and are ultimately more effective in raising prices, so they have greater impact."

15   Much of the research on beverage taxes comes from the Rudd Center for Food Policy and Obesity at Yale. Its projections indicate that taxes become significant at the equivalent of about a penny an ounce, a level at which three very good things should begin to happen: the consumption of sugar-sweetened beverages should decrease, as should the incidence of disease and therefore public health costs; and money could be raised for other uses.

16   Even in the current antitax climate, we'll probably see new, significant soda taxes soon, somewhere; Philadelphia, New York (city and state) and San Francisco all considered them last year, and the scenario for such a tax spreading could be similar to that of legalized gambling: once the income stream becomes apparent, it will seem irresistible to cash-strapped governments.

17   Currently, instead of taxing sodas and other unhealthful food, we subsidize them (with, I might note, tax dollars!). Direct subsidies to farmers for crops like corn (used, for example, to make now-ubiquitous high-fructose corn syrup) and soybeans (vegetable oil) keep the prices of many unhealthful foods and beverages artificially low. There are indirect subsidies as well, because prices of junk foods don't reflect the costs of repairing our health and the environment.

18   Other countries are considering or have already started programs to tax foods with negative effects on health. Denmark's saturated-fat tax is going into effect Oct. 1, and Romania passed (and then un-passed) something similar; earlier this month, a French minister raised the idea of tripling the value added tax on soda. Meanwhile, Hungary is proposing a new tax on foods with "too much" sugar, salt or fat, while increasing taxes on liquor and soft drinks, all to pay for state-financed health care; and Brazil's Fome Zero (Zero Hunger) program features subsidized produce markets and state-sponsored low-cost restaurants.

19   Putting all of those elements together could create a national program that would make progress on a half-dozen problems at once—disease, budget, health care, environment, food access and more—while paying for itself. The benefits are staggering, and though it would take a level of political will that's rarely seen, it's hardly a moonshot.

20   The need is dire: efforts to shift the national diet have failed, because education alone is no match for marketing dollars that push the very foods that are the worst for us. (The fast-food industry alone spent more than $4 billion on marketing in 2009; the Department of Agriculture's Center for Nutrition Policy and Promotion is asking for about a third of a percent of that in 2012: $13 million.) As a result, the percentage of obese adults has more than doubled over the last 30 years; the percentage of obese children has tripled. We eat nearly 10 percent more animal products than we did a generation or two ago, and though there may be value in eating at least some animal products, we could perhaps live with reduced consumption of triple bacon cheeseburgers.

Government and Public Health

21   Health-related obesity costs are projected to reach $344 billion by 2018— with roughly 60 percent of that cost borne by the federal government. For a precedent in attacking this problem, look at the action government took in the case of tobacco.

22   The historic 1998 tobacco settlement, in which the states settled health-related lawsuits against tobacco companies, and the companies agreed to curtail marketing and finance antismoking efforts, was far from perfect, but consider the results. More than half of all Americans who once smoked have quit and smoking rates are about half of what they were in the 1960s.

23   It's true that you don't need to smoke and you do need to eat. But you don't need sugary beverages (or the associated fries), which have been linked not only to Type 2 diabetes and increased obesity but also to cardiovascular diseases and decreased intake of valuable nutrients like calcium. It also appears that liquid calories provide less feeling of fullness; in other words, when you drink a soda it's probably in addition to your other calorie intake, not instead of it.

24   To counter arguments about their nutritional worthlessness, expect to see "fortified" sodas—à la Red Bull, whose vitamins allegedly "support mental and physical performance"—and "improved" junk foods (Less Sugar! Higher Fiber!). Indeed, there may be reasons to make nutritionally worthless foods less so, but it's better to decrease their consumption.

25   Forcing sales of junk food down through taxes isn't ideal. First off, we'll have to listen to nanny-state arguments, which can be countered by the acceptance of the anti-tobacco movement as well as a dozen other successful public health measures. Then there are the predictions of job loss at soda distributorships, but the same predictions were made about the tobacco industry, and those were wrong. (For that matter, the same predictions were made around the nickel deposit on bottles, which most shoppers don't even notice.) Ultimately, however, both consumers and government will be more than reimbursed in the form of cheaper healthy staples, lowered health care costs and better health. And that's a big deal.

The Resulting Benefits

26   A study by Y. Claire Wang, an assistant professor at Columbia's Mailman School of Public Health, predicted that a penny tax per ounce on sugar-sweetened beverages in New York State would save $3 billion in health care costs over the course of a decade, prevent something like 37,000 cases of diabetes and bring in $1 billion annually. Another study shows that a two-cent tax per ounce in Illinois would reduce obesity in youth by 18 percent, save nearly $350 million and bring in over $800 million taxes annually.

27   Scaled nationally, as it should be, the projected benefits are even more impressive; one study suggests that a national penny-per-ounce tax on sugar-sweetened beverages would generate at least $13 billion a year in income while cutting consumption by 24 percent. And those numbers would swell dramatically if the tax were extended to more kinds of junk or doubled to two cents an ounce. (The Rudd Center has a nifty revenue calculator online that lets you play with the numbers yourself.)

28   A 20 percent increase in the price of sugary drinks nationally could result in about a 20 percent decrease in consumption, which in the next decade could prevent 1.5 million Americans from becoming obese and 400,000 cases of diabetes, saving about $30 billion.

29   It's fun—inspiring, even—to think about implementing a program like this. First off, though the reduced costs of healthy foods obviously benefit the poor most, lower prices across the board keep things simpler and all of us, especially children whose habits are just developing, could use help in eating differently. The program would also bring much needed encouragement to farmers, including subsidies, if necessary, to grow staples instead of commodity crops.

30   Other ideas: We could convert refrigerated soda machines to vending machines that dispense grapes and carrots, as has already been done in Japan and Iowa. We could provide recipes, cooking lessons, even cookware for those who can't afford it. Television public-service announcements could promote healthier eating. (Currently, 86 percent of food ads now seen by children are for foods high in sugar, fat or sodium.)

31   Money could be returned to communities for local spending on gyms, pools, jogging and bike trails; and for other activities at food distribution centers; for Meals on Wheels in those towns with a large elderly population, or for Head Start for those with more children; for supermarkets and farmers' markets where needed. And more.

32   By profiting as a society from the foods that are making us sick and using those funds to make us healthy, the United States would gain the same kind of prestige that we did by attacking smoking. We could institute a national, comprehensive program that would make us a world leader in preventing chronic or "lifestyle" diseases, which for the first time in history kill more people than communicable ones. By doing so, we'd not only repair some of the damage we have caused by first inventing and then exporting the Standard American Diet, we'd also set a new standard for the rest of the world to follow.

Attacking the Obesity Epidemic by First Figuring Out Its Cause

By Jane E. Brody
New York Times, September 12, 2011

1   If you have gained a lot of unwanted pounds at any time during the last 30-odd years, you may be relieved to know that you are probably not to blame. At least not entirely.

2   Many environmental forces, from economic interests of the food and beverage industries to the way our cities and towns are built, have conspired to subvert the body's natural ability to match calories in with calories out.

3   And the solution to the nation's most pressing health problem—the ever-rising epidemic of overweight and obesity at all ages—lies in the answer to this question: Why did this happen in the first place?

4   That is the conclusion of an impressive team of experts who spent the last two years examining obesity-promoting forces globally. They recently published their findings online in a series of reports in The Lancet.

5   But as has happened with smoking, it will take many years, a slew of different tactics and the political will to overcome powerful lobbying by culpable industries to turn the problem around and begin to bring the prevalence of overweight and obesity back to the levels of the 1970s.

What Changed?

6   When I was growing up in the 1940s and '50s, I had to walk or bike many blocks to buy an ice cream cone. There were no vending machines dispensing candy and soda, and no fast-food emporiums or shopping malls with food courts. Nor were we constantly bombarded with televised commercials for prepared foods and drinks laden with calories of fats and sugars.

7   Yes, we kids had our milk and cookies after school, but then we went out to run around and play until dark. Television watching (through my father's business, my family acquired an early TV with a seven-inch screen) was mostly a weekend family affair, not a nightly ritual with constant noshing.

8   Most meals were prepared and eaten at home, even when both parents worked (as mine did). Eating out was a special event. "Convenience" foods were canned fruits and vegetables, not frozen lasagna or Tater Tots. A typical breakfast was hot or cold cereal sweetened with raisins or fresh fruit, not a Pop-Tart, jelly doughnut or 500-calorie bagel with 200 calories of cream cheese.

9   Before a mass exodus to the suburbs left hordes of Americans totally car-dependent, most people lived in cities and towns where feet served as a main means of transportation.

10   Since 1900, the energy requirements for daily life have decreased substantially with the advent of labor-saving devices and automobiles, yet American weights remained stable until the 1970s. Dr. Boyd A. Swinburn, an obesity researcher at Deakin University in Melbourne, Australia, and his co-authors in one Lancet paper call that decade the "tipping point."

11   As more women entered the work force, the food industry, noting a growing new market, mass-produced convenience foods with palate appeal. The foods were rich in sugar, salt and fat, substances that humans are evolutionarily programmed to crave.

12   "Women were spending a lot less time on food preparation, but the industry figured out ways to make food more readily available for everybody," Steven L. Gortmaker, a sociologist at the Harvard School of Public Health, said in an interview. "The industry made it easier for people to consume more calories throughout the day."

13   As Dr. Swinburn and his co-authors wrote, "The 1970s saw a striking rise in the quantity of refined carbohydrates and fats in the U.S. food supply, which was paralleled by a sharp increase in the available calories and the onset of the obesity epidemic. Energy intake rose because of environmental push factors, i.e., increasingly available, cheap, tasty, highly promoted obesogenic foods."

14   During a morning run in Ohio some years ago, I passed five fast-food and family restaurants in one long block, including one that advertised a "Texas-size breakfast" of three scrambled eggs, two fried potato cakes, a buttered croissant and a choice of three sausage links, three ounces of ham or four strips of bacon—enough to produce a Texas-size heart attack, and for $1.99. Americans are not known for resisting such temptations, especially if money is tight.

15   The Lancet authors reported that to bring the weights of Americans back to 1978 levels, steep reductions in caloric intake are needed: about 240 calories a day less for the average person and double that amount for obese adults, whose body mass index is 35 or higher.

'Systems Approach' Needed

16   Several coordinated, complementary policies are needed to turn the epidemic around, Dr. Gortmaker and his co-authors wrote in one report. He pointed out that four interventions worked together to drive smoking rates down to 20 percent from 40 percent.

17   First, tobacco advertising was banned from television. Then tobacco taxes were increased, the nicotine patch became available and smoking was banned in more and more public places.

18   Just as the decline in smoking did not happen overnight, a reduction in the rates of overweight and obesity will take a while, Dr. Gortmaker said. He emphasized the importance of taking action immediately, before the increase in life expectancy that Americans have enjoyed is reversed by obesity-caused diseases.

19   He and his co-authors listed three of the most cost-saving and health-saving measures: a 10 percent tax on unhealthy foods and drinks (like sugar-sweetened beverages, a proposal defeated in New York State by industry pressure); more obvious nutrition labeling of packaged foods, like a red, yellow or green traffic light on package fronts; and reduced advertising of "junk foods and beverages to children."

20   "Marketing of food and beverages is associated with increasing obesity rates and is especially effective among children," they wrote. Dr. Gortmaker pointed out that "very few children are born obese," but most American children grow up in an obesogenic environment. For those who become obese by age 10 or 11, he and his co-authors said, family-based programs are needed to keep overweight from carrying over into adulthood. (In Scotland recently, authorities went so far as to remove two children from a family that had failed to control the youngsters' girth.)

21   "Children aged 2 to 19 consume seven trillion calories of sugar-sweetened beverages a year. It's a $24 billion industry just for kids alone," Dr. Gortmaker said.

22   He called a tax on sugared drinks a "no-brainer," noting that it could raise billions of dollars a year for cash-starved states. California, for example, could bring in $1.5 billion a year with a 1-cent-per-ounce excise tax on sugar-sweetened drinks, he said.

23   But Dr. Gortmaker and his co-authors noted, "Almost all food policies recommended as priority actions, including front-of-pack traffic light labeling, have been heavily contested by the food industry." Although there has been some reduction in unhealthy food advertisements on children's television, the decline has been minimal.

24   Also needed—and less controversial—are school-based programs to encourage healthier eating and exercise habits and to reduce television watching, the authors said. Schools that introduce healthful foods in the classroom have shown that they are more likely to be eaten in the lunchroom and at home.

25   Of course, the rising overweight and obesity rate is not just an American problem. The effect is being seen globally, even in low- and middle-income countries. This month the United Nations General Assembly will focus on noncommunicable diseases, with the "wicked problem" (as Brian Head, a social scientist at the University of Queensland in Australia, put it) of the global obesity epidemic front and center.

No Lunch Left Behind

By Alice Waters and Katrina Heron
New York Times, February 19, 2009

1   This new era of government bailouts and widespread concern over wasteful spending offers an opportunity to take a hard look at the National School Lunch Program. Launched in 1946 as a public safety net, it has turned out to be a poor investment. It should be redesigned to make our children healthier.

2   Under the program, the United States Department of Agriculture gives public schools cash for every meal they serve—$2.57 for a free lunch, $2.17 for a reduced-price lunch and 24 cents for a paid lunch. In 2007, the program cost around $9 billion, a figure widely acknowledged as inadequate to cover food costs. But what most people don't realize is that very little of this money even goes toward food. Schools have to use it to pay for everything from custodial services to heating in the cafeteria.

3   On top of these reimbursements, schools are entitled to receive commodity foods that are valued at a little over 20 cents per meal. The long list of options includes high-fat, low-grade meats and cheeses and processed foods like chicken nuggets and pizza. Many of the items selected are ready to be thawed, heated or just unwrapped—a necessity for schools without kitchens. Schools also get periodic, additional "bonus" commodities from the U.S.D.A., which pays good money for what are essentially leftovers from big American food producers.

4   When school districts allow fast-food snacks in the lunchroom they provoke widespread ire, and rightfully so. But food distributed by the National School Lunch Program contains some of the same ingredients found in fast food, and the resulting meals routinely fail to meet basic nutritional standards. Yet this is how the government continues to "help" feed millions of American schoolchildren, a great many of them from low-income households.

5   Some Americans are demanding better. Parent advocacy groups like Better School Food have rejected the National School Lunch Program and have turned instead to local farmers for fresh alternatives. Amid steep budgetary challenges, these community-supported coalitions are demonstrating that schools can be the masters of their own menus. Schools here in Berkeley, for example, continue to use U.S.D.A. commodities, but cook food from scratch and have added organic fruits and vegetables from area farms. They have cut costs by adopting more efficient accounting software and smart-bulk policies (like choosing milk dispensers over individual cartons), and by working with farmers to identify crops that they can grow in volume and sell for reasonable prices.

6   Many nutrition experts believe that it is possible to fix the National School Lunch Program by throwing a little more money at it. But without healthy food (and cooks and kitchens to prepare it), increased financing will only create a larger junk-food distribution system. We need to scrap the current system and start from scratch. Washington needs to give schools enough money to cook and serve unprocessed foods that are produced without pesticides or chemical fertilizers. When possible, these foods should be locally grown.

7   How much would it cost to feed 30 million American schoolchildren a wholesome meal? It could be done for about $5 per child, or roughly $27 billion a year, plus a one-time investment in real kitchens. Yes, that sounds expensive. But a healthy school lunch program would bring long-term savings and benefits in the areas of hunger, children's health and dietary habits, food safety (contaminated peanuts have recently found their way into school lunches), environmental preservation and energy conservation.

8   The Agriculture Department will have to do its part, by making good on its fledgling commitment to back environmentally sound farming practices and by realizing a separate program to deliver food, especially fresh fruits and vegetables, from farms to schools. It will also need to provide adequate support for kitchens and healthy meal planning. Congress has an opportunity to accomplish some of these goals when it takes up the Child Nutrition and Women Infants and Children Reauthorization Act, which is set to expire in September.

9   But the Department of Education should take some initiative, too. After all, eating well requires education. We can teach students to choose good food and to understand how their choices affect their health and the environment. The new school lunch program should be partly financed by the Department of Education, and Arne Duncan, the secretary of education, should oversee it. Vice President Joseph Biden should also come to the table by making school lunch a priority of his White House Task Force on Middle Class Working Families.

10   Every public school child in America deserves a healthful and delicious lunch that is prepared with fresh ingredients. Cash-strapped parents should be able to rely on the government to contribute to their children's physical well-being, not to the continued spread of youth obesity, Type 2 diabetes and other diet-related problems. Let's prove that there is such a thing as a good, free lunch.

Alice Waters is the president of The Chez Panisse Foundation. Katrina Heron is a director of the foundation and a co-producer of civileats.com.

Juvenile Justice

Kids Are Kids—Until They Commit Crimes

By Marjie Lundstrom
Sacramento Bee, March 1, 2001

1   A week from now, a judge in Florida will decide how old Lionel Tate really is.

2   Never mind that he is indisputably twelve at the time of "the incident." Is he a boy? Or a man?

3   It is a vexing question these days for the under-eighteen crowd, the group we routinely write off as "only kids." It's why they can't smoke, or drink, or go to R movies without our OK. It's why they don't vote. It's why they have curfews. It's why we fret over their Internet access and fuss about driving privileges.

4   Hey, they're only kids.

5   That is, until they foul up. Until they commit crimes. And the bigger the crime, the more eager we are to call them adults.

6   It's a glaring inconsistency that's getting more glaring by the hour as children as young as twelve and thirteen are being charged as adults in America's courts.

7   A California appeals court recently stuck its nose into the quandary of when to charge young offenders as adults, returning that power to judges, not prosecutors.

8   Meanwhile, in Texas, a lawmaker has had it. You want to throw the adult book at kids? Fine, says Democratic state Rep. Ron Wilson of Houston.

9   Lower the voting age to fourteen.

10   And really, in light of things, how wacky is that? Today we are witness to criminal defendants—facing life sentences without parole—who cannot shave, still play with fire trucks and love to act out scenes from television or video games.

11   On March 9, Lionel Tate—who was twelve when he savagely beat to death a six-year-old girl—will likely learn if he must spend life in prison after his lawyer unsuccessfully tried to put pro wrestling on trial. Now fourteen and convicted as an adult of first-degree murder, Tate supposedly was imitating his World Wrestling Federation heroes when he pummeled his playmate, less than a third his size.

12   Last month in Sacramento, a fifteen-year-old Yuba City youth who reportedly claimed he was mimicking a TV program about little girls who rob a bank was given a 26-years-to-life prison term. Tried as an adult, Thomas A. Preciado was fourteen when he stabbed to death a minimart clerk.

13   In April, Court TV will air live daily coverage of the trial of Nathaniel Brazill, now fourteen, charged as an adult with first-degree murder. Brazill was thirteen and already in trouble for throwing water balloons when he returned to his Lake Worth, Fla., middle school and shot to death an English teacher, who would not let him say good-bye to two girls on the final day of classes.

14   This is not to say that the boys' crimes were not heinous, or that they should go unpunished. No one's talking about coddling here. But the zeal to corral wildly troubled, ever-younger kids and ram them through the adult system belies everything the juvenile justice system is all about: that kids are different. Their reasoning is not fully developed.

15   They are not adults.

16   "We've created this image that teenagers are something to be feared," said Dan Macallair of the Center on Juvenile and Criminal Justice in San Francisco.

17   This warped vision of America's youth was given an unfortunate boost with the recent arrest of two seemingly "good kids" in the brutal slayings of two Dartmouth College professors. Before they were even arrested, prosecutors had charged the teenagers, sixteen and seventeen, as adults.

18   Trouble is, statistics don't bear out the hysteria. While politicians and prosecutors press for hard-line stands against youthful offenders—nearly every state has moved to make it easier to charge kids as adults—juvenile crime is way down.

19   The nation's juvenile arrest rate for murder fell 68 percent from 1993 to 1999, hitting its lowest level since 1966, according to the Justice Department. The juvenile arrest rate for violent crime overall fell 36 percent from 1994 to 1999.

20   Macallair believes the excitable media have perpetuated and fueled the youth-violence scare of the 1980s. In fact, California voters were so persuaded by tough-on-crime rhetoric they passed Proposition 21 last March, shifting the power from judges to prosecutors in deciding which juveniles to charge as adults in certain crimes.

21   Sensibly, the 4th District Court of Appeals in San Diego disagreed, finding that the provision violated the separation-of-powers principle. The San Diego district attorney has vowed to appeal.

22   But the fact remains, politics and demagoguery do not make good public policy. Research suggests that adolescents squeezed through the adult system are more likely to come out as violent career criminals than similar kids handled on the juvenile side.

23   More lives, lost.

24   So what, then, to do about Lionel Tate—a kid who apparently still doesn't understand that "pile-driving" fellow inmates is not a good thing?

25   In another week, he will find out who tucks him in at night. And where.

Startling Finds on Teenage Brains

By Paul Thompson
Sacramento Bee, Friday, May 25, 2001

1   Emotions ran high at the trial of Nathaniel Brazill in West Palm Beach, Fla., two weeks ago. Friends of slain teacher Barry Grunow called for the death penalty, while a growing crowd of demonstrators outside the courthouse wielded hastily written placards reading, "A child is not a man." Jurors returned with their verdict May 16: Fourteen-year-old Brazill, charged in last May's shooting of middle-school teacher Grunow, was found guilty of second-degree murder.

2   A Florida grand jury had previously ruled that Brazill, who frequently looked dazed during the trial, would be tried as an adult, and if he had been convicted of first-degree murder he would have faced life in prison without parole. But Brazill's immaturity was evident throughout this incident—from the act itself of Brazill's shooting a teacher he considered one of his favorites, to his subsequent inability to give a reason for doing so, to the various quizzical looks that came across his face as the verdicts were read.

3   In terms of cognitive development, as research on the human brain has shown, Brazill—and any other young teen—is far from adulthood.

4   Over the last several years, as school shootings have seemed to occur with disturbing frequency, startling discoveries have emerged about the teenage brain. The White House held a televised conference on adolescent development in May of last year, and a flurry of papers on the teen brain has appeared in top science journals. Reporters and teen advocates ask: Do the studies help explain the impulsive, erratic behavior of teens? The biggest surprise in recent teen-brain research is the finding that a massive loss of brain tissue occurs in the teen years.

5   Specifically, my own research group at the University of California, Los Angeles, and our colleagues at the National Institutes of Health have developed technology to map the patterns of brain growth in individual children and teenagers. With repeated brain scans of kids from three to twenty, we pieced together "movies" showing how brains grow and change.

6   Some changes make perfect sense: Language systems grow furiously until age twelve and then stop, coinciding with the time when children learn foreign languages fastest. Mathematical brain systems grow little until puberty, corresponding with the observation that kids have difficulty with abstract concepts before then. Basically, the brain is like a puzzle, and growth is fastest in the exact parts the kids need to learn skills at different times. So far, all well and good.

7   But what really caught our eye was a massive loss of brain tissue that occurs in the teenage years. The loss was like a wildfire, and you could see it in every teenager. Gray matter, which brain researchers believe supports all our thinking and emotions, is purged at a rate of 1 percent to 2 percent a year during this period. Stranger still, brain cells and connections are only being lost in the areas controlling impulses, risk-taking, and self-control. These frontal lobes, which inhibit our violent passions, rash actions, and regulate our emotions, are vastly immature throughout the teenage years.

8   The implications are tantalizing. Brazill was only thirteen when he committed his crime. He said he made a "stupid mistake," but prosecutors argued that by bringing a gun to school he planned the crime.

9   Does "planning" mean the same thing for a thirteen-year-old, with his diminished capacity for controlling erratic behavior, as it means for an adult? The verdict, in this case, seems to line up with the research. The jurors, by returning a verdict of second-degree murder instead of first, indicated that they believe Brazill's actions, while not accidental, were not fully thoughtout, either.

10   Linking this maelstrom of normal brain change with legal or moral accountability is tough: Even though normal teens are experiencing a wildfire of tissue loss in their brains, that does not remove their accountability. What is clear from the research is that the parts of the frontal lobes that inhibit reckless actions restructure themselves with startling speed in the teen years. Given this delicate—and drastic—reshaping of the brain, teens need all the help they can get to steer their development onto the right path.

11   While research on brain-tissue loss can help us to understand teens better, it cannot be used to excuse their violent or homicidal behavior. But it can be used as evidence that teenagers are not yet adults, and the legal system shouldn't treat them as such.

Paul Thompson is an assistant professor of neurology at the University of California, Los Angeles, School of Medicine.

On Punishment and Teen Killers

By Jennifer Jenkins
Juvenile Justice Information Exchange, Aug 2, 2011

1   "Some persons will shun crime even if we do nothing to deter them, while others will seek it out even if we do everything to reform them. Wicked people exist. Nothing avails except to set them apart from innocent people."
     — James Q. Wilson, Harvard Professor and Crime Expert

2   My youngest sister was the joy of our close family. When a teenager murdered her and her husband in 1990 in suburban Chicago, she was pregnant with their first child. She begged for the life of her unborn child as he shot her. He reported to a friend, who testified at his trial, about his "thrill kill" that he just wanted to "see what it would feel like to shoot someone."

3   This offender is now serving three life sentences in the Illinois Department of Corrections. According to Charles Stimson, a leading expert in criminal law at the Heritage Foundation's Center for Legal and Judicial Studies, he is one of 1,300 cases nationally of a teen killer sentenced as an adult to life, sometimes called JLWOP (Juvenile Life without Parole).

4   There are advocates who wish to minimize these offenders' culpability simply because of their age. As a high school teacher, I have worked lovingly with teens all my life and I understand how hard it is to accept the reality that a 16 or 17 year old is capable of forming such requisite criminal intent.

5   We in America have to own this particular problem, with weapons so easily available to our youth, and the violence-loving culture in which we raise them. The Innuit people of northern Canada had no juvenile crime at all until 1980 and the introduction of television into their culture.

6   Both sides in the debate about JLWOP agree: Teens are being tried as adults and sentenced to prison for murder at alarming rates in the United States. But this actually disproves juvenile advocates' reliance on the "underdeveloped brain" argument. If brain development were the reason, then teens would kill at roughly the same rates all over the world. They do not. Advocates often repeat, but truly misunderstand brain research on this issue. The actual science does not, according to experts such as Professor Stephen Morse, and others, in any way negate criminal culpability.

7   The offender in our case was a serial killer in the making. He came from privilege. Whenever he got in trouble, his parents fixed it. After a series of other crimes, he planned the murders for months, carefully and privately. He did not act on impulse or because of peer pressure. He was not mentally disabled—in fact was quite intelligent. But he got a rush out of breaking the law and ultimately started work on his other plan for mass murder at a local bank. Bragging to friends led to his arrest.

8   There are no words adequate to describe what this kind of traumatic loss does to a victim's family. So few who work on the juvenile offender side can truly understand what the victims of their crimes sometimes go through. Some never recover.

9   The nationwide campaign to end JLWOP has spent millions of dollars advocating for these convicted murderers to be set free. Not a dime has been allocated for victim outreach or support.

10   With absolutely no regard to the impact on victims' families, they have published glossy "reports" widely distributed to the media and legislators. They feature propaganda photos of 7- and 8- year-old child models on the cover, with misleading headlines that the United States was "sentencing children to die in prison."

11   For the record, the nation is NOT sentencing children to die in prison. This photo is pure propaganda.

12   The juvenile death penalty was abolished here years ago and a life sentence still allows a great deal of good living to be done—even from behind bars—far more than these teen killers gave to our murdered loved ones.

13   Many JLWOP offenders are repeat violent offenders and many have killed multiple people. The propaganda campaign by the well-funded juvenile advocates attempts to paint a different picture.

14   Consistently, they don't talk about the facts of the crimes, just the "poor children in prison." And while we respect their right to advocate for reform, some of which is needed, we have begged them to embrace the victims of these crimes as well, and take a truly inclusive and restorative justice approach to their advocacy. Our pleas have fallen on mostly deaf ears.

15   The offender advocates have also promoted another horrible lie—that the United States is the only nation that sentences teens to life for murder. In fact, at least 11 other nations do, according to Stimson's research. Many nations do the equivalent and far worse—the juvenile death penalty, selling teens into sexual slavery, forced labor, sexual mutilation and the list goes on. Many nations do not have separate juvenile justice systems such as the enlightened system we have here, and many nations torture offenders of all ages without regard for human rights.

16   Legislative proposals for reforming JLWOP have been retroactive but without any victim notification, in full violation of constitutionally protected victims' rights. Advocates who wish to believe in the nobility of their actions cannot wrong murder victims' family members in this way without losing all credibility. Restorative Justice shows us the way out—a conversation focused on victims needs, with all stakeholders at the table.

Juveniles Don't Deserve Life Sentences

By Gail Garinger
New York Times, March 14, 2012

1   In the late 1980s, a small but influential group of criminologists predicted a coming wave of violent juvenile crime: "superpredators," as young as 11, committing crimes in "wolf packs." Politicians soon responded to those fears, and to concerns about the perceived inadequacies of state juvenile justice systems, by lowering the age at which children could be transferred to adult courts. The concern was that offenders prosecuted as juveniles would have to be released at age 18 or 21.

2   At the same time, "tough on crime" rhetoric led some states to enact laws making it easier to impose life without parole sentences on adults. The unintended consequence of these laws was that children as young as 13 and 14 who were charged as adults became subject to life without parole sentences.

3   Nationwide, 79 young adolescents have been sentenced to die in prison—a sentence not imposed on children anywhere else in the world. These children were told that they could never change and that no one cared what became of them. They were denied access to education and rehabilitation programs and left without help or hope.

4   But the prediction of a generation of superpredators never came to pass. Beginning in the mid-1990s, violent juvenile crime declined, and it has continued to decline through the present day. The laws that were passed to deal with them, however, continue to exist. This month, the United States Supreme Court will hear oral arguments in two cases, Jackson v. Hobbs and Miller v. Alabama, which will decide whether children can be sentenced to life without parole after being convicted of homicide.

5   The court has already struck down the death penalty for juveniles and life without parole for young offenders convicted in nonhomicide cases. The rationale for these earlier decisions is simple and equally applicable to the cases to be heard: Young people are biologically different from adults. Brain imaging studies reveal that the regions of the adolescent brain responsible for controlling thoughts, actions and emotions are not fully developed. They cannot be held to the same standards when they commit terrible wrongs.

6   Homicide is the worst crime, but in striking down the juvenile death penalty in 2005, the Supreme Court recognized that even in the most serious murder cases, "juvenile offenders cannot with reliability be classified among the worst offenders": they are less mature, more vulnerable to peer pressure, cannot escape from dangerous environments, and their characters are still in formation. And because they remain unformed, it is impossible to assume that they will always present an unacceptable risk to public safety.

7   The most disturbing part of the superpredator myth is that it presupposed that certain children were hopelessly defective, perhaps genetically so. Today, few believe that criminal genes are inherited, except in the sense that parental abuse and negative home lives can leave children with little hope and limited choices.

8   As a former juvenile court judge, I have seen firsthand the enormous capacity of children to change and turn themselves around. The same malleability that makes them vulnerable to peer pressure also makes them promising candidates for rehabilitation.

9   An overwhelming majority of young offenders grow out of crime. But it is impossible at the time of sentencing for mental health professionals to predict which youngsters will fall within that majority and grow up to be productive, law-abiding citizens and which will fall into the small minority that continue to commit crimes. For this reason, the court has previously recognized that children should not be condemned to die in prison without being given a "meaningful opportunity to obtain release based on demonstrated maturity and rehabilitation."

10   The criminologists who promoted the superpredator theory have acknowledged that their prediction never came to pass, repudiated the theory and expressed regret. They have joined several dozen other criminologists in an amicus brief to the court asking it to strike down life without parole sentences for children convicted of murder. I urge the justices to apply the logic and the wisdom of their earlier decisions and affirm that the best time to decide whether someone should spend his entire life in prison is when he has grown to be an adult, not when he is still a child.

Gail Garinger, a juvenile court judge in Massachusetts from 1995 to 2008, is the state's child advocate, appointed by the governor.

Greg Ousley Is Sorry for Killing His Parents. Is That Enough?

By Scott Anderson
New York Times, July 19, 2012

1. For 19 years, Greg Ousley has sought to make sense of the event that has haunted and dictated his life, but the answer, if such a simple thing exists, has remained forever beyond his grasp. In its place, he has hunches and half-formed theories. He can lay out a chronology of moments leading up to the event, but some of these are contradictory, others are mere fragments and all are trivial when stacked against what came next. Occasionally, though, he stumbles upon something that is raw and true, like when he describes what happened on the afternoon of Tuesday, Feb. 23, 1993, four days before he murdered his parents.

2. It was a normal day at his junior high school, but when Greg came home, he fought with his parents and defiantly locked himself in his bedroom. Greg's father, Jobie, knocked on the door for a minute or two, and when that had no effect, he returned to the couch to watch television.

3. In the prison where Greg told me this story, he gave a quick chuckle. "Well, there's no way my mom was gonna let that stand," he said, "so after she had a try and I still wouldn't come out, she got a hairpin and just picked the lock."

4. Bonnie Ousley found Greg lying on his stomach, refusing to speak or even look at her. She sat on the edge of the bed and began stroking his back. In the telling, Greg slid into present tense, pantomiming his mother's caress. "And she keeps saying: 'What's wrong, honey? What's going on with you? Talk to me. Just talk to me.'"

5. The 14-year-old boy told his mother that he was scared, that all he ever thought about was murder and suicide.

6. "And as soon as I say that, she takes her hand off my back." Greg, who is now 33, yanked his hand into the air, as if scalded. "She jumps up—'You're just watching too many movies'—and walks out the room."

7. His face crumpled. Over the many hours I had spent with him, he rarely showed emotion, and the abruptness with which this came on seemed to startle and embarrass him. He took a minute to compose himself, then said: "I remember lying there thinking: Man, this is just never going to change. Mom and Dad, they are never, ever gonna listen to me. I've got no choice, I've got to go through with it."

8. "Go through with it?" I asked.

9. Greg gave a slow shrug of his shoulders. "Kill them."

10   **Four nights later,** at about 11:30, Greg went into his parents' bedroom with a 12-gauge shotgun and shot his father once in the head. Moments later, as his mother rushed for the telephone in the dining room, he killed her with two more shots. Greg then drove the family pickup truck to his best friend's house three miles away. He told his friend what he had done and swore him to secrecy. Then he drove back to his home around 4 a.m., parked the pickup in the garage, placed the gun in the kitchen doorway and ran to a neighbor's house to raise the alarm.

11   The story Greg told the police—that he returned home from a late-night joy ride to find the shotgun on the floor and his mother lying dead just beyond—had holes in it from the outset, and those holes became gaping once his friend revealed what he knew to investigators. By midafternoon the next day, Greg finally broke down at the Kosciusko County sheriff's office in Warsaw, Ind., and provided a full confession.

12   "I had been thinking about killing them every time I get mad," he told his interrogator. "They don't seem to understand me." Indicative of either his youth or his mental state at that moment, Greg made a forlorn request of the detective: "Please don't tell my family."

13   Despite Greg's age, his case was swiftly waived into the adult justice system. Facing the possibility of life in prison, he accepted a plea agreement of guilty but mentally ill. In early 1994, Greg, then 15, entered the Indiana penitentiary system to begin serving a 60-year sentence. He was one of the youngest adult inmates in the state's history.

14   Today there are well more than 2,500 juveniles serving time in adult prisons in the United States—enough, in Indiana's case, to fill a dedicated Y.I.A. (Youth Incarcerated as Adults) wing at Wabash Valley Correctional Facility. The United States is the only Western nation to routinely convict minors as adults, and the practice has set off a growing disquiet even in conservative legal circles. In 2005, the Supreme Court ruled that the death penalty for juveniles was unconstitutional, and just last month it similarly banned mandatory sentencing of life without parole in juvenile homicide cases.

15   But in this controversy, Greg Ousley is an unlikely representative for sentencing reform. He is not a 16-year-old doing 20 years for his third drug felony or a 13-year-old who found his father's loaded handgun and shot a playmate. What he is, or was, is a teenage boy who planned and carried out a crime so unthinkable that to most people it is not just a moral transgression but almost a biological one.

16   I first learned of Greg's crime in the spring of 2009, and I wrote him a letter asking if he would be willing to talk to me. I wasn't sure what I expected to find, but I wanted to understand how a man who had served 16 years for killing his parents made sense of what he had done and what his life could still be. The first time I saw him, that April, Greg was at Westville Correctional Facility, a sprawling medium-security complex set in the cornfields just east of Valparaiso. He was slighter than I expected—about 5-foot-10, with the wiry frame of a wrestler or a distance runner—and a good deal perkier, possessed

of a quick-witted cheerfulness that was out of sync with his surroundings. Even more surprising, given the nature of his crimes, was the setting for our meeting. Rather than speaking in a visitors' hall or a monitored media room, Greg and I were led to a small conference room where we were allowed to visit, without supervision and Greg free of any restraints, for as long as we wished.

17   "I work across the hall from the superintendent," Greg explained, "so they all know me." He pointed out a window to a high fence topped with concertina wire, the innermost ring of Westville's many barriers to the outside. "And let's be honest," he said, "where am I gonna go?" We talked that day for about five hours and nearly as long the next, the first of scores of conversations we would have in person or by phone over the next three years.

18   For a host of reasons, Greg's story is a confounding one. Despite the media attention they often garner, instances of a child's murdering a parent or stepparent—juvenile parricide, as it is legalistically known—are among the rarest of homicides, probably accounting for fewer than 75 of the some 15,000 murders committed in the United States in any given year. Seldom are both parents murdered.

19   Perhaps just as confounding as his crime, however, is the journey Greg has taken inside prison. To say that he has spent his entire adulthood behind bars doesn't begin to capture the isolation he has experienced. While he had frequent visitors in the first few years of his incarceration, that number quickly trailed off. By the time of my appearance in April 2009, he had just three or four visitors in the previous decade, none of them family members. I realized after my first two conversations with him that those 9 or 10 hours constituted about half of all his contact with the outside world since he turned 20. Yet during this same period, Greg somehow managed to become a model inmate. After earning his high-school equivalency and attending nearly every anger- and stress-management workshop the penal system had to offer, he pursued a bachelor's degree in liberal arts through Indiana State University's correspondence program. In 2004, he graduated magna cum laude. ("I was a bit disappointed with that," he told me. "I was hoping for summa cum laude, but I screwed up on this one class.")

20   Just before I met Greg, his appeals lawyer petitioned the prosecutor for a sentence modification, a procedure in which, on a prosecutor's recommendation, an Indiana judge might amend a sentence and grant an early release for a prisoner whose behavior and record in prison suggest complete rehabilitation. The prosecutor had previously rejected a handwritten appeal from Greg, but in early 2009 he agreed to allow the modification process to move forward, provided that none of the victims' next of kin—meaning Greg's two sisters and five aunts and uncles—objected. It suddenly opened up the possibility that, at 30, Greg might be released from prison years before his official eligibility date of March 2019.

21   "I'm really confident it's going to happen," he told me at our first meeting. "I have one aunt who might be a problem, but I'm pretty sure everyone else will totally support it."

22   It was tempting to dismiss this as wishful thinking, except that the corrections officials I spoke with—and no group of professionals is more jaded, working as they do in an environment where nearly everyone is trying to work some angle—appeared to be the biggest supporters of Greg's campaign. This was evident in the extraordinary freedom we were allowed in our discussions and also in the array of Westville officials, ranging from Greg's casework manager, Dennis Hood, up to the prison superintendent, William Wilson, who made themselves available to extol the virtues of the bright and personable young man in their midst.

23   "He's just a great worker," Hood offered, "enthusiastic, solves problems on his own, never complains. I have no doubt he'll succeed in whatever he puts his mind to when he's released."

24   His former work supervisor, Cindy Estes, was more explicit. "This kid has jumped through every hoop the state has put in front of him," she told me. "He deserves to come out. There's absolutely nothing to be gained by keeping him in there for another 10 years."

25   Along with happy anticipation at the prospect of soon walking out into a world he hadn't seen in 16 years, Greg was also clear on what he wanted to do there. "I want to work with young people," he said. "I want to use my life as an example of what can go wrong, of how important it is when you're that age to get help if you feel things closing in on you." He recognized the cliché and gave a knowing laugh. "Yeah, I know, me and every other guy in here, right? But in my case, it's true." He grew more thoughtful. "It comes down to hope. That's what I didn't have at 14. I learned it in here. That's what I can teach them."

26   **Since Freud, it** has been generally assumed that the only way to unlock the mysteries of the psyche is to dissect your childhood, especially the formative influence of your parents. In Greg's case, that process can quickly sound like the ultimate blame-the-victim excuse. It might also complicate one of his greatest goals, which is to reconcile with his extended family. As a result, he tends to intersperse negative anecdotes about his parents with statements like, "But that doesn't mean they deserved what I did to them," or with accounts of better times. He likes to talk about an essay he had to write in the fifth grade, on the person he most admired, and how he chose his mother.

27   "When I was little, she was just the greatest mom around," he told me, "always playing with me, going to all my sports events. She was just so much fun."

28   He had a far more distant relationship with his father. Greg says Jobie could go days without uttering a single word and can recall only one occasion when he told Greg that he loved him—and this, Greg says, occurred when Jobie was quite drunk. Chancy Schmucker, the friend Greg visited on the night of the murders, used the phrase "good ol' boy" to describe Jobie. "He'd always be out in that workshed they had there, sitting in his old, ratty armchair, a cigarette in one hand, a can of beer in the other, listening to country music. If Greg and I came in, it was, 'Hey boys, how's it going?' and that was about it."

29   Although they first met in Indiana, Jobie and Bonnie were transplants from the same impoverished corner of southeastern Kentucky coal country, late travelers on the so-called Hillbilly Highway that, beginning after World War II, saw the mass exodus of poor whites out of Appalachia for the industrial cities of the Midwest. In Kosciusko County, a pleasant stretch of rolling farmland and lakes in northeastern Indiana, they prospered. With Jobie working as a press operator for R. R. Donnelley, a commercial printer in Warsaw, and Bonnie as a packer for Kimble Glass, they were able to provide a comfortable middle-class home for the three children who came along in the 1970s: Angie, Tammy and Greg. Around 1980, they moved into a three-bedroom ranch on a five-acre parcel of farmland two miles south of Pierceton, later adding a large deck in back and an aboveground pool.

30   Greg remembers his early childhood being a content one—long afternoons spent tramping through the surrounding woods with his friends, family vacations to the Indiana Dunes on Lake Michigan and to visit the extended Ousley clan back in Kentucky. It was neither a materially deprived existence nor a physically abusive one. Like most other kids growing up in rural Indiana, Greg got the occasional spanking, administered by his father, but rarely anything more severe than that. Yet even at a young age, he was aware of the profoundly circumscribed orbit in which his family moved. Sociologists have long noted a tendency among many of the Appalachian transplants to the Midwest to remain separate from the larger community. The Ousleys appear to have been an extreme example of this, rarely socializing with anyone other than three sets of relatives, all first cousins of Jobie's, and all of whom lived nearby. If easy and familiar in some ways, such tight social compacts can lead to a kind of pressure-cooker environment in times of family discord, and by the late 1980s, the Ousleys were living in constant discord.

31   Sometimes the arguments were between Greg's parents—usually centered on Jobie's drinking—but more frequently they were between Bonnie and her two teenage daughters, squabbles that occasionally escalated to slapping and hair-pulling. Much of the family strife may have had roots in the sad conditions of Bonnie's own childhood. Abandoned by her father at a young age, she was barely a teenager when her mother died. Essentially orphaned, she and her two siblings—a sister, one year older, and a brother, a couple of years younger—were sent north to Indiana to live with an aunt. The sorrows didn't end there. In the early '70s, her brother was killed in a motorcycle accident. As her own two daughters came of age and prepared to escape the fractious family home, Bonnie's history of loss seemed to manifest itself in rages at her daughters, interspersed with accusations of abandonment.

32   As the youngest child, Greg was largely an observer to these battles. That ended when first Angie moved out of the house, and then Tammy followed her in the summer of 1991. "That's when everything with my mom went from tense but manageable to sheer hell," Greg said. "I remember this one day when Tammy was moving out. She and Mom were fighting again, and I was kind of off in a corner smirking about it, and Tammy turned to me: 'Don't laugh, because it's all going to fall on you now. You're it.' And, man, was she right."

33   Given the small statistical pool from which to draw, the few scholarly studies devoted to juvenile parricide all come with an implied asterisk. But criminologists have isolated a set of characteristics that are likely to be found in the killer's home. Not all of these markers were present in the Ousley house—Greg was neither physically nor sexually abused, for example—but others certainly were: family strife; social isolation. Perhaps most intriguing are those things often absent from such households: juvenile delinquency on the part of the killer and a history of police intervention with the family, both of which were absent from the Ousley home.

34   With his sisters gone from the house, 12-year-old Greg was suddenly burdened with perhaps the most significant parricidal marker of all: a recent event that has made the child/killer the central focus of the parents' abuse and/or attention. Within months of Tammy's departure, Greg began telling a seventh-grade friend that he was going to kill his parents.

35   **Tony Phillips is** a science teacher and coach at Whitko Middle School and an Air Force veteran. He exudes that calm, slightly stern manner that certain troubled kids gravitate toward as a sign of stability and strength. As in other schools across the country, teachers at Whitko find that much of their time is taken up dealing with problems that have little to do with education ("We don't teach anymore," Phillips commented on several occasions, "we parent"), and they have become adept at looking for the bruises or body language that might indicate abuse or turmoil in the home. The number of children that Phillips has helped in such situations over the years is a source of pride to him.

36   "Sometimes you have to push a little," he said, "because kids this age aren't that communicative. But show you genuinely care, and they'll usually crack right open."

37   Phillips might be especially vigilant in this regard because of what he sees as his failure with one particular student two decades ago. From the autumn of 1990 until February 1993, he was Greg's coach and teacher. Fourteen years after the murders, Phillips remained so troubled by his experience with Greg that he finally took a day off from Whitko to make the 90-minute drive out to Westville to see him.

38   "I think I was hoping for the golden key, so to speak," he told me. "What didn't I see? Was there something I didn't pick up on that could have prevented it?"

39   Phillips first encountered Greg at the beginning of sixth grade, and he remembers him as a bright, polite student. Among the extended clan scattered around the Pierceton area, Ousley boys had a reputation for being star athletes, but Greg had little interest in baseball and was absolutely useless in basketball, *the* sport in Indiana. With some coaxing, though, Phillips managed to steer him into wrestling, where the small but lithe sixth grader proved something of a standout.

40   By the beginning of seventh grade, though, Greg's interest in sports had waned, and he was frequently making elaborate excuses to avoid practice. He had started to wear his hair in a mullet and donned the black garb of his favorite heavy-metal bands. To Phillips, none of this was cause for alarm. "Kids at this age are constantly redefining themselves, and what their friends think is more important than anything else," he said. "So sure, Greg had become more standoffish, he'd decided sports were a waste of time, but what did that mean?"

41   What Phillips couldn't see was that Greg's behavior masked a rapidly deteriorating home life, where he was now the sole focus of his mother's rages. Almost daily, Greg told me, his mother would rip into him about something—his grades, his appearance, his choice of friends—ferocious tirades that often culminated in her telling him, "I know you're going to leave me just like your sisters did." Once her anger passed, Bonnie would usually apologize to her son, but after a time Greg didn't even hear it anymore.

42   "I just knew it was going to happen all over again tomorrow, so what did it mean?" he said.

43   At the same time, he was becoming increasingly convinced that his father's remoteness was less a sign of disinterest in him than outright disgust: disgust in his physical appearance, disgust in his lack of athletic prowess. Indicative of this, at least in Greg's mind, was Jobie's reaction when Greg ran away from home in the fall of 1991 and sought refuge with his sister Angie, who lived 10 miles down the road.

44   "My dad came in his pickup truck to get me," Greg recalled, "opened the passenger door—'Get in'—and that was it. The whole way home, not another word. It was like he didn't even care enough to be mad at me."

45   The process by which a disturbed individual moves from generalized despair or anger toward a plan of action is known in the mental-health community as ideation, and by the spring of 1992, Greg was displaying clear signs of it. On one occasion, while his mother hung laundry in the backyard, he took a rifle down from the gun cabinet and aimed it at her head, imagining what would happen if he pulled the trigger. He quickly put the gun away, terrified by his own thoughts.

46   Equally ominous, from a psychological standpoint, was when he decided he needed a more convincing reason to get out of wrestling practice than the excuses he was trading in. His solution was to shoot himself in the foot. Instead of destroying his foot, the antique rifle backfired, leaving him with an intermittent ringing in one ear.

47   Perhaps hastening this ideation process, Greg and his friends had begun getting high, which for 12-year-olds in rural Indiana often meant turning to inhalants: gasoline, paint thinner, model glue. Huffing is well known to cause brain damage in adolescents, and among his group of Whitko pals, Greg quickly developed the reputation of a hard-core huffer.

48   "He'd do anything he could get his hands on," said his former best friend, Chancy. "I remember him once taking WD-40 and huffing that."

49   In the early summer of 1992, something occurred that compounded the pressures mounting on the troubled 13-year-old boy. Walking into the family garage one afternoon, he found his mother in a kissing embrace with his father's best friend. For a time, Greg kept the knowledge to himself: when he finally confronted his mother, she tearfully admitted to the kiss but insisted there was nothing more to it. When Bonnie refused to tell Jobie, as Greg demanded she do, the boy saw that he was stuck, that his father now might very well blame him for having withheld the information from him for so long. Stuck, but also handed a potential weapon. Greg told his mother that if she didn't get off his back and let him do as he pleased, he would tell his father about "the affair."

50   "Basically I blackmailed her," Greg explained. "I know it was an awful thing to do—I knew it even then—but it worked. All of sudden, I felt like I could breathe again, that now I had this escape hatch."

51   But the episode also marked a turning point in Greg's relationship with his parents. Whatever respect he still held for them was now gone; his mother was no longer just a "bitch" but a "whore," his father a clueless cuckold. All manageable, perhaps, as long as Greg could run free, but then on Feb. 20, 1993, the escape hatch slammed shut. In the face of another of his blackmailing demands, Bonnie called her son's bluff; if Greg wanted to tell his father about the illicit kiss in the garage, he could go ahead.

52   "And that was it," he recalled. "All I could see was that it was going to be like this forever. Well, at least until I got out of high school and left home, but that was four and a half more years away, so it might as well have been forever."

53   Over the next week, Greg planned his parents' murder and told his best friend that it was coming soon. Days before the killings, his thoughts had become so consuming, and so frightening, that he made that last, missed overture to his mother. Two days later, during his third-period study hall, he opened his school notebook and penned a message. "This weekend," it began, "I am going to kill my parents."

54   Yet in Greg's mental reconstruction, even at this late date, there remained one last chance for the whole plan to be scuttled. It came on that Friday afternoon when he shouted an obscenity at his girlfriend and Tony Phillips stopped him. After scolding the eighth grader for using such language at school, Phillips detained Greg long enough to ask what was going on with him.

55   "I almost told him right then," Greg said. "If he or anyone else had just pushed me a little bit more, because I was so upset and scared by what was about to happen, I just know I would've crumbled right there."

56   Instead, Greg gave the stock response of most every 14-year-old boy— "nothing"—and the moment passed.

57 It is this account that Greg related to Phillips on that day in 2007 when his former teacher showed up at Westville hoping to discover the "golden key." And it is the same account, if more detailed, that he told Phillips and me in November 2009 when we went to Westville together. During the drive back to Kosciusko County after that meeting, Phillips was quiet for a very long time. "You know what's the scariest aspect to all this?" he finally said. "I don't remember that conversation at all. Ever since Greg told me about it, I've racked my brain trying to remember, but I just can't."

58 **For the long-term prisoner,** hope is a tricky property, something that needs to be constantly monitored and managed. Bereft of it, the inmate can quickly descend into a state of apathetic despair and turn to the fast-at-hand reliefs— drug use, gang allegiance—that all but ensure his stay will be lengthened. But to nurture out too much hope is to invite repeated and crushing disappointment, which can be just a slower way to get to the same place. The proper balance, it seems, is to work toward a goal—reconciliation with a family member, winning a legal appeal—while constantly reminding yourself that it probably won't happen.

59 At Westville, Greg is allowed to call people on an approved contact list, and after my first visit in 2009 we began staying in touch through weekly hourlong phone conversations. His calls invariably came at precisely the scheduled time, but on those occasions when I was unable to pick up, Greg shrugged off the lost opportunity with equanimity. "No problem," he would say the following week. "I know you've got other things going on."

60 Through his first few years in prison, Greg's fear alone acted as something of a distraction, the time eased by occasional visits from his sisters and their young children. Then things became routine, the visits stopped and the enormity of what lay ahead—a minimum of 28 years if he did everything just right; he'd be a man in his 40s when he got out—gradually dawned on him. Greg remembers those as the very worst years, a period when he occasionally turned to prison dope and moonshine for brief relief and when he got written up a number of times for minor infractions.

61 During this period, though, he set out on a painful journey of self-examination, trying to understand what he had done and why. One of the crueler paradoxes of his situation is that if he had been remanded into Indiana's juvenile justice system, Greg would have received help in this process; Indiana places an emphasis on youthful offenders' undergoing intensive behavioral and psychological therapy as a way for them to understand their actions and, it's hoped, correct their course in the future.

62 But Greg entered an adult system where whatever psychological counseling existed was primarily geared toward helping an inmate cope with his incarceration, not examining how he got there in the first place. Going it alone, Greg began putting his thoughts to paper. His first effort, a 40-page handwritten essay begun when he was 19, took him 15 months to write and was titled, "Why I Killed My Parents."

63   "For a long time," he wrote, "I searched for the reason of why I did what I did, and today I am finding it. Although there are other things that I remember, but don't know how to explain yet, basically it all comes down to one thing: acceptance. In my case, it was not being accepted by my parents for trying to be myself."

64   Six years later, at 25, he embarked on a far more mature and pained effort, keeping a journal in which he frequently addressed passages directly to his dead parents. That journal coincided not only with his pursuit of a bachelor's degree but with something else, as well. It is one of the few aspects of his life Greg is reluctant to discuss, but it seems to hold the key to his fortitude. "I've never been particularly religious," he told me during one of our visits, "and I've never really fallen for all that mystical stuff, but I had these two different dreams, about three months apart, where first my father and then my mother came to me. They were so vivid, lifelike, and for the first time since it happened, I could hear their voices, see their faces. And they forgave me. They hugged me, and forgave me for what I did." Greg paused and kneaded his fingers. "People might think that I'm just letting myself off the hook, but after that, everything changed. I still have the guilt, but I truly believe they have forgiven me, and that's kind of allowed me to move on, to think about what comes next because I feel that's what they want now."

65   **In Greg's memory,** it was the best night he ever spent with his parents.

66   He made plans to spend that Saturday night at Chancy's house, but that day, Greg was confronted by his parents and admitted pocketing the deposit for a canceled school trip and using the money to buy guitar strings for his father's old guitar. He called Chancy with the news that he was grounded but said he would sneak over later that night once his parents were asleep. The day took an unusual turn when Jobie told Greg to bring out the guitar strings, and father and son together restrung the guitar. Later, as Greg sat strumming in the family room, Jobie came in and briefly listened to him play.

67   "My father said, 'Wow, you're pretty good,' " Greg recalled. "It was weird, because I couldn't think of the last time he'd complimented me about anything."

68   Jobie took up the guitar and taught his son a few chords of an old bluegrass favorite. The two were joined by Bonnie, and for the next several hours, Greg and his parents sat in the family room singing and playing together.

69   "It was so strange," Greg said, "because this had just never, ever happened before. It was almost like. . . ." He groped for the right words "I don't know, like on some level he knew, like he was trying to make amends or head it off somehow."

70   At about 10:30, Jobie and Bonnie went to bed. For the next hour, Greg sat on the couch and stared at the television—it was tuned to an old-movie channel, he recalled, though he has no memory of what was playing—and tried to find a reason to not go through with it. On the one hand, maybe that evening was a sign of better times to come. But weighted against this was a concern so perverse that only an adolescent mind might come up with it: already having a reputation among his friends as a liar, he was sure that if he didn't do this now, no one would ever believe him about anything again. At about 11:30, he rose from the couch and made for the gun cabinet.

71   Around 4 a.m., Chloe and Michael Neer, the Ousleys' closest neighbors, were awakened by a frantic pounding on their front door. It was Greg.

72   "He was saying, 'My mother's been killed, someone's killed my mother,' " Chloe Neer remembers. Greg was friends with Chloe's three sons, and after she called 911, she went to hug the sobbing boy. "And as soon as I did, I knew he'd done it," she told me. "I can't explain why—a mother's intuition, I guess—but I just knew."

73   A 12-gauge slug fired from close range inflicts horrific damage on a human body, and the two that killed Bonnie Ousley—one to her right side, the other to the back of her head—struck with such force that blood and tissue were sprayed on the ceiling and a wall nearly 20 feet away. Police officers found a similarly gory scene in the master bedroom where Jobie lay dead.

74   While one aspect of Greg's story checked out—that he had gone to see his friend Chancy that night—it was just about all that did. Shortly after daybreak, he was transported to the Kosciusko County sheriff's office in downtown Warsaw, where the authorities faced a legal wrinkle. Under Indiana law, minors can waive their Miranda rights only with parental consent, but with Greg's parents dead, it meant a legal guardian had to be appointed before the boy could be interviewed. Among the relatives who gathered outside the Ousley household that morning, one of the most distraught was Bonnie's sister; to several officers, she made a comment that she had lost the only family she had left. At the sheriff's office, authorities quickly moved to make her and her husband Greg's guardians, an arrangement that all parties agreed to.

75   The county sheriff was nervous enough about the legality of this maneuver— in Indiana, guardianship can be conferred only by the courts, and no judge had been anywhere near this case yet—that he ordered investigators to halt their questioning. It soon became a moot point, however. By noon, the police had found the notebook in which Greg wrote of killing his parents, and his friend Chancy had related Greg's account of the killings, details that precisely matched up with the murder scene. Shortly after 3 p.m., Greg broke down and confessed.

76   Two days later, Greg was taken into court for a hearing on whether his case should be routed into the adult legal system. His court-appointed lawyer might have asked for a preliminary psychiatric examination, a procedure that would have at least slowed the process down, but he declined to do so. He might have also asserted that the presence of premeditation—the prosecutor's chief argument for taking it to adult court—was a particularly poor standard in the context of juvenile parricide; given the physical and psychological power imbalance inherent in child-parent relationships, a not uncommon feature to such murders is premeditation. He declined to do that as well. And so in a single 20-minute hearing held less than 72 hours after the murders, it was decided that the 14-year-old would stand as an adult.

77   Having accepted a plea agreement of guilty but mentally ill, Greg appeared for his sentencing hearing in early January 1994. A panel of three psychological examiners hired by the defense unanimously argued against simple incarceration, urging instead for "treatment which would deal with the traumas and deficiencies noted in his development."

78   Daniel Hampton, the Kosciusko County deputy prosecutor (he declined to be interviewed for this article), argued for a severe penalty. "Greg," he stated, "will eventually set an example for other juveniles."

79   Greg was sentenced to two consecutive 30-year prison terms.

80   **In 2009, letters** were sent by Greg's lawyer to Greg's two sisters and five aunts and uncles asking their views on his modification petition. Of the six relatives who replied, five were in favor of early release, but one, his mother's sister, was opposed. Greg got the bad news in the form of a letter from the prosecutor, Daniel Hampton: "It is on that basis that the State of Indiana will be objecting to any modification in this case."

81   When Greg next called, I expected him to be morose. Instead, he was remarkably upbeat. "So maybe it doesn't all come together the first time out," he said, "but this starts the process, and eventually it will. I have to believe that. I've gone too far to lose hope now."

82   In fact, he had come up with another idea: a family mediation session. His vision was for a kind of family reunion inside the prison walls, a chance for all his relatives to sit and ask him anything they wanted, to vent, to curse him, whatever.

83   "Even the ones who said, 'Yeah, sure, let him out,' I'd like them to come," he said in one of our phone calls. "I want them to see I'm not the crazy 14-year-old kid they remember, because one of the problems here is that I'm frozen in time to them. I need for them to see what I've become." He paused. "And I hope [my aunt] comes, too. I really don't blame her for opposing my release—I took away the most important person in her life—but if I've learned one thing from all this, it's that you can't keep things bottled up. Even if it doesn't sway her one bit, I think it'd help her to see my face."

84   It took over a year to organize the mediation session. Part of the delay was because Greg was transferred from Westville to another medium-security prison, Miami Correctional Facility, about an hour north of Indianapolis. Another obstacle was the difficulty finding the required outside mediator to officiate. One after another, those approached demurred or simply went silent once they heard the nature of Greg's crimes. Finally Rick Russell, a family therapist living about an hour away from the prison, agreed to do it, and the mediation session was scheduled for mid-November 2010.

85   When the day arrived, only a single uncle, Jobie's older brother Eddie, accompanied by his fourth wife, Patricia, made the journey to Miami. Prison visits always have an awkward, forced quality to them, and so it was with the mediation session, the five of us—Greg and Rick Russell, Eddie and Patricia and me—arrayed in a semicircle in a large visitation hall, two prison guards keeping watch from a respectful distance.

86   Greg was intensely anxious in the days leading up to the meeting—he hadn't seen Eddie since immediately after the murders—and he prepared a kind of soliloquy for the occasion, an accounting of all that had brought him to that awful day. Five or six minutes into the speech, though, it proved too much, and Greg fell apart and began to sob. Russell intervened and advised him to take his time, to let the conversation wander where it wanted to go. Soon the conversation settled into an easier rhythm, one in which the grim recollections were interspersed with happier reminiscences.

87   At one point, while talking about Jobie's aloofness even when they were kids, Eddie said, "If you could get two words out of Jobie, you were doing real well." Then he told Greg: "He was proud of you. I know, because he used to brag on you to me. Problem was, he just didn't know how to express it."

88   This came to Greg with the force of revelation, appearing to please and sadden him simultaneously. He described that last night with his parents, came to the part where his father took up his old guitar. "He tried to teach me the chords to this old bluegrass song, really pretty song, and all these years I've been trying to remember what it was. It kind of went like this." Greg looked at the group and hummed a few bars.

89   "'Wildwood Flower,'" Eddie said, grinning. "Our father used to play it all the time." And for the next few moments, he and Greg sat humming the tune together.

90   I returned to the prison the next day and met with Greg alone. He was emotionally exhausted from the experience and was focused on getting some photographs of his parents that Eddie promised to send.

91   "I've only ever had this one photo of them," he said, "but you can't see their eyes in it, so I feel like I can't really remember what they look like. I just really want to be able to see their eyes."

92   When those photos arrived, though, Greg was devastated. "I have only been able to look at them a few times [since] the night I received them," he wrote to me in an e-mail. "I feel pretty bad, man. It has me feeling all kinds of screwed-up things. Just seeing my parents and really seeing them as real people. I mean there are pictures in there from the early '80s. They were all happy. We were all happy."

93   Shortly after that, Greg went quiet for a long time. When our contact resumed, the weekly phone calls became monthly phone calls, my e-mails to him going unanswered for long stretches. "Sorry, man," he offered, when I finally confronted him about it in a phone call, "I've just been really busy."

94   "Busy? In prison?"

95   We shared a laugh—but a soft one lest the hypersensitive prison phone system cut us off.

96   **Mark Sevier, a** powerfully built man with close-cropped hair, is the superintendent of Miami Correctional. By coincidence, he was an inmate counselor in the winter of 1994 at Wabash Valley, the prison in southwestern Indiana where the 15-year-old Greg Ousley was sent to start serving his 60-year sentence. Sevier was assigned to his case.

97   "I remember when he came in," Sevier told me. "He was just so young and little—and he's not a big guy even now—but back then he was like, what, 130 pounds? It was like putting a baby in among all these grown men."

98   Their new charge presented the Wabash Valley staff with a formidable challenge. All cells at Wabash were two-man units, and while Greg was slated to enter the general population, that population included nearly 200 maximum-security inmates. "We thought very carefully about who to put him in with," Sevier recalled. "I think we also tapped some of the other guys on the block to watch out for him. It's better now, because they've got a special unit down there to house all the under-age guys who've come in, but back then there was nothing like that."

99   Despite his earlier intentions, Greg hasn't had another family mediation session since the one in 2010 with his uncle Eddie. As grueling as that meeting was, he felt it helped him gain a new perspective on his parents, especially his father. He now suspects that what he interpreted in his father as disinterest, even disgust, more likely stemmed from a paralyzing self-consciousness. Jobie found solace from this torment by shutting himself away in his workshed.

100   That, and probably he was bone tired. "You know, my parents worked so damned hard," Greg says, "and they were constantly being moved from one shift to another, so their sleep was always messed up. How much of it was maybe just that they were tired? Even that afternoon when I told my mom that I was scared, maybe it was, 'O.K., I know this is important, but right at this moment, I just can't deal.' But when you're 13, 14, everything's about you, you don't get any of that."

101   Over the past two years, Greg's isolation has eased. While he's yet to be visited by his sisters, he is now in e-mail contact with them and regularly receives letters from two nieces. Chloe Neer, his old neighbor in Pierceton, recently began visiting him in Miami. "I try to get down at least once a month," she says.

102   As for winning an early release, Greg now knows that is very unlikely, unless there occurs some unforeseeable change of heart by his aunt or by the prosecutor, Daniel Hampton. At the end of my meeting with Sevier, he asked how much more time Greg had to serve. In prisons, both inmates and officers have a habit of thinking of doing time in terms of stamina, as if it were a long-distance race, and when I told Sevier seven years, he briefly pondered before giving a sharp nod.

103   "He can do that. He's a strong guy."

104   Strong or not, Greg's case is a telling one in the national debate over just what is accomplished by sentencing juveniles to long prison sentences. In the case of juvenile parricide, there is an added paradox. Because it is among the most target-specific of crimes, criminologists believe that an abused juvenile who killed a parent is likely to be at low risk of future criminality if he gets treatment and has a strong social support system when he is released. Certainly society might recoil at the notion that a child who murders his parents should be "let off" by a juvenile detention that might end at 18 or 21, but attached to this is the question of when the thirst for punishment becomes counterproductive to all concerned. After all, Greg Ousley, like 95 percent of other prison inmates, is going to come out some day, and is it better for society that he do so when he's in his 30s and still has the potential of patching together a somewhat-normal life, or not until his 40s when his options will be far more limited?

105   This debate seems a long way off in Kosciusko County. In April 2010, two young boys from a rural corner of the county, Colt Lundy, 15, and Paul Gingerich, 12, shot to death Lundy's stepfather, Phillip Danner. Days later, at the urging of the county prosecutor, Daniel Hampton, the boys' cases were waived into the adult system, where, facing up to 65 years in prison, both entered plea agreements. On Jan. 4, 2011, almost 17 years to the day that Greg Ousley was sentenced in the same county courthouse, Paul Gingerich was sentenced to 25 years. Considered by prison officials to be too vulnerable for even the youth as adults wing of Wabash Valley prison, Gingerich is currently being temporarily housed at a juvenile facility. He is the youngest adult inmate in Indiana.

Scott Anderson is a contributing writer to the magazine and the author of the novel *Moonlight Hotel.* He is at work on a book about World War I.

Language, Gender, and Culture

Honor Code

By David Brooks
New York Times, July 5, 2012

1. Henry V is one of Shakespeare's most appealing characters. He was rambunctious when young and courageous when older. But suppose Henry went to an American school.

2. By about the third week of nursery school, Henry's teacher would be sending notes home saying that Henry "had another hard day today." He was disruptive during circle time. By midyear, there'd be sly little hints dropped that maybe Henry's parents should think about medication for attention deficit hyperactivity disorder. Many of the other boys are on it, and they find school much easier.

3. By elementary school, Henry would be lucky to get 20-minute snatches of recess. During one, he'd jump off the top of the jungle gym, and, by the time he hit the ground, the supervising teachers would be all over him for breaking the safety rules. He'd get in a serious wrestling match with his buddy Falstaff, and, by the time he got him in a headlock, there'd be suspensions all around.

4. First, Henry would withdraw. He'd decide that the official school culture is for wimps and softies and he'd just disengage. In kindergarten, he'd wonder why he just couldn't be good. By junior high, he'd lose interest in trying and his grades would plummet.

5. Then he'd rebel. If the official high school culture was über-nurturing, he'd be über-crude. If it valued cooperation and sensitivity, he'd devote his mental energies to violent video games and aggressive music. If college wanted him to be focused and tightly ambitious, he'd exile himself into a lewd and unsupervised laddie subculture. He'd have vague high ambitions but no realistic way to realize them. Day to day, he'd look completely adrift.

6. This is roughly what's happening in schools across the Western world. The education system has become culturally cohesive, rewarding and encouraging a certain sort of person: one who is nurturing, collaborative, disciplined, neat, studious, industrious and ambitious. People who don't fit this cultural ideal respond by disengaging and rebelling.

7. Far from all, but many of the people who don't fit in are boys. A decade or so ago, people started writing books and articles on the boy crisis. At the time, the evidence was disputable and some experts pushed back. Since then, the evidence that boys are falling behind has mounted. The case is closed. The numbers for boys get worse and worse.

8. By 12th grade, male reading test scores are far below female test scores. The eminent psychologist Michael Thompson mentioned at the Aspen Ideas Festival a few days ago that 11th-grade boys are now writing at the same level as 8th-grade girls. Boys used to have an advantage in math and science, but that gap is nearly gone.

9. Boys are much more likely to have discipline problems. An article as far back as 2004 in the magazine Educational Leadership found that boys accounted for nearly three-quarters of the D's and F's.

10   Some colleges are lowering the admissions requirements just so they can admit a decent number of men. Even so, men make up just over 40 percent of college students. Two million fewer men graduated from college over the past decade than women. The performance gap in graduate school is even higher.

11   Some of the decline in male performance may be genetic. The information age rewards people who mature early, who are verbally and socially sophisticated, who can control their impulses. Girls may, on average, do better at these things. After all, boys are falling behind not just in the U.S., but in all 35 member-nations of the Organization for Economic Cooperation and Development.

12   But the big story here is cultural and moral. If schools want to re-engage Henry, they can't pretend they can turn him into a reflective Hamlet just by feeding him his meds and hoping he'll sit quietly at story time. If schools want to educate a fiercely rambunctious girl, they can't pretend they will successfully tame her by assigning some of those exquisitely sensitive Newbery award-winning novellas. Social engineering is just not that easy.

13   Schools have to engage people as they are. That requires leaders who insist on more cultural diversity in school: not just teachers who celebrate cooperation, but other teachers who celebrate competition; not just teachers who honor environmental virtues, but teachers who honor military virtues; not just curriculums that teach how to share, but curriculums that teach how to win and how to lose; not just programs that work like friendship circles, but programs that work like boot camp.

14   The basic problem is that schools praise diversity but have become culturally homogeneous. The education world has become a distinct subculture, with a distinct ethos and attracting a distinct sort of employee. Students who don't fit the ethos get left out.

15   Little Prince Hal has a lot going on inside. He's not the unfeeling, uncommunicative, testosterone-driven cretin of common boy stereotype. He's just inspired by a different honor code. He doesn't find much inspiration in school, but he should.

phylosophe

By Judith Butler
Transcript of *YouTube* clip, February 23, 2007

1   There's a story—that came out around, I don't know, eight years ago—of a young man who lived in Maine, and he walked down the street of his small town where he had lived his entire life. And he walks with what we call a "swish"—a kind of . . . his hips move back and forth in a "feminine" way. And as he grew older—14, 15, 16—that swish, that walk became more pronounced, OK, and it was more dramatically feminine, and he started to be harassed by the boys in the town. And soon two or three boys stopped his walk, and they fought with him.

2   And they ended up throwing him over a bridge and they killed him.

3   So then we have to ask: Why would someone be killed for the way they walk? Why would that walk be so upsetting to those other boys that they would feel that they must negate this person, they must expunge the trace of this person, they must stop that walk, no matter what, they must eradicate the possibility of that person ever walking again?

4   It seems to me that we are talking about an extremely deep panic or fear, an anxiety that pertains to gender norms.

5   And if someone says you must comply with the norm of masculinity, otherwise you will die, or I kill you now because you do not comply, then we have to start to question what the relation is between complying with gender and coercion.

The Transformation of Silence into Language and Action*

By Audre Lorde
An excerpt from *The Cancer Journals*

(handwritten: Such a Powerful Woman)

1   I would like to preface my remarks on the transformation of silence into language and action with a poem. The title of it is "A Song for Many Movements" and this reading is dedicated to Winnie Mandela. Winnie Mandela is a South African freedom fighter who is in exile now somewhere in South Africa. She had been in prison and had been released and was picked up again after she spoke out against the recent jailing of black school children who were singing freedom songs, and who were charged with public violence... "A Song for Many Movements":

2   Nobody wants to die on the way
        caught between ghosts of whiteness
        and the real water
        none of us wanted to leave
        our bones
        on the way to salvation
        three planets to the left
        a century of light years ago
        our spices are separate and particular
        but our skins sing in complimentary keys
        at a quarter to eight mean time
        we were telling the same stories
        over and over and over.

(handwritten: even the mighty fall)

3   Broken down gods survive
        in the crevasses and mudpots
        of every beleaguered city
        where it is obvious
        there are too many bodies
        to cart to the ovens
        or gallows
        and our uses have become
        more important than our silence
        after the fall

(handwritten: Too many have died)

        too many empty cases
        of blood to bury or burn
        there will be no body left
        to listen
        and our labor
        has become more important
        than our silence.

* Originally given as a speech, December 28, 1977, at the Lesbian and Literature Panel of the Modern Language Association.

4   Our labor
           has become more important
           than our silence.

           (from Audre Lorde's *The Black Unicorn,* W.W. Norton & Co., 1978)

5   I have come to believe over and over again that what is most important to me
      must be spoken, made verbal and shared, even at the risk of having it bruised
      or misunderstood. That the speaking profits me, beyond any other effect. I am
      standing here as a black lesbian poet, and the meaning of all that waits upon
      the fact that I am still alive, and might not have been. Less than two months
      ago, I was told by two doctors, one female and one male, that I would have
      to have breast surgery, and that there was a 60 to 80 percent chance that the
      tumor was malignant. Between that telling and the actual surgery, there was
      a three week period of the agony of an involuntary reorganization of my entire
      life. The surgery was completed, and the growth was benign.

6   But within those three weeks, I was forced to look upon myself and my living
      with a harsh and urgent clarity that has left me still shaken but much stronger.
      This is a situation faced by many women, by some of you here today. Some of
      what I experienced during that time has helped elucidate for me much of what
      I feel concerning the transformation of silence into language and action.

7   In becoming forcibly and essentially aware of my mortality, and of what I
      wished and wanted for my life, however short it might be, priorities and
      omissions became strongly etched in a merciless light, and what I most
      regretted were my silences. Of what had I *ever* been afraid? To question or
      to speak as I believed could have meant pain, or death. But we all hurt in so
      many different ways, all the time, and pain will either change, or end. Death,
      on the other hand, is the final silence. And that might be coming quickly, now,
      without regard for whether I had ever spoken what needed to be said, or had
      only betrayed myself into small silences, while I planned someday to speak, or
      waited for someone else's words. And I began to recognize a source of power
      within myself that comes from the knowledge that while it is most desirable
      not to be afraid, learning to put fear into a perspective gave me great strength.

8   I was going to die, if not sooner then later, whether or not I had ever spoken
      myself. My silences had not protected me. Your silence will not protect you.
      But for every real word spoken, for every attempt I had ever made to speak
      those truths for which I am still seeking, I had made contact with other women
      while we examined the words to fit a world in which we all believed, bridging
      our differences. And it was the concern and caring of all those women which
      gave me strength and enabled me to scrutinize the essentials of my living.

9   The women who sustained me through that period were black and white, old
      and young, lesbian, bisexual, and heterosexual, and we all shared a war against
      the tyrannies of silence. They all gave me a strength and concern without
      which I could not have survived intact. Within those weeks of acute fear came
      the knowledge—within the war we are all waging with the forces of death,
      subtle and otherwise, conscious or not—I am not only a casualty, I am also a
      warrior.

[Handwritten margin notes: "Thank god"; "such deep words"; "such an interesting quote 'death is the final silence'"; "don't be afraid to stand up"; "she had support from the suppression"; "she isn't just a martyr"]

10   What are the words you do not yet have? What do you need to say? What are the tyrannies you swallow day by day and attempt to make your own, until you will sicken and die of them, still in silence? Perhaps for some of you here today, I am the face of one of your fears. Because I am woman, because I am black, because I am lesbian, because I am myself, a black woman warrior poet doing my work, come to ask you, are you doing yours?

11   And, of course, I am afraid—you can hear it in my voice—because the transformation of silence into language and action is an act of self-revelation and that always seems fraught with danger. But my daughter, when I told her of our topic and my difficulty with it, said, "Tell them about how you're never really a whole person if you remain silent, because there's always that one little piece inside of you that wants to be spoken out, and if you keep ignoring it, it gets madder and madder and hotter and hotter, and if you don't speak it out one day it will just up and punch you in the mouth."

12   In the cause of silence, each one of us draws the face of her own fear—fear of contempt, of censure, or some judgment, or recognition, of challenge, of annihilation. But most of all, I think, we fear the very visibility without which we also cannot truly live. Within this country where racial difference creates a constant, if unspoken, distortion of vision, black women have on one hand always been highly visible, and so, on the other hand, have been rendered invisible through the depersonalization of racism. Even within the women's movement, we have had to fight and still do, for that very visibility which also renders us most vulnerable, our blackness. For to survive in the mouth of this dragon we call america, we have had to learn this first and most vital lesson—that we were never meant to survive. Not as human beings. And neither were most of you here today, black or not. And that visibility which makes us most vulnerable is that which also is the source of our greatest strength. Because the machine will try to grind you into dust anyway, whether or not we speak. We can sit in our corners mute forever while our sisters and our selves are wasted, while our children are distorted and destroyed, while our earth is poisoned, we can sit in our safe corners mute as bottles, and we still will be no less afraid.

13   In my house this year we are celebrating the feast of Kwanza, the African-American festival of harvest which begins the day after Christmas and lasts for seven days. There are seven principles of Kwanza, one for each day. The first principle is Umoja, which means unity, the decision to strive for and maintain unity in self and community. The principle for yesterday, the second day, was Kujichagulia—self-determination—the decision to define ourselves, name ourselves, and speak for ourselves, instead of being defined and spoken for by others. Today is the third day of Kwanza, and the principle for today is Ujima—collective work and responsibility—the decision to build and maintain ourselves and our communities together and to recognize and solve our problems together.

14   Each of us is here now because in one way or another we share a commitment to language and to the power of language, and to the reclaiming of that language which has been made to work against us. In the transformation of silence into language and action, it is vitally necessary for each one of us to establish or examine her function in that transformation, and to recognize her role as vital within that transformation.

15   For those of us who write, it is necessary to scrutinize not only the truth of what we speak, but the truth of that language by which we speak it. For others, it is to share and spread also those words that are meaningful to us. But primarily for us all, it is necessary to teach by living and speaking those truths which we believe and know beyond understanding. Because in this way alone we can survive, by taking part in a process of life that is creative and continuing, that is growth.

[handwritten: write with the intention to tell the truth]

16   And it is never without fear; of visibility, of the harsh light of scrutiny and perhaps judgment, of pain, of death. But we have lived through all of those already, in silence, except death. And I remind myself all the time now, that if I were to have been born mute, or had maintained an oath of silence my whole life long for safety, I would still have suffered, and I would still die. It is very good for establishing perspective.

[handwritten: If you're silent she would've still suffered.]

[handwritten margin: ★ notice] (17)   And where the words of women are crying to be heard, we must each of us recognize our responsibility to seek those words out, to read them and share them and examine them in their pertinence to our lives. That we not hide behind the mockeries of separations that have been imposed upon us and which so often we accept as our own: for instance, "I can't possibly teach black women's writing—their experience is so different from mine," yet how many years have you spent teaching Plato and Shakespeare and Proust? Or another: "She's a white woman and what could she possibly have to say to me?" Or, "She's a lesbian, what would my husband say, or my chairman?" Or again, "This woman writes of her sons and I have no children." And all the other endless ways in which we rob ourselves of ourselves and each other.

[handwritten: write for those who cannot speak stand up for those who won't]

18   We can learn to work and speak when we are afraid in the same way we have learned to work and speak when we are tired. For we have been socialized to respect fear more than our own needs for language and definition, and while we wait in silence for that final luxury of fearlessness, the weight of that silence will choke us.

19   The fact that we are here and that I speak now these words is an attempt to break that silence and bridge some of those differences between us, for it is not difference which immobilizes us, but silence. And there are so many silences to be broken.

[handwritten: (1-sentence) Summary: Silence will be your downfall and it will always choke you with a kosh.]

His Politeness Is Her Powerlessness

By Deborah Tannen
An excerpt from *You Just Don't Understand: Women and Men in Conversation*

1   There are many kinds of evidence that women and men are judged differently even if they talk the same way. This tendency makes mischief in discussions of women, men, and power. If a linguistic strategy is used by a woman, it is seen as powerless; if it is done by a man, it is seen as powerful. Often, the labeling of "women's language" as "powerless language" reflects the view of women's behavior through the lens of men's.

2   Because they are not struggling to be one-up, women often find themselves framed as one-down. Any situation is ripe for misinterpretation, because status and connections are displayed by the same moves. This ambiguity accounts for much misinterpretation, by experts as well as nonexperts, by which women's ways of talking, uttered in a spirit of rapport, are branded powerless. Nowhere is this inherent ambiguity clearer than in a brief comment in a newspaper article in which a couple, both psychologists, were jointly interviewed. The journalist asked them the meaning of "being very polite." The two experts responded simultaneously, giving different answers. The man said, "Subservience." The woman said, "Sensitivity." Both experts were right, but each was describing the view of a different gender.

3   Experts and nonexperts alike tend to see anything women do as evidence of powerlessness. The same newspaper article quotes another psychologist as saying, "A man might ask a woman, 'Will you please go to the store?' where a woman might say, 'Gee, I really need a few things from the store, but I'm so tired.'" The woman's style is called "covert," a term suggesting negative qualities like being "sneaky" and "underhanded." The reason offered for this is power: The woman doesn't feel she has a right to ask directly.

4   Granted, women have lower status than men in our society. But this is not necessarily why they prefer not to make outright demands. The explanation for a woman's indirectness could just as well be her seeking connection. If you get your way as a result of having demanded it, the payoff is satisfying in terms of status: You're one-up because others are doing as you told them. But if you get your way because others happened to want the same thing, or because they offered freely, the payoff is in rapport. You're neither one-up nor one-down but happily connected to others whose wants are the same as yours. Furthermore, if indirectness is understood by both parties, then there is nothing covert about it: That a request is being made is clear. Calling an indirect communication covert reflects the view of someone for whom the direct style seems "natural" and "logical"—a view more common among men.

5   Indirectness itself does not reflect powerlessness. It is easy to think of situations where indirectness is the prerogative of those in power. For example, a wealthy couple who know that their servants will do their bidding need not give direct orders, but can simply state wishes: The woman of the house says, "It's chilly in here," and the servant sets about raising the temperature. The man of the house says, "It's dinner time," and the servant

sees about having dinner served. Perhaps the ultimate indirectness is getting someone to do something without saying anything at all: The hostess rings a bell and the maid brings the next course; or a parent enters the room where children are misbehaving and stands with hands on hips, and the children immediately stop what they're doing.

6   Entire cultures operate on elaborate systems of indirectness. For example, I discovered in a small research project that most Greeks assumed that a wife who asked, "Would you like to go to the party?" was hinting that she wanted to go. They felt that she wouldn't bring it up if she didn't want to go. Furthermore, they felt, she would not state her preference outright because that would sound like a demand. Indirectness was the appropriate means for communicating her preference.

7   Japanese culture has developed indirectness to a fine art. For example, a Japanese anthropologist, Harumi Befu, explains the delicate exchange of indirectness required by a simple invitation to lunch. When his friend extended the invitation, Befu first had to determine whether it was meant literally or just pro forma, much as an American might say, "We'll have to have you over for dinner some time" but would not expect you to turn up at the door. Having decided the invitation was meant literally and having accepted, Befu was then asked what he would like to eat. Following custom, he said anything would do, but his friend, also following custom, pressed him to specify. Host and guest repeated this exchange an appropriate number of times, until Befu deemed it polite to answer the question—politely—by saying that tea over rice would be fine. When he arrived for lunch, he was indeed served tea over rice—as the last course of a sumptuous meal. Befu was not surprised by the feast, because he knew that protocol required it. Had he been given what he had asked for, he would have been insulted. But protocol also required that he make a great show of being surprised.

8   This account of mutual indirectness in a lunch invitation may strike Americans as excessive. But far more cultures in the world use elaborate systems of indirectness than value directness. Only modern Western societies place a priority on direct communication, and even for us it is more a value than a practice.

9   Evidence from other cultures also makes it clear that indirectness does not in itself reflect low status. Rather, our assumptions about the status of women compel us to interpret anything they do as reflecting low status. Anthropologist Elinor Keenan, for example, found that in a Malagasy-speaking village on the island of Madagascar, it is women who are direct and men who are indirect. And the villagers see the men's indirect way of speaking, using metaphors and proverbs, as the better way. For them, indirectness, like the men who use it, has high status. They regard women's direct style as clumsy and crude, debasing the beautiful subtlety of men's language. Whether women or men are direct or indirect differs; what remains constant is that the women's style is negatively evaluated—seen as lower in status than the men's.

Prelude: The Barbershop

By Vershawn Ashanti Young
Preface from *Your Average Nigga: Performing Race, Literacy, and Masculinity*

1   While sitting in the only black barbershop in Cedar Rapids, Iowa, on the morning of writing this prelude, trying to think of the best way to acquaint you with what this book is about and who I am as the author behind it, I was struck with just how different I am from a lot of other black men, and yet again I was compelled to acknowledge my desire to be like them. The men I observed walked with that lanky dip I wish I could perfect; they talked casually but passionately about sports, basketball especially, with the deep resonance that reverberates in my hungry ears. Many spoke a spicy black lingo, the hip linguistics that even white kids from Iowa crave. The men wore pants that sagged. Their feet were adorned with the latest two-hundred-dollar sneakers endorsed by Allen Iverson or Shaq. Their self-assurance made me want to mimic them, to give a gender performance that would say unequivocally to everybody—white folks, black folks, everybody—that I too am a black male with balls. That's part of why I was at the barbershop—and to get that fresh bald fade, one of the trendy hallmarks of black masculinity.

I notice this in one of my friends

2   However, because this barbershop is located smack dab in the middle of Mostly White, Iowa—a state that unapologetically leads in incarcerating black men—my vicarious revel in black masculinity was sobered by the statistics: while only 2 percent of those who live in Iowa are black, blacks comprise 25 percent of the state's prison population. Thus in addition to enchantment, I felt a conflicting fusion of fortune and tribulation—fortune because my language and demeanor often mark me as educated, separating me from those who exemplify the stigmatized (and paradoxically romanticized) black male profile, and consequently excusing me, though certainly not always, from the plight that follows that image. I am troubled because the black men who suffer most from the educational and judicial systems are poor, from the underclass, from the ghetto, like me. And although many flee the big city, looking for a small haven in mid-America, they sometimes find that their situation gets worse. I both identify with their predicament and disidentify with it because I am and am not exactly one of them, and both do and do not want to be.

He's stuck in limbo

I can sort of connect w/ being b/c because I'm either not gay enough or straight enough not Chunk I

3   To embrace my blackness, my heritage, my manliness, I identify with men who represent the ghetto. I no longer want to deny my class background or the racial experience associated with it. I identify to belong. I disidentify to escape racism, to avoid the structures that oppress black men. But I also disidentify to retaliate against black men—to punish them for what I perceive as their efforts to disown me. This ambivalence provokes me to imitate and just as often to dissociate from the black men I envy. Both efforts fail. Neither alleviates my racial anxiety. Instead, they heighten the angst I experience. As a result I am hyperaware of how masculine I am (not) and how black I (don't) act.

You are torn between a love and hatred for your white.

4   I can't neatly explain why my visit to the barbershop brings all this to mind and spurs my unease. I mean, the barbers are only courteous. They take me ahead of clients who come less frequently. They even call me sir, although I'm not much older than they are and tell them to use my first name. Still, I can't shake the way I feel. For although I know that some of my discomfort is self-induced, a consequence of not conversing much with the barbers and their customers about their racial and gender performances and not allowing them to give their take on mine, I also know there's reason for my worry, that my experience is *Chunk II* not unique.

5   Shelly Eversley aptly summarizes part of the reason for my concern in her book *The Real Negro.* Offering an anecdote about the time she felt uncomfortable in a black barbershop in Baltimore, Eversley concludes that the barbershop is "a racial and cultural distinction" from the university campus, the site where we both trained as intellectuals and currently work as professors. Because we participate in both sites, we suffer from the conflict that exists between them. So in order to get along on the (white) campus and in the barbershop, we must alter not the color of our skin but the ways we perform race in each location. These racial performances are most often carried out through language, the way we communicate.

Values her as an author & knows she goes through the same thing

6   Eversley, for instance, was "uneasy in her barber's chair" as "she listened to the men ... discussing their plans to [participate in and] make a political statement" during the Million Man March. In what she terms "her best graduate-student speak," she expressed her belief that the march perpetuated the oppression of black women and gays. "For a few seconds, the men ... seemed to listen," she writes, "[but] then continued with their conversation." Prompted by her barber to persist (he whispered: "Try it again, college girl"), "she offered a picture of her thoughts." She explained that the "sexism and homophobia" of the march "mirrored the logic of white supremacy." As she left, the men told her she was "still 100 percent black." As she made her way to campus, however, she says she "felt triumphant and sad" —triumphant because, although the men "had read the education in her language as proof of her 'imitation whiteness,'" she was able "to shed her academic self-consciousness" and belong, to be seen as "part of the group, as authentic." She was sad because, "when she arrived on campus," her performance of black authenticity lost its cachet; she realized that the benefits she garnered in the shop were now distinct disadvantages.

another confliction

such heavy words

7   Why did Eversley feel split in two? Had she become the twenty-first-century incarnation of Du Bois's double consciousness, an embodiment of racial schizophrenia? One moment she spoke as an "imitation white woman," and after a switch of the tongue, she became an authentically black one. What endowed the barbers with the authority to make her feel race-fake and then authentic? Did her linguistic performance really have such transformative power? Whatever the answers to these questions are, it's clear that Eversley was compelled to contend with the consequence of her performance: the *Chunk III* transformation of her political commitments into identity ambivalence.

8   This racial ambivalence is what makes me so self-conscious about and analytical of other men in the barbershop—because my linguistic performance is rated in relation to theirs. And not only do I feel as if my racial performance is judged, but I know my gender performance is too. Because the barbershop is a masculine space, the performance of heterosexuality is the gold standard. Talking sufficiently black is not enough for me to be heard; I must also speak and act acceptably masculine. This performance is even more difficult for those who are gay or are taken as gay, as I sometimes am, because we are often estranged in these spaces. Quincy Mills offers Eric as an example in this regard in his ethnography of a black barbershop on the South Side of Chicago.

such depth, he seems to hurt for him

9   Mills describes Eric as "one of the regulars in the shop." But unlike other patrons, "his identity is shrouded in suspicion and innuendo," because "the barbers and many customers assume that Eric is gay." As a result, unlike other regulars who become key players in the discourse community, Mills writes that Eric "is silenced as an agenda setter. . . . When [he] would initiate conversations, the men would turn away, ignore him, or patronize him for a short while only to move quickly to other topics." Instead of engaging Eric, they would "act annoyed by his mannerisms and voice."

10 Mills doesn't describe the particulars of Eric's voice and manner, but it's conclusive that for the others his masculine performance is insufficiently heterosexual. What's interesting about the other men's perception of Eric's sexuality is that it's not based on facts but on how he acts. On this Mills is clear: "Eric never came out to me" or to the other men, he says. "There was no confirmation of his sexual identity in the months I spent at the shop." Eric's insufficient heterosexual performance cast him "outside the boundaries of blackness because his demeanor and speech," Mills writes, "are beyond the narrow definitions of masculinity."

chunk IV

11 My personal history is replete with anecdotes like Eversley's and experiences like Eric's, and I'm trying to keep them from adding up, which is why I keep my mouth closed in the barbershop. It's also why I was nervous about reading the novel I brought with me to help pass the wait. It's not that novel reading itself is off-limits in the shop. I've seen other men read. But given my past, my profession, and my dubious masculine performance, I hesitate.

12 Literacy habits, like reading novels of a certain kind and speaking what might appear to be standard English, have always made me seem more queer, more white identified, and more middle class than I am. When I fail to meet the class, gender, and racial notions that others ascribe to me, I'm punished. In some ways, living in a mostly white town and being an assistant professor at a Big Ten school heightens—not lessens, as I had hoped—the conflict that stems from the sometimes converging, but oftentimes diverging, racial and gender expectations that are held out for black men and that we hold for each other.

such depth & understanding and acknowledges that he does it too

chunk V

13   I recognize the problem, and I'm working so that it doesn't consume me. "Hell," I say to encourage myself, "I'm an English professor; that justifies my reading a novel in a barbershop. And what's this nonsense of trying to fit in, to avoid alienation, to avoid name-calling: 'Sissy!' 'Faggot!'" But I wonder: What does not fitting in cost me? This issue of trying to fit in but never succeeding, of being perpetually on the margins of various communities and never finding a way into any one of them, is the trope of my life, making me something of a black Sisyphus. Academic literacy is my heavy rock.

14   You see, my Sisyphean experience in Iowa is a continuation of troubles that began while I was growing up in Chicago, in the late 1970s and '80s, in the notorious Governor Henry Horner Homes, the same site that Alex Kotlowitz writes about in his journalistic ethnography, *There Are No Children Here*. In fact, as Kotlowitz was gathering material for his book, I was still living there. But unlike his subjects, Lafeyette and Pharoah, who are portrayed as boys who must fight the criminalizing lure of the ghetto in order to succeed in school, I was seen as an anomaly. Kotlowitz sees Lafeyette and Pharoah as having identities compatible with the ghetto even as he describes their striving to get out. My identity, however, was atypical, alienating me from my neighbors and hood and excluding me from representations of "authentic" ghetto life. Thus I didn't have to fight to get out of the ghetto. I was kicked out.

Chunk II

15   It might seem like a good thing that I was kicked out. It might seem as if this exile expedited the leave I was seeking. But the problem that this bit of personal history presents, the problem that my monograph theorizes, the problem that my trip to the barbershop illustrates is this: because I ain't no homeboy—though I long to be and would do anything short of killing to gain that identity—I'm not ghetto enough for the ghetto. Because I'm not a white boy, I'm not white enough for white folks. And because I wasn't born into the middle class, I'm not completely accepted by the mainstream. And sometimes, if you can believe it, I'm not ghetto enough for the mainstream or middle class enough for the ghetto or black enough for white folks! The psychoemotional pain that this liminal existence creates, the pain of negotiating multiple cultural and racial worlds, is far too great for many. I've been doing it for a long time and have been able to cope only by transforming my personal problem into an intellectual one. In some ways I'm chipping away at the burden. But far too many are not able to do this. And why should they have to?

16   Perhaps some black men in that barbershop are also trying to avoid racial and cultural punishment. Instead of negotiating two worlds, maybe they have chosen to live in only one—a microcosm, a subculture of white society that accepts and mandates a certain sociolinguistic performance of masculinity. Because they have chosen and are accepted by a community, perhaps they have no need to envy me as I do them. But then what do they lose when they don't try to imitate what I represent? It's my desire to reconcile my ghetto past with my middleclass aspirations and possibly be of assistance to others in the process. I want to expose the factors that make black racial identity incompatible with literacy, especially for males. Thus masculine panic, racial anxiety, and their relation to language and academic literacy (as the prescribed means for class climbing) constitute the three-part theme that I explore in this book.

Chunk VII

1984

That's No Phone. That's My Tracker.

By Peter Maass and Megha Rajagopalan
New York Times, July 13, 2012

1   The device in your purse or jeans that you think is a cellphone—guess again. It is a tracking device that happens to make calls. Let's stop calling them phones. They are trackers.

2   Most doubts about the principal function of these devices were erased when it was recently disclosed that cellphone carriers responded 1.3 million times last year to law enforcement requests for call data. That's not even a complete count, because T-Mobile, one of the largest carriers, refused to reveal its numbers. It appears that millions of cellphone users have been swept up in government surveillance of their calls and where they made them from. Many police agencies don't obtain search warrants when requesting location data from carriers.

3   Thanks to the explosion of GPS technology and smartphone apps, these devices are also taking note of what we buy, where and when we buy it, how much money we have in the bank, whom we text and e-mail, what Web sites we visit, how and where we travel, what time we go to sleep and wake up— and more. Much of that data is shared with companies that use it to offer us services they think we want.

4   We have all heard about the wonders of frictionless sharing, whereby social networks automatically let our friends know what we are reading or listening to, but what we hear less about is frictionless surveillance. Though we invite some tracking—think of our mapping requests as we try to find a restaurant in a strange part of town—much of it is done without our awareness.

5   "Every year, private companies spend millions of dollars developing new services that track, store and share the words, movements and even the thoughts of their customers," writes Paul Ohm, a law professor at the University of Colorado. "These invasive services have proved irresistible to consumers, and millions now own sophisticated tracking devices (smartphones) studded with sensors and always connected to the Internet."

6   Mr. Ohm labels them tracking devices. So does Jacob Appelbaum, a developer and spokesman for the Tor project, which allows users to browse the Web anonymously. Scholars have called them minicomputers and robots. Everyone is struggling to find the right tag, because "cellphone" and "smartphone" are inadequate. This is not a semantic game. Names matter, quite a bit. In politics and advertising, framing is regarded as essential because what you call something influences what you think about it. That's why there are battles over the tags "Obamacare" and "death panels."

7   In just the past few years, cellphone companies have honed their geographic technology, which has become almost pinpoint. The surveillance and privacy implications are quite simple. If someone knows exactly where you are, they probably know what you are doing. Cellular systems constantly check and record the location of all phones on their networks—and this data is particularly treasured by police departments and online advertisers. Cell companies typically retain your geographic information for a year or longer, according to data gathered by the Justice Department.

8   What's the harm? The United States Court of Appeals for the District of Columbia Circuit, ruling about the use of tracking devices by the police, noted that GPS data can reveal whether a person "is a weekly church goer, a heavy drinker, a regular at the gym, an unfaithful husband, an outpatient receiving medical treatment, an associate of particular individuals or political groups—and not just one such fact about a person, but all such facts." Even the most gregarious of sharers might not reveal all that on Facebook.

9   There is an even more fascinating and diabolical element to what can be done with location information. New research suggests that by cross-referencing your geographical data with that of your friends, it's possible to predict your future whereabouts with a much higher degree of accuracy.

10   This is what's known as predictive modeling, and it requires nothing more than your cellphone data.

11   If we are naïve to think of them as phones, what should we call them? Eben Moglen, a law professor at Columbia University, argues that they are robots for which we—the proud owners—are merely the hands and feet. "They see everything, they're aware of our position, our relationship to other human beings and other robots, they mediate an information stream around us," he has said. Over time, we've used these devices less for their original purpose. A recent survey by O2, a British cell carrier, showed that making calls is the fifth-most-popular activity for smartphones; more popular uses are Web browsing, checking social networks, playing games and listening to music. Smartphones are taking over the functions that laptops, cameras, credit cards and watches once performed for us.

12   If you want to avoid some surveillance, the best option is to use cash for prepaid cellphones that do not require identification. The phones transmit location information to the cell carrier and keep track of the numbers you call, but they are not connected to you by name. Destroy the phone or just drop it into a trash bin, and its data cannot be tied to you. These cellphones, known as burners, are the threads that connect privacy activists, Burmese dissidents and coke dealers.

13   Prepaids are a hassle, though. What can the rest of us do? Leaving your smartphone at home will help, but then what's the point of having it? Turning it off when you're not using it will also help, because it will cease pinging your location to the cell company, but are you really going to do that? Shutting it down does not even guarantee it's off—malware can keep it on without your realizing it. The only way to be sure is to take out the battery. Guess what? If you have an iPhone, you will need a tiny screwdriver to remove the back cover. Doing that will void your warranty.

14   Matt Blaze, a professor of computer and information science at the University of Pennsylvania, has written extensively about these issues and believes we are confronted with two choices: "Don't have a cellphone or just accept that you're living in the Panopticon."

15   There is another option. People could call them trackers. It's a neutral term, because it covers positive activities—monitoring appointments, bank balances, friends—and problematic ones, like the government and advertisers watching us.

16   We can love or hate these devices—or love *and* hate them—but it would make sense to call them what they are so we can fully understand what they do.

Peter Maass and Megha Rajagopalan are reporters on digital privacy for *ProPublica,* the nonprofit investigative newsroom.

Long Beach Police to Use 400 Cameras Citywide to Fight Crime

Tapping into hundreds of privately owned cameras, the system synchronizes law enforcement data with real-time video feeds from parks, beaches and business corridors.

By Richard Winton
Los Angeles Times, August 15, 2012

1   Long Beach police now have eyes everywhere.

2   Battling a worsening budget and seeking to make Long Beach one of the safest big cities, Police Chief Jim McDonnell is turning to more than 400 cameras citywide as a solution.

3   Although the city has a few dozen cameras across the community, McDonnell has set up a system to tap into hundreds of privately owned cameras that are part of the city's streetscape. The new program synchronizes law enforcement data with real-time video feeds from parks, beaches, business corridors and even some retail centers.

4   Dubbed Long Beach Common Operating Picture, or Long Beach COP, the "state-of-the-art program" was unveiled this week by McDonnell and Mayor Bob Foster.

5   "We are using every technology advantage to improve safety in this city. Long Beach officers will now know even before they arrive what potential threats they face," McDonnell said. "It will help us to respond to crimes better and prevent other crimes."

6   With Long Beach experiencing a 40-year low in serious crimes, McDonnell said he is looking for every advantage he can get to keep the city safe.

7   Said Foster: "We're putting more eyes on the street without putting more bodies out there."

8   The chief said it won't be a case of "big brother is watching," because a central control center will enlist the private cameras only when police know an incident is unfolding in a certain area.

9   "We are not running a camera-monitoring center, but it will allow us to see what happened or is occurring on a street or intersection," McDonnell said. "It is designed to make us more efficient in combating crime and to promote greater community and officer safety."

10   McDonnell said that when crimes occur, a quick examination of camera recordings in the moments before and after can reveal vital clues or suspects. He said London's extensive camera system helped capture terrorist bombers there.

11   Private security cameras are already connected to their owners electronically, and the department has been able to access such feeds when needed, he said.

12   The cameras are connected to a city operations center with computer terminals that can access an array of databases from the Justice Department, Department of Motor Vehicles and other agencies, allowing staff to chase down the slimmest of clues, such as a partial license plate in a bank robbery getaway, he said.

13   The center can also receive live feeds of pursuits from Police Department helicopters. The system will be used heavily during crisis situations and on Friday and Saturday nights when calls and incidents tend to peak, McDonnell said.

14   He said the center and new technologies were paid for by federal grants; he hopes one day to download images from the system to officers in their patrol cars.

15   The program debuts as the city and department face a budget squeeze that could slash the police agency's budget by nearly $9 million.

Bullying: A Research Project

Students' Perspectives on Cyber Bullying

By Patricia W. Agatston, Ph.D.[a],*, Robin Kowalski, Ph.D.[b], and Susan Limber, Ph.D.[c]

a   Cobb County School District, Prevention/Intervention Center, Marietta, Georgia
b   Department of Psychology, Clemson University, Clemson, South Carolina
c   Institute on Family and Neighbor Life, Clemson University, Clemson, South Carolina

Journal of Adolescent Health

Abstract

1   The aim of this study was to gain a better understanding of the impact of cyber bullying on students and the possible need for prevention messages targeting students, educators, and parents. A total of 148 middle and high school students were interviewed during focus groups held at two middle and two high schools in a public school district. The focus groups were approximately 45 minutes in length. Students were divided by gender and asked a series of scripted questions by a same-gender student assistance counselor. We found that students' comments during the focus groups suggest that students—particularly females—view cyber bullying as a problem, but one rarely discussed at school, and that students do not see the school district personnel as helpful resources when dealing with cyber bullying. Students are currently experiencing the majority of cyber bullying instances outside of the school day; however there is some impact at school. Students were able to suggest some basic strategies for dealing with cyber bullying, but were less likely to be aware of strategies to request the removal of objectionable websites, as well as how to respond as a helpful bystander when witnessing cruel online behavior. We conclude that school districts should address cyber bullying through a combination of policies and information that are shared with students and parents. Schools should include cyber bullying as part of their bullying prevention strategies and include classroom lessons that address reporting and bystander behavior. © 2007 Society for Adolescent Medicine. All rights reserved.

Keywords: Cyber bullying; Internet; Prevention; Students

2   Young people are very sophisticated users of technology and often lead the way in adapting new technologies to everyday use. Their technological savvy, combined with the ability to be online without much adult supervision, can lead to behaviors that are high risk. Such high risk behaviors include exposure to pornography, drugs, violence, and cyber bullying (i.e., using the Internet to harass and bully others). In a study involving 3767 students in grades 6–8, Kowalski and Limber found that although 78% of the students surveyed had no experience with cyber bullying, 11% were victims of cyber bullying, 7% were bully/victims, and 4% were bullies [1].

*   Address correspondence to: Patricia W. Agatston, Ph.D., Cobb County School District, Prevention/Intervention Center, 514 Glover Street, Marietta, GA 30080.
     E-mail address: pagatston@bellsouth.net

3   In addition to rates of cyber bullying reported by youth, it is helpful to gain an understanding of how concerned youth are about cyber bullying and whether or not the prevention of cyber bullying is being addressed in the school and community setting. This article will discuss findings from focus groups conducted in the Cobb County School District of Marietta, Georgia. Despite frequent offcampus origination, some cyber bullying incidents come to the attention of school district personnel because they are disruptive to the school day. The rationale for the focus groups was to gain a better understanding of the impact of cyber bullying on students and the possible need for prevention messages targeting students, educators, and parents. In addition students' responses would provide input for policy development governing students' use of the Internet and other mobile devices on campus.

Methods

4   Approximately 150 students participated in focus groups at two middle schools and two high schools. Although income demographic level information was not collected for individual students, middle and high schools were selected in part based on diverse socioeconomic (SES) data. One high school had a rate of 13% of students eligible for free or reduced-cost lunches, and the other had a rate of 42%. The two middle schools had free/reduced-cost lunch rates of 25% and 48% respectively. Student participants' ages ranged from 12–17 years. The students were divided by gender during the focus groups. Cyber bullying was defined for the students as "using the Internet or other digital technologies such as cellular phones and personal digital assistants to be intentionally mean or to harass others."

Results

5   Students in the groups indicated that they were very familiar with technology. The majority of them own cellular phones and have Internet access at home. A majority of the female students indicated that cyber bullying was a problem at their schools, although male students were somewhat less likely to agree that this was a problem. Students indicated that the majority of the incidents occurred outside of the school day, with the exception of cyber bullying via text messaging. Students indicated that they were unlikely to report cyber bullying to the adults at school, as it frequently occurs via cellular phone use, and it is against the school policy to have cellular phones on during school hours. When students were asked if they placed text messages or used their cellular phone during the school day, the majority of the students interviewed indicated that they did despite the policy. Students also indicated that they did not think the adults at school could help them if they were experiencing cyber bullying. Students were more likely to report cyber bullying to parents than adults at school, particularly if the bullying was threatening in nature. However students also indicated that they were reluctant to report cyber bullying to parents because they feared the loss of online privileges.

6   When asked whether they could circumvent the school filters to access MySpace or other social networking sites, e-mail, or instant messaging programs, students were able to describe ways to effectively circumvent the school district filters. This knowledge was more apparent at the high school level, but some middle school students were aware of ways to circumvent filters. The students indicated that because no one else was on MySpace or instant messaging at the same time, there was not much incentive to go to these sites during the school day.

7   Students were able to suggest strategies for dealing with cyber bullying, such as to block the sender or ignore the message rather than respond in a manner that would encourage retaliation. Students were less likely to be aware of strategies to request the removal of objectionable websites, as well as how to respond as helpful bystanders when witnessing cruel online behavior.

Discussion

8   The focus group and interviews conducted suggest that students—particularly female students—view cyber bullying as a problem but one rarely discussed at school, and the students do not see the school district personnel as helpful resources for dealing with cyber bullying. Students are currently experiencing the majority of cyber bullying instances outside of the school day, with the possible exception of text messaging via cellular phone. It is possible that with greater ease of access to MySpace and to the Internet in general with increasingly sophisticated cellular phones, we may see an increase in cyber bullying during the school day through the use of such phones. It is recommended that school districts that allow cellular phones on campus prepare for this potential by ensuring that cellular phone policies are enforced with consistent consequences for students who use their phones during the school day. It is also recommended that school districts have parents and students read and sign the school districts' policies regarding acceptable use of technology, and accompany these policies with literature for parents on cyber bullying. Finally, schools are encouraged to adopt bullying prevention programs that include classroom lessons on cyber bullying to ensure that students understand that targeting classmates through negative messages or images online or through cellular phones is a form of bullying [2]. Classroom lessons should include steps that bystanders can take to report and respond to cyber bullying, whether it occurs on campus or in the community.

Acknowledgment

9   The authors acknowledge Michael Carpenter, Ph.D., of the Cobb County School District, for his assistance with student interviews for this project.

References

[1]   Kowalski RM, Limber SP. Cyber bullying among middle school students. J Adolesc Health 2007;41(Suppl):S22–S30.

[2]   Kowalski RM, Limber S, Agatston P. Cyber Bullying: Bullying in the Digital Age. Malden, Massachusetts: Blackwell, 2007.

Bullying in Schools

By Ron Banks
ERIC Digest

1   Bullying in schools is a worldwide problem that can have negative consequences for the general school climate and for the right of students to learn in a safe environment without fear. Bullying can also have negative lifelong consequences--both for students who bully and for their victims. Although much of the formal research on bullying has taken place in the Scandinavian countries, Great Britain, and Japan, the problems associated with bullying have been noted and discussed wherever formal schooling environments exist.

2   Bullying is comprised of direct behaviors such as teasing, taunting, threatening, hitting, and stealing that are initiated by one or more students against a victim. In addition to direct attacks, bullying may also be more indirect by causing a student to be socially isolated through intentional exclusion. While boys typically engage in direct bullying methods, girls who bully are more apt to utilize these more subtle indirect strategies, such as spreading rumors and enforcing social isolation (Ahmad and Smith 1994; Smith and Sharp 1994). Whether the bullying is direct or indirect, the key component of bullying is that the physical or psychological intimidation occurs repeatedly over time to create an ongoing pattern of harassment and abuse (Batsche and Knoff 1994; Olweus 1993).

Extent of the Problem

3   Various reports and studies have established that approximately 15 percent of students are either bullied regularly or are initiators of bullying behavior (Olweus 1993). Direct bullying seems to increase through the elementary years, peak in the middle school/junior high school years, and decline during the high school years. However, while direct physical assault seems to decrease with age, verbal abuse appears to remain constant. School size, racial composition, and school setting (rural, suburban, or urban) do not seem to be distinguishing factors in predicting the occurrence of bullying. Finally, boys engage in bullying behavior and are victims of bullies more frequently than girls (Batsche and Knoff 1994; Nolin, Davies, and Chandler 1995; Olweus 1993; Whitney and Smith 1993).

Characteristics of Bullies and Victims

4   Students who engage in bullying behaviors seem to have a need to feel powerful and in control. They appear to derive satisfaction from inflicting injury and suffering on others, seem to have little empathy for their victims, and often defend their actions by saying that their victims provoked them in some way. Studies indicate that bullies often come from homes where physical punishment is used, where the children are taught to strike back physically as a way to handle problems, and where parental involvement and warmth are frequently lacking. Students who regularly display bullying behaviors are generally defiant or oppositional toward adults, antisocial, and apt to break school rules. In contrast to prevailing myths, bullies appear to have little anxiety and to possess strong self-esteem. There is little evidence to support the contention that they victimize others because they feel bad about themselves (Batsche and Knoff 1994; Olweus 1993).

5   Students who are victims of bullying are typically anxious, insecure, cautious, and suffer from low self-esteem, rarely defending themselves or retaliating when confronted by students who bully them. They may lack social skills and friends, and they are often socially isolated. Victims tend to be close to their parents and may have parents who can be described as overprotective. The major defining physical characteristic of victims is that they tend to be physically weaker than their peers--other physical characteristics such as weight, dress, or wearing eyeglasses do not appear to be significant factors that can be correlated with victimization (Batsche and Knoff 1994; Olweus 1993).

Consequences of Bullying

6   As established by studies in Scandinavian countries, a strong correlation appears to exist between bullying other students during the school years and experiencing legal or criminal troubles as adults. In one study, 60 percent of those characterized as bullies in grades 6-9 had at least one criminal conviction by age 24 (Olweus 1993). Chronic bullies seem to maintain their behaviors into adulthood, negatively influencing their ability to develop and maintain positive relationships (Oliver, Hoover, and Hazler 1994).

7   Victims often fear school and consider school to be an unsafe and unhappy place. As many as 7 percent of America's eighth-graders stay home at least once a month because of bullies. The act of being bullied tends to increase some students' isolation because their peers do not want to lose status by associating with them or because they do not want to increase the risks of being bullied themselves. Being bullied leads to depression and low self-esteem, problems that can carry into adulthood (Olweus 1993; Batsche and Knoff 1994).

Perceptions of Bullying

8   Oliver, Hoover, and Hazler (1994) surveyed students in the Midwest and found that a clear majority felt that victims were at least partially responsible for bringing the bullying on themselves. Students surveyed tended to agree that bullying toughened a weak person, and some felt that bullying "taught" victims appropriate behavior. Charach, Pepler, and Ziegler (1995) found that students considered victims to be "weak," "nerds," and "afraid to fight back." However, 43 percent of the students in this study said that they try to help the victim, 33% said that they should help but do not, and only 24 percent said that bullying was none of their business.

9   Parents are often unaware of the bullying problem and talk about it with their children only to a limited extent (Olweus 1993). Student surveys reveal that a low percentage of students seem to believe that adults will help. Students feel that adult intervention is infrequent and ineffective, and that telling adults will only bring more harassment from bullies. Students report that teachers seldom or never talk to their classes about bullying (Charach, Pepler, and Ziegler 1995). School personnel may view bullying as a harmless right of passage that is best ignored unless verbal and psychological intimidation crosses the line into physical assault or theft.

Intervention Programs

10 Bullying is a problem that occurs in the social environment as a whole. The bullies' aggression occurs in social contexts in which teachers and parents are generally unaware of the extent of the problem and other children are either reluctant to get involved or simply do not know how to help (Charach, Pepler, and Ziegler 1995). Given this situation, effective interventions must involve the entire school community rather than focus on the perpetrators and victims alone. Smith and Sharp (1994) emphasize the need to develop whole-school bullying policies, implement curricular measures, improve the schoolground environment, and empower students through conflict resolution, peer counseling, and assertiveness training. Olweus (1993) details an approach that involves interventions at the school, class, and individual levels. It includes the following components:

11 • An initial questionnaire can be distributed to students and adults. The questionnaire helps both adults and students become aware of the extent of the problem, helps to justify intervention efforts, and serves as a benchmark to measure the impact of improvements in school climate once other intervention components are in place.

12 • A parental awareness campaign can be conducted during parent-teacher conference days, through parent newsletters, and at PTA meetings. The goal is to increase parental awareness of the problem, point out the importance of parental involvement for program success, and encourage parental support of program goals. Questionnaire results are publicized.

13 • Teachers can work with students at the class level to develop class rules against bullying. Many programs engage students in a series of formal role-playing exercises and related assignments that can teach those students directly involved in bullying alternative methods of interaction. These programs can also show other students how they can assist victims and how everyone can work together to create a school climate where bullying is not tolerated (Sjostrom and Stein 1996).

14 • Other components of anti-bullying programs include individualized interventions with the bullies and victims, the implementation of cooperative learning activities to reduce social isolation, and increasing adult supervision at key times (e.g., recess or lunch). Schools that have implemented Olweus's program have reported a 50 percent reduction in bullying.

Conclusion

15 Bullying is a serious problem that can dramatically affect the ability of students to progress academically and socially. A comprehensive intervention plan that involves all students, parents, and school staff is required to ensure that all students can learn in a safe and fear-free environment.

A Resource List on This Topic is Also Available.

References

Ahmad, Y., & Smith, P. K. (1994). Bullying in schools and the issue of sex differences. In John Archer (Ed.), Male Violence. London: Routledge.

Batsche, G. M., & Knoff, H. M. (1994). Bullies and their victims: Understanding a pervasive problem in the schools. School Psychology Review, 23 (2), 165–174. EJ 490 574.

Charach, A., Pepler, D., & Ziegler, S. (1995). Bullying at school—a Canadian perspective: A survey of problems and suggestions for intervention. Education Canada, 35 (1), 12–18. EJ 502 058.

Nolin, M. J., Davies, E., & Chandler, K. (1995). Student Victimization at School. National Center for Education Statistics—Statistics in Brief (NCES 95-204). ED 388 439.

Oliver, R., Hoover, J. H., & Hazler, R. (1994). The perceived roles of bullying in small-town Midwestern schools. Journal of Counseling and Development, 72 (4), 416–419. EJ 489 169.

Olweus, D. (1993). Bullying at School: What We Know and What We Can Do. Cambridge, MA: Blackwell. ED 384 437.

Sjostrom, Lisa, & Stein, Nan. (1996). Bully Proof: A Teacher's Guide on Teasing and Bullying for Use with Fourth and Fifth Grade Students. Boston, MA: Wellesley College Center for Research on Women and the NEA Professional Library. PS 024 450.

Smith, P. K., & Sharp, S. (1994). School Bullying: Insights and Perspectives. London: Routledge. ED 387 223.

Whitney, I., & Smith, P. K. (1993). A survey of the nature and extent of bullying in junior/middle and secondary schools. Educational Research, 35 (1), 3–25. EJ 460 708.

References identified with an ED (ERIC document), EJ (ERIC journal), or PS number are cited in the ERIC database. Most documents are available in ERIC microfiche collections at more than 900 locations worldwide and can be ordered through EDRS: (800) 443-ERIC. Journal articles are available from the original journal, interlibrary loan services, or article reproduction clearinghouses such as UnCover (800-787-7979), UMI (800-732-0616), or ISI (800-523-1850). The Eric Identifier for this article is ED407154. ERIC Digests are in the public domain and may be freely reproduced.

A Profile of Bullying at School

By Dan Olweus
Educational Leadership

1   Bullying and victimization are on the increase, extensive research shows. The attitudes and routines of relevant adults can exacerbate or curb students' aggression toward classmates.

2   Bullying among schoolchildren is a very old and well-known phenomenon. Although many educators are acquainted with the problem, researchers only began to study bullying systematically in the 1970s (Olweus 1973, 1978) and focused primarily on schools in Scandinavia. In the 1980s and early 1990s, however, studies of bullying among schoolchildren began to attract wider attention in a number of other countries, including the United States.

What Is Bullying?

3   Systematic research on bullying requires rigorous criteria for classifying students as bullies or as victims (Olweus 1996; Solberg and Olweus, in press). How do we know when a student is being bullied? One definition is that a student is being bullied or victimized when he or she is exposed, repeatedly and over time, to negative actions on the part of one or more other students. (Olweus 1993, p. 9)

4   The person who intentionally inflicts, or attempts to inflict, injury or discomfort on someone else is engaging in negative actions, a term similar to the definition of aggressive behavior in the social sciences. People carry out negative actions through physical contact, with words, or in more indirect ways, such as making mean faces or gestures, spreading rumors, or intentionally excluding someone from a group.

5   Bullying also entails an imbalance in strength (or an asymmetrical power relationship), meaning that students exposed to negative actions have diffi culty defending themselves. Much bullying is proactive aggression, that is, aggressive behavior that usually occurs without apparent provocation or threat on the part of the victim.

Some Basic Facts

6   In the 1980s, questionnaire surveys of more than 150,000 Scandinavian students found that approximately 15 percent of students ages 8–16 were involved in bully/victim problems with some regularity—either as bullies, victims, or both bully and victim (bully-victims) (Olweus 1993). Approximately 9 percent of all students were victims, and 6–7 percent bullied other students regularly. In contrast to what is commonly believed, only a small proportion of the victims also engaged in bullying other students (17 percent of the victims or 1.6 percent of the total number of students).

7   In 2001, when my colleagues and I conducted a new large-scale survey of approximately 11,000 students from 54 elementary and junior high schools using the same questions that we used in 1983 (Olweus 2002), we noted two disturbing trends. The percentage of victimized students had increased by approximately 50 percent from 1983, and the percentage of students who were involved (as bullies, victims, or bully-victims) in frequent and serious bullying problems—occurring at least once a week—had increased by approximately 65 percent. We saw these increases as an indication of negative societal developments (Solberg and Olweus, in press).

8   The surveys showed that bullying is a serious problem affecting many students in Scandinavian schools. Data from other countries, including the United States (Nansel et al. 2001; Olweus and Limber 1999; Perry, Kusel, and Perry 1988)—and in large measure collected with my Bully/Victim Questionnaire (1983, 1996)—indicate that bullying problems exist outside Scandinavia with similar, or even higher, prevalence (Olweus and Limber 1999; Smith et al. 1999). The prevalence figures from different countries or cultures, however, may not be directly comparable. Even though the questionnaire gives a detailed definition of bullying, the prevalence rates obtained may be affected by language differences, the students' familiarity with the concept of bullying, and the degree of public attention paid to the phenomenon.

9   Boys bully other students more often than girls do, and a relatively large percentage of girls—about 50 percent—report that they are bullied mainly by boys. A somewhat higher percentage of boys are victims of bullying, especially in the junior high school grades. But bullying certainly occurs among girls as well. Physical bullying is less common among gifts, who typically use more subtle and indirect means of harassment, such as intentionally excluding someone from the group, spreading rumors, and manipulating friendship relations. Such forms of bullying can certainly be as harmful and distressing as more direct and open forms of harassment. Our research data (Olweus 1993), however, clearly contradict the view that girls are the most frequent and worst bullies, a view suggested by such recent books as *Queen Bees and Wannabes* (Wiseman 2002) and *Odd Girl Out* (Simmons 2002).

Common Myths About Bullying

10   Several common assumptions about the causes of bullying receive little or no support when confronted with empirical data. These misconceptions include the hypotheses that bullying is a consequence of large class or school size, competition for grades and failure in school, or poor selfesteem and insecurity. Many also believe erroneously that students who are overweight, wear glasses, have a different ethnic origin, or speak with an unusual dialect are particularly likely to become victims of bullying.

11   All of these hypotheses have thus far failed to receive clear support from empirical data. Accordingly, we must look for other factors to find the key origins of bullying problems. The accumulated research evidence indicates that personality characteristics or typical reaction patterns, in combination with physical strength or weakness in the case of boys, are important in the development of bullying problems in individual students. At the same time, environmental factors, such as the attitudes, behavior, and routines of relevant adults—in particular, teachers and principals—play a crucial role in determining the extent to which bullying problems will manifest themselves in a larger unit, such as a classroom or school. Thus, we must pursue analyses of the main causes of bully/victim problems on at least two different levels: individual and environmental.

Victims and the Bullying Circle

12   Much research has focused on the characteristics and family backgrounds of victims and bullies. We have identified two kinds of victims, the more common being the passive or submissive victim, who represents some 80–85 percent of all victims. Less research information is available about provocative victims, also called bully-victims or aggressive victims, whose behavior may elicit negative reactions from a large part of the class. The dynamics of a classroom with a provocative victim are different from those of a classroom with a submissive victim (Olweus 1978, 1993).

13   Bullies and victims naturally occupy key positions in the configuration of bully/victim problems in a classroom, but other students also play important roles and display different attitudes and reactions toward an acute bullying situation. Figure 1 outlines "The Bullying Circle" and represents the various ways in which most students in a classroom with bully/victim problems are involved in or affected by them (Olweus 2001a, 2001b).

The Olweus Bullying Prevention Program

14   The Olweus Bullying Prevention Program,[1] developed and evaluated over a period of almost 20 years (Olweus 1993, 1999), builds on four key principles derived chiefly from research on the development and identification of problem behaviors, especially aggressive behavior. These principles involve creating a school—and ideally, also a home—environment characterized by

- warmth, positive interest, and involvement from adults;
- firm limits on unacceptable behavior;
- consistent application of nonpunitive, nonphysical sanctions for unacceptable behavior or violations of rules; and
- adults who act as authorities and positive role models.

15   We have translated these principles into a number of specific measures to be used at the school, classroom, and individual levels (Olweus 1993, 2001b). Figure 2 lists the set of core components that our statistical analyses and experience with the program have shown are particularly important in any implementation of the program.

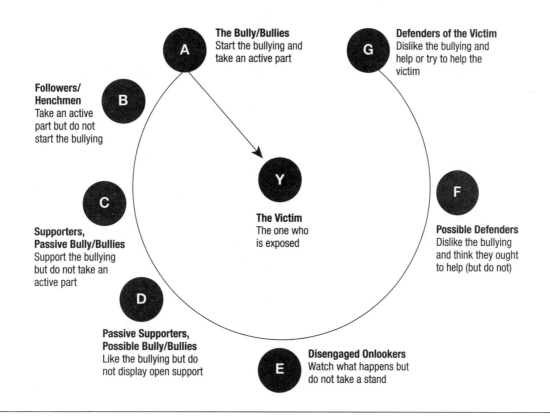

FIGURE 1
The Bullying Circle
Students' Modes of Reaction/Roles in an Acute Bullying Situation

A — **The Bully/Bullies** Start the bullying and take an active part

B — **Followers/Henchmen** Take an active part but do not start the bullying

C — **Supporters, Passive Bully/Bullies** Support the bullying but do not take an active part

D — **Passive Supporters, Possible Bully/Bullies** Like the bullying but do not display open support

E — **Disengaged Onlookers** Watch what happens but do not take a stand

F — **Possible Defenders** Dislike the bullying and think they ought to help (but do not)

G — **Defenders of the Victim** Dislike the bullying and help or try to help the victim

Y — **The Victim** The one who is exposed

FIGURE 2
The Olweus Bullying Prevention Program

General Prerequisite
- Awareness and involvement of adults

Measures at the School Level
- Administration of the Olweus Bully/Victim Questionnaire (filled out anonymously by students)
- Formation of a Bullying Prevention Coordinating Committee
- Training of staff and time for discussion groups
- Effective supervision during recess and lunch periods

Measures at the Classroom Level
- Classroom and school rules about bullying
- Regular classroom meetings
- Meetings with students' parents

Measures at the Individual Level
- Individual meetings with students who bully
- Individual meetings with victims of bullying
- Meetings with parents of students involved
- Development of individual intervention plans

16   The program's implementation relies mainly on the existing social environment. Teachers, administrators, students, and parents all play major roles in carrying out the program and in restructuring the social environment. One possible reason for this intervention program's effectiveness is that it changes the opportunity and reward structures for bullying behavior, which results in fewer opportunities and rewards for bullying (Olweus 1992).

Research-Based Evaluations

17   The first evaluation of the effects of the Olweus Bullying Prevention Program involved data from approximately 2,500 students in 42 elementary and junior high schools in Bergen, Norway, and followed students for two and one-half years, from 1983 to 1985 (Olweus 1991, in press; Olweus and Alsaker 1991). The findings were significant:

- Marked reductions—by 50 percent or more—in bully/victim problems for the period studied, measuring after eight and 20 months of intervention.

- Clear reductions in general antisocial behavior, such as vandalism, fighting, pilfering, drunkenness, and truancy.

- Marked improvement in the social climate of the classes and an increase in student satisfaction with school life.

18   The differences between baseline and intervention groups were highly significant. The research concluded that the registered changes in bully/victim problems and related behavior patterns were likely to be a consequence of the intervention program and not of some other factor. Partial replications of the program in the United States, the United Kingdom, and Germany have resulted in similar, although somewhat weaker, results (Olweus and Limber, 1999; Smith and Sharp 1994).

19   In 1997–1998, our study of 3,200 students from 30 Norwegian schools again registered clear improvements with regard to bully/victim problems in the schools with intervention programs. The effects were weaker than in the first project, with averages varying between 21 and 38 percent. Unlike the first study, however, the intervention program had been in place for only six months when we made the second measurement. In addition, we conducted the study during a particularly turbulent year in which Norway introduced a new national curriculum that made heavy demands of educators' time and resources.

20   Nonetheless, the intervention schools fared considerably better than the comparison schools. Surveys of the comparison schools, which had set up anti-bullying efforts according to their own plans, showed very small or no changes with regard to "being bullied" and a 35 percent increase for "bullying other students" (Olweus, in press). Because we have not yet analyzed the questionnaire information, we cannot fully explain this result, but it is consistent with findings from a number of studies showing that inexpert interventions intended to counteract delinquent and antisocial behavior often have unexpectedly negative effects (Dishion, McCord, and Poulin 1999; Gottfredson 1987; Lipsey 1992).

21   In the most recent (1999–2000) evaluation of the Olweus Bullying Prevention Program among approximately 2,300 students from 10 schools—some of which had large percentages of students with immigrant backgrounds— we found an average reduction by around 40 percent with regard to "being bullied" and by about 50 percent for "bullying other students" (Olweus, in press).

The Need for Evidence-Based Intervention Programs

22   Coping with bully/victim problems has become an official school priority in many countries, and many have suggested ways to handle and prevent such problems. But because most proposals have either failed to document positive results or have never been subjected to systematic research evaluation, it is difficult to know which programs or measures actually work and which do not. What counts is how well the program works for students, not how much the adults using the program like it.

23   Recently, when a U.S. committee of experts used three essential criteria (Elliott 1999) to systematically evaluate more than 500 programs ostensibly designed to prevent violence or other problem behaviors, only 11 of the programs (four of which are school-based) satisfied the specified criteria.[2] The U.S. Department of Justice's office of Juvenile Justice and Delinquency Prevention and other sources are now providing financial support for the implementation of these evidence-based "Blueprint" programs in a number of sites.

24   In Norway, an officially appointed committee recently conducted a similar evaluation of 56 programs being used in Norway's schools to counteract and prevent problem behavior (Norwegian Ministry of Education, Research, and Church Affairs 2000) and recommended without reservation only one program for further use. The Olweus Bullying Prevention Program is one of the 11 Blueprint programs and the program selected by the Norwegian committee.

Norway's New National Initiative Against Bullying

25   In late 2000, Norway's Department of Education and Research and Department of Children and Family Affairs decided to offer the Olweus Bullying Prevention Program on a large scale to Norwegian elementary and junior high schools over a period of several years. In building the organization for this national initiative, we have used a four-level train-the-trainer strategy of dissemination. At Norway's University of Bergen, the Olweus Group Against Bullying at the Research Center for Health Promotion trains and supervises specially selected instructor candidates, each of whom trains and supervises key persons from a number of schools. The key persons are then responsible for leading staff discussion groups at each participating school. These meetings typically focus on key components and themes of the program (Olweus 1993, 2001b).

26   The training of the instructor candidates consists of 10–11 whole-day assemblies over 16 months. In between the whole-day meetings, the instructor candidates receive ongoing consultation from the Olweus Group by telephone or through e-mail.

27   In implementing this train-the-trainer model in the United States with financial support from the U.S. Department of Justice and the U.S. Department of Health and Human Services, we have made some modifications to accommodate cultural differences and practical constraints. In particular, we have reduced the number of whole-day assemblies to four or five and have granted greater autonomy to individual schools' Bullying Prevention Coordinating Committees than is typical in Norway.

28   So far, 75 instructor candidates have participated in training, and more than 225 schools participate in the program. Recently, Norway's government substantially increased our funding to enable us to offer the program to more schools starting in 2003.

29   We see Norway's national initiative as a breakthrough for the systematic, long-term, and research-based work against bully/victim problems in schools. We hope to see similar developments in other countries.

Notes

1   More information about the Olweus Bullying Prevention Program is available at www.colorado.edu/cspv/blueprints/model/BPPmaterials.html or by contacting sentell@ clemson.edu or olweus@psych.uib.no.

2   The four school-based programs are Life Skills Training, Promoting Alternative Thinking Strategies (PATHS), the Incredible Years, and the Olweus Bullying Prevention Program. For more information about the Blueprints for Violence Prevention's model programs, visit www.colorado.edu/cspv/blueprints/model/overview.html.

References

Dishion, T. J., McCord, J., & Poulin, F. (1999). When interventions harm: Peer groups and problem behavior. *American Psychologist, 54,* 755-764.

Elliott, D. S. (1999). Editor's introduction. In D. Olweus & S. Limber, *Blueprints for Violence Prevention: Bullying Prevention Program.* Boulder, CO: Institute of Behavioral Science.

Gottfredson, G. D. (1987). Peer group interventions to reduce the risk of delinquent behavior: A selective review and a new evaluation. *Criminology, 25,* 671-714.

Lipsey, M. W. (1992). Juvenile delinquency treatment: A meta-analytic inquiry into the variability of effects. In T. D. Cook, H. Cooper, D. S. Corday, H. Hartman, L. V. Hedges, R. J. Light, T. A. Louis, & F. Mosteller (Eds.), *Meta-analysis for explanation.* A casebook (pp. 83-125). New York: Russell Sage.

Nansel, T. R., Overpeck, M., Pilla, R. S., Ruan, W. J., Simons-Morton, B., & Scheidt, P. (2001). Bullying behaviors among U.S. youth: Prevalence and association with psychosocial adjustment. *Journal of the American Medical Association, 285,* 2094-2100.

Norwegian Ministry of Education, Research, and Church Affairs. (2000). Rapport 2000: *Vurdering av program og tiltak for å redusere problematferd og utvikle sosial kompetanse. (Report 2000: Evaluation of programs and measures to reduce problem behavior and develop social competence.)* Oslo, Norway: Author.

Olweus, D. (1973). *Hackkycklingar och översittare. Forskning om skolmobbing. (Victims and bullies: Research on school bullying.)* Stockholm: Almqvist & Wicksell.

Olweus, D. (1978). *Aggression in the schools: Bullies and whipping boys.* Washington, DC: Hemisphere Press (Wiley).

Olweus, D. (1983). The Olweus Bully/Victim Questionnaire. Mimeo. Bergen, Norway: Research Center for Health Promotion, University of Bergen.

Olweus, D. (1991). Bully/victim problems among schoolchildren: Basic facts and effects of a school-based intervention program. In D. Pepler & K. Rubin (Eds.), *The development and treatment of childhood aggression* (pp. 411-448). Hillsdale, NJ: Erlbaum.

Olweus, D. (1992). Bullying among schoolchildren: Intervention and prevention. In R. D. Peters, R. J. McMahon, & V. L. Quincy (Eds.), *Aggression and violence throughout the life span.* Newbury Park, CA: Sage.

Olweus, D. (1993). *Bullying at school: What we know and what we can do.* Cambridge, MA: Blackwell. (Available from AIDC, P.O. Box 20, Williston, VT 05495; (800) 216-2522)

Olweus, D. (1996). The Revised Olweus Bully/Victim Questionnaire. Mimeo. Bergen, Norway: Research Center for Health Promotion, University of Bergen.

Olweus, D. (1999). Norway. In P. K. Smith, Y. Morita, J. Junger-Tas, D. Olweus, R. Catalano, & P. Slee (Eds.), *The nature of school bullying: A cross-national perspective* (pp. 28-48). London: Routledge.

Olweus, D. (2001a). Peer harassment: A critical analysis and some important issues. In J. Juvonen & s. Graham (Eds.), *Peer harassment in school* (pp. 3-20). New York: Guilford Publications.

Olweus, D. (2001b). *Olweus' core program against bullying and antisocial behavior: A teacher handbook.* Bergen, Norway: Research Center for Health Promotion, University of Bergen.

Olweus, D. (2002). Mobbing i skolen: Nye data om omfang og forandring over tid. (Bullying at school: New data on prevalence and change over time.) Manuscript. Research Center for Health Promotion, University of Bergen, Bergen, Norway.

Olweus, D. (in press). *Bullying at school: Prevalence estimation, a useful evaluation design, and a new national initiative in Norway.* Association for Child Psychology and Psychiatry Occasional Papers.

Olweus, D., & Alsaker, F. D. (1991). Assessing change in a cohort longitudinal study with hierarchical data. In D. Magnusson, L. R. Bergman, G. Rudinger, & B. Törestad (Eds.), *Problems and methods in longitudinal research* (pp. 107-132). New York: Cambridge University Press.

Olweus, D., & Limber, S. (1999). *Blueprints for violence prevention: Bullying Prevention Program.* Boulder, CO: Institute of Behavioral Science.

Perry, D. G., Kusel, S. J., & Perry, L. C. (1988). Victims of peer aggression. *Developmental Psychology, 24,* 807-814.

Simmons, R. (2002). *Odd girl out.* New York: Harcourt.

Smith, P. K., Morita, Y., Junger-Tas, J., Olweus, D., Catalano, R., & Slee, P. (Eds.). (1999). *The nature of school bullying: A cross-national perspective.* London: Routledge.

Smith, P. K., & Sharp, S. (Eds.). (1994). *School bullying: Insights and perspectives.* London: Routledge.

Solberg, M., & Olweus, D. (in press). *Prevalence estimation of school bullying with the Olweus Bully/Victim Questionnaire. Aggressive Behavior.*

Wiseman, R. (2002). *Queen bees and wannabes.* New York: Crown. Copyright © 2003 Dan Olweus.

How to Handle a Bully

By Kathiann Kowalski
Current Health, Originally published September 8, 1997.
Links last updated September 8, 2004.

Getting Along

1   Meanness comes in many forms, and you can stop them all.

2   'I don't want to talk about it!' Ted snapped. His face was scratched up when he got home from school. It seems another boy bragged he could make a 'ninja' sword by folding paper. Then he demonstrated the weapon— by lashing out at Ted.

3   Bullying can start at an early age and grow more intense in the teen years.

4   Bullying is repeated aggressive behavior or, quite simply, unprovoked meanness. It's a form of intimidation, which is behavior designed to threaten, frighten, or coerce someone.

5   'Bullying doesn't stop when you get out of the third grade,' says Jean O'Neil of the National Crime Prevention Council (NCPC). Later, it may be called power-tripping, harassing, or disrespecting. Sexual harassment— unwanted and unwelcome behavior of a sexual nature—is also a form of bullying.

6   When teens intimidate each other, they may attack with bats, knives, guns, or other weapons. The psychological stakes are high too. Physical assaults, vicious taunts, and exclusion from groups can—and have—led to depression and even suicide.

7   Intimidation peaks in junior high. It continues through high school and even into the workplace. Intimidation is not just 'boys being boys.' Studies show that girls intimidate other students at least as much as boys. Boys use more physical force. Girls rely more on teasing, taunting, or excluding others from groups.

8   Intimidation occurs for different reasons. Hate, prejudice, immaturity, a distorted self-image, or lack of respect can underlie harassing behavior. Some teens pick on others simply to increase their own sense of power.

9   In any case, bullying is caused by bullies, not their victims. No one deserves to be intimidated. Everyone has a responsibility to stop intimidation.

10   How you handle intimidation depends on the situation and your personal style. Don't feel you have to suffer in silence. And don't be afraid to get help when necessary.

11   "I'm a big fan of immediately dealing with the situation," says Lisa Lybbert at the NCPC. But dealing with the situation doesn't mean aggravating it, says Lybbert. "Escalating the situation too often leads to violence."

12   "There are alternatives to violence," says sixteen-year-old Jovon Hill of Philadelphia, Pennsylvania. "Really think for yourself, because there are ways to get out of situations."

13   Here's how some teens would handle these bullying situations. How would you respond?

14   Suppose a teen keeps tripping you at school. "First, I would ask the student to stop," says Jovon. "Then if he or she continues, I would take it to one of the proper authorities at school."

15   Frances McNamara of Ventura, California, wouldn't argue with the other person. The seventeen-year-old says, "I would probably go to my counselor or my principal about it."

16   "I would refer it to mediation," says seventeen-year-old Gekeita Hill of Violet, Louisiana. Gekeita is a peer mediator at St. Bernard High School. She likes how the program provides a forum to talk maturely about feelings and resolve problems.

17   Suppose someone badmouths you or spreads rumors. "The way I handle it is [to] ignore it," says Frances. Brushing it off, laughing, or briefly telling taunters to get a life are all ways of refusing to take the bait. They keep you from feeling cowed and deprive the *bully* of any power rush.

18   Controlled confrontation is another strategy. "I would go to the student personally," says Jovon, "and ask if there is a problem with me or something." "If you are saying these things about me, I would like to know why," agrees Gekeita, "because I don't have a problem with you, and I don't like to make enemies."

19   Suppose someone demands that you hand over your jacket. If you're threatened with a weapon, hand it over. Then tell someone later. The jacket is not worth your life.

20   Otherwise, use good judgment. Frances and Gekeita said they'd probably object verbally and would definitely report the incident to school authorities. "I wouldn't wear an expensive jacket to school anyway," adds Gekeita.

21   Jovon said he'd offer to contact social services if the other person really needed a jacket. Staying calm helps him in tough situations.

22   Suppose a group of kids makes offensive sexual comments about your body. "I'm just going to let them know that's not on my mind at this moment," says Jovon, "and that I would really appreciate it if they would stop."

23   Frances might ignore minor comments. But she'd report it "if it was really offensive and really hurtful."

24   "I would probably go to the disciplinarian," says Gekeita. Sexual harassment violates civil rights laws, and schools have an obligation to stop it. She might also pursue peer mediation. "If they know how you feel about it and how much it's hurting you," Gekeita says, "they'd probably stop it."

25   Even if you're not the immediate target of a *bully*, intimidation cheapens the quality of life in your school and community. Don't let harassers have their way.

26   "Cut it out." "Leave them alone." A few words from you might make intimidators back down.

27   If you're uncomfortable speaking out directly, tell school authorities confidentially about a problem. That's what someone did after Ted was attacked with the paper knife. That got the problem resolved without revenge or reprisals.

28   On a broader level, get some students together to develop or revise your school's code of conduct. "Work with the administration, and set up some standards," recommends NCPC's O'Neil. One example of an important standard is: "We treat each other with respect at all times."

29   When students help develop school codes of conduct, everyone knows what's expected. It empowers bullied victims to stand up for themselves. And it tells bullies that intimidation won't be tolerated.

School Bullies Are Often Also Victims; Feeling Safe Reduces Youth Bullying

By Pamela Kan-Rice
UC Agriculture and Natural Resources News and Information Outreach

1   OAKLAND, Calif.—School bullies are often themselves the victims of bullying, according to University of California Cooperative Extension researchers who conducted a study of Oakland middle school students aged eleven to fourteen.

2   In response to the 1999 Columbine High School shooting in Littleton, Colorado, many educators began trying to "bully-proof" their schools. UC Cooperative Extension youth development advisors Charles Go and Shelley Murdock surveyed Oakland middle school students to get a clearer picture of the bullies and their victims. Based on the responses of 1,137 students, 1 out of 10 youth reported having been threatened with a weapon in the last 12 months. But interestingly, half of these teens reported perpetrator behaviors such as using a weapon and selling drugs.

3   In response to the questions indicating bullying behavior, 36 percent of the youth reported having been in a physical fight; 9 percent used a weapon to threaten someone; 6 percent sold drugs and 11 percent had been arrested in school at least once during the past year.

4   Responding to victimization questions, 10 percent had been threatened with a weapon within the past year. About 20 percent of the youth reported they were offered, sold or given drugs at least once in school. Also within the past year, 24 percent had been teased about their race and 29 percent had had property stolen from them or damaged at school.

5   The boys were more likely to be perpetrators than girls were, but were just as likely to be victims. Boys were no more likely than girls were to feel safe at school. Perhaps surprisingly, the bullies didn't feel safer than their victims did. "It is most likely because they know their victims may retaliate," Go said.

6   Go and Murdock, who are based at UC Cooperative Extension in Alameda and Contra Costa counties, respectively, concluded there are myriad factors that influence bullying, such as the youth's home life and racial tension. "If a parent tells the kid to hit people who are messing with them, then you need to talk to the parent," Go explained. Youths who have been beaten because of their race may join gangs for protection.

7   Quelling school violence is not as simple as weeding out the bullies and "fixing" them, according to Go. A youth who has been bullied may get caught retaliating or picking on someone else. "It's easy to label one a bully," Go said, "but it really depends on where you catch them in the cycle. Perpetrators get victimized too."

8   A more effective approach may be to ask the individual, "Why are you doing this?" then to try to break the circle of bullying. Go suggests teaching youth different ways of negotiating the situation, such as conducting teen conflict resolution education programs, providing alternative creative venues such as physical education in resolving conflicts, or providing positive adult mentors to help teens deal with their problems.

9   Another effective approach may be to work in helping our teens feel safer in school. Go and Murdock found that 84 percent of the middle school students reported feeling very safe or safe in their own neighborhoods, but that figure dropped to 70 percent when the students were asked how they felt in school. Thirteen percent claimed they stayed home one or more days because they were afraid to go to school. Interestingly, they also found that when the teens felt safe in their schools, both the youth perpetrator and victim behaviors tended to decrease.

10   If schools send a message about the type of behavior that is unacceptable, it establishes ground rules, says Go. They need to make clear the consequences. If a school protects all its students, then they feel safer and don't have to defend themselves.

11   Bullying behavior is part of adolescent development, according to Go. "They're trying to figure out what they can get away with. And it can be a search for identity, to learn social relationships and peer relations," he said. Go cited the classic example of a child who pesters the bigger kids until he gets whopped. Some might call that learning the hard way.

12   "One thing that this study elucidates is that there is no magic bullet for stopping bullying," Murdock said. "As with most societal issues, it is more complex and requires a more complex intervention than a simple curriculum."

13   The researchers chose to focus on middle school students because in 1998, nearly 60 percent of all students suspended in Oakland Unified School District were in middle school. Four times as many 6th graders were suspended as fifth graders. The questionnaire was anonymous and confidential and available in English, Spanish, and Vietnamese.

Key Policy Letters from the Education Secretary

June 14, 2011

Dear Colleagues:

1   Harassment and bullying are serious problems in our schools, and lesbian, gay, bisexual, and transgender (LGBT) students are the targets of disproportionate shares of these problems. Thirty-two percent of students aged 12-18 experienced verbal or physical bullying during the 2007-2008 school year;[1] and, according to a recent survey, more than 90 percent of LGBT students in grades 6 through 12 reported being verbally harassed—and almost half reported being physically harassed—during the 2008-2009 school year.[2] High levels of harassment and bullying correlate with poorer educational outcomes, lower future aspirations, frequent school absenteeism, and lower grade-point averages.[3] Recent tragedies involving LGBT students and students perceived to be LGBT only underscore the need for safer schools.

2   Gay-straight alliances (GSAs) and similar student-initiated groups addressing LGBT issues can play an important role in promoting safer schools and creating more welcoming learning environments. Nationwide, students are forming these groups in part to combat bullying and harassment of LGBT students and to promote understanding and respect in the school community. Although the efforts of these groups focus primarily on the needs of LGBT students, students who have LGBT family members and friends, and students who are perceived to be LGBT, messages of respect, tolerance, and inclusion benefit all our students. By encouraging dialogue and providing supportive resources, these groups can help make schools safe and affirming environments for everyone.

3   But in spite of the positive effect these groups can have in schools, some such groups have been unlawfully excluded from school grounds, prevented from forming, or denied access to school resources. These same barriers have sometimes been used to target religious and other student groups, leading Congress to pass the Equal Access Act.

4   In 1984, Congress passed and President Ronald Reagan signed into law the Equal Access Act, requiring public secondary schools to provide equal access for extracurricular clubs. Rooted in principles of equal treatment and freedom of expression, the Act protects student-initiated groups of all types. As one of my predecessors, Secretary Richard W. Riley, pointed out in guidance concerning the Equal Access Act and religious clubs more than a decade ago, we "protect our own freedoms by respecting the freedom of others who differ from us."[4] By allowing students to discuss difficult issues openly and honestly, in a civil manner, our schools become forums for combating ignorance, bigotry, hatred, and discrimination.

5   The Act requires public secondary schools to treat all student-initiated groups equally, regardless of the religious, political, philosophical, or other subject matters discussed at their meetings. Its protections apply to groups that address issues relating to LGBT students and matters involving sexual orientation and gender identity, just as they apply to religious and other student groups.

6   Today, the U.S. Department of Education's General Counsel, Charles P. Rose, is issuing a set of legal guidelines affirming the principles that prevent unlawful discrimination against any student-initiated groups. We intend for these guidelines to provide schools with the information and resources they need to help ensure that all students, including LGBT and gender nonconforming students, have a safe place to learn, meet, share experiences, and discuss matters that are important to them.

7   Although specific implementation of the Equal Access Act depends upon contextual circumstances, these guidelines reflect basic obligations imposed on public school officials by the Act and the First Amendment to the U.S. Constitution. The general rule, approved by the U.S. Supreme Court, is that a public high school that allows at least one noncurricular student group to meet on school grounds during noninstructional time (e.g., lunch, recess, or before or after school) may not deny similar access to other noncurricular student groups, regardless of the religious, political, philosophical, or other subject matters that the groups address.

8   I encourage every school district to make sure that its administrators, faculty members, staff, students, and parents are familiar with these principles in order to protect the rights of all students—regardless of religion, political or philosophical views, sexual orientation, or gender identity. I also urge school districts to use the guidelines to develop or improve district policies. In doing so, school officials may find it helpful to explain to the school community that the Equal Access Act requires public schools to afford equal treatment to all noncurricular student organizations, including GSAs and other groups that focus on issues related to LGBT students, sexual orientation, or gender identity. Officials need not endorse any particular student organization, but federal law requires that they afford all student groups the same opportunities to form, to convene on school grounds, and to have access to the same resources available to other student groups.

9   The process of revising or developing an equal-access policy offers an opportunity for school officials to engage their community in an open dialogue on the equal treatment of all noncurricular student organizations. It is important to remember, therefore, that the Equal Access Act's requirements are a bare legal minimum. I invite and encourage you to go beyond what the law requires in order to increase students' sense of belonging in the school and to help students, teachers, and parents recognize the core values behind our principles of free speech. As noted in our October 2010 Dear Colleague Letter and December 2010 guidance regarding anti-bullying policies, I applaud such policies as positive steps toward ensuring equal access to education for all students.

10   Thank you for your work on behalf of our nation's children.

Sincerely,

Arne Duncan

Enclosure

[1] Dinkes, R., Kemp, J., and Baum, K. (2010). Indicators of School Crime and Safety: 2010. (NCES 2010-012/NCJ 228478). 42 National Center for Education Statistics: Washington, DC.

[2] Kosciw, J. G., Greytak, E. A., Diaz, E. M., and Bartkiewicz, M. J. (2010). The 2009 National School Climate Survey: The experiences of lesbian, gay, bisexual and transgender youth in our nation's schools, 26, New York: GLSEN.

[3] GLSEN, at 46-8.

[4] U.S. Department of Education, "Secretary's Guidelines on Religious Expression in Public Schools," August 1995, http://www2.ed.gov/Speeches/08-1995/religion.html.

Life After Bullying

By Mark Brown
PTA

Emmy-nominated Mark Brown is a youth motivational speaker who, as part of a national outreach program sponsored by QSP, the educational fundraising arm of Reader's Digest, talks to young people about the harmful effects of bullying. To see and hear Brown firsthand, log onto www.rd.com/bully.

1   Billy has a thyroid disorder; no matter how fun-loving he is, the other kids cannot see past his being overweight. Liz has been dubbed "trailer trash" by the local kids because she lives on the "wrong side of town." Eleven-yearold Matt came home with black and blue marks, the result of a classmate convincing others to have a punching contest on the "new kid's" arm.

2   Bullying is a serious problem today. In a recent Reader's Digest poll, 70 percent of all parents surveyed said their children have been bullied at school. In fact, according to the National Education Association, 160,000 kids stay home from school each day to avoid torment.

3   As I travel the country teaching the lesson of tolerance and respect to victims and bullies alike, I have learned something myself. With the proper guidance from family and the school community, children can survive a hurtful experience like bullying and grow in many ways never imagined.

A victim finds her "inner light"

4   Sue Stapleton and I met in February 2000 when she was substitute teaching at a middle school in Connecticut. Sue said her daughter Katelyn, then 10 years old, "had always been the child in the classroom who was picked on, teased, even physically abused." It started in kindergarten with taunts about her weight, her glasses, even the size of her nose, and it escalated through the years—from kids throwing rocks at her to locking her in a fenced-in area after gym. It got to the point where Katelyn did not want to go to school.

5   On that day four years ago, Sue began her crusade to help rebuild Katelyn's self-esteem. Katelyn became a Girl Scout and lived the Girl Scout promise of being good to other people. She began to expect nothing less for herself. The family's ties to their place of worship also helped nurture Katelyn's inner strength, as did her parent's unending efforts to help their daughter know how loved she was.

6   This past fall, 150 students heard Katelyn's message of hope as she shared her story in a special assembly at her high school. As a victim of bullying, Katelyn spoke about her inner light that burns bright and cannot be snuffed out by the mean actions and words of others.

Words as weapons

7   Molly was in the 8th grade when we met. She never considered herself a victim, but there were times other kids had picked on her for her disinterest in makeup and fashion, and her passion for athletics. She never considered herself a bully, either, but she could remember having called other kids names.

8   I explained to Molly and her schoolmates that words can actually be used as weapons. They were taken aback by this notion. Molly recalls that day, "So many kids were so emotional because it had never occurred to them that their words could be so hurtful to others."

9   Molly thought about Emily, a classmate with cerebral palsy, whom most students avoided because of her disability. Molly and her best friend decided to reach out to Emily, thus finding a new friend.

10   Today Molly is a college freshman with a far different perspective. She's studying to be a nurse so that she can help people.

11   Sue, Katelyn, and Molly personify why it is important that every parent, educator, and child work together to create a safe and caring school.

Creating a caring school environment

12   Here are some ways parents can help combat bullying and create a more caring school environment for their children:

- Always take bullying seriously and never dismiss it as merely a rite of passage.
- Keep the lines of communication open with your children and reassure them that they are loved and valued.
- Involve your child in character-building activities and be involved in these kinds of activities yourself.
- Establish PTA-sponsored programs in your school that reinforce the importance of tolerance and respect.
- Encourage school special assemblies and bring in outside speakers to raise awareness about this issue.
- If one doesn't already exist, establish a peer mediation program where students can present their grievances with one another in a nonthreatening environment.

Excerpts from
The Bully, the Bullied, and the Bystander

By Barbara Coloroso

1　In a study conducted in 2001 by the Kaiser Foundation, a U.S. health care philanthropy organization, in conjunction with the Nickelodeon TV network and Children Now, a youth advocacy group, almost three-quarters of preteens interviewed said bullying is a regular occurrence at school and that it becomes even more pervasive as kids start high school; 86 percent of children between the ages of twelve and fifteen said that they get teased or bullied at school—making bullying more prevalent than smoking, alcohol, drugs, or sex among the same age group. More than half of children between the ages of eight and eleven said that bullying is a "big problem" at school. "It's a big concern on kids' minds. It's something they're dealing with every day," report Lauren Asher of the Kaiser Foundation.

2　Dr. Debra J. Pepler and her colleagues at the La Marsh Centre for Research on Violence and Conflict Resolution at York University conducted a descriptive study on bullying at the request of the Toronto Board of Education. Drawing on answers given by the 211 students in fourteen classes from grades four through eight, their teachers, and their parents, two other researchers, S. Zeigler and M. Rosenstein-Manner (1991), compiled the following statistics:

- 35 percent of the kids were directly involved in bullying incidents.
- Bulling peaked in the eleven- to twelve-year-old age group.
- 38 percent of students identified as special education students were bullied, compared with 18 percent of other students.
- 24 percent reported that race-related bullying occurred now and then or often.
- 23 percent of the students bullied and 71 percent of the teachers reported that teachers intervened often or almost always. (page 12)

. . . .

3　Individual incidents of verbal, physical, or relational bullying can appear trivial or insignificant, nothing to be overly concerned about, part of the school culture. But it is the imbalance of power, the intent to harm, the threat of further aggression, and the creation of an atmosphere of terror that should raise red flags and signal a need for intervention. Sadly, even when the[se] four markers of bullying are clearly in evidence, adults have been known to minimize or dismiss the bullying, underestimate its seriousness, blame the bullied child, and/or heap on additional insult to injury. (page 22)

. . . .

(Racist Bullying)

4　Racist bullying doesn't just happen. Kids have to be taught to be racist before they can engage in racist bullying. Racist bullying takes place in a climate where children are taught to discriminate against a group of people, where differences are seen as bad, and where the common bonds of humanity are not celebrated.

5   Children systematically learn the language of racial slurs and the rules of bigoted behavior through thought (stereotype), feeling (prejudice), and action (discrimination). First, children are taught to *stereotype*—that is, to generalize about an entire group of people without regard to individual differences: [insert a group] are hot-tempered, ugly, lazy, stupid, no good, crazy. . .

6   Second, children are taught to *prejudge* a person based on this stereotype. Prejudice is a feeling: We don't like [------].

7   Combine racist thought and feeling and you get children willing to *discriminate* against individuals in that group: You can't play with us. You can't come to our party. We don't want you on our team. Get out of here, you creep!

8   This is bullying and needs to be addressed as such. It is only a short walk from racist discrimination to scapegoating a particular child—selecting someone to suffer in place of others or attaching blame or wrongdoing to a specific child when it is not clear who is at fault. Rangi was accused of starting the fight because "his kind" has hot tempers. (page 30)

     . . . .

     (Sexual Bullying)

9   Just as racist attitudes can collide with bullying, so, too, can sexist attitudes. And all three forms of bullying—physical, verbal, and relational—can be wrapped in sexual overtones. Because our sexuality is an integral part of who we are, sexual bullying cuts at the core of our being and can have devastating consequences. Peer-to-peer sexual bullying is one of the most widespread forms of violence in our schools today. According to the 1993 "Hostile Hallways" study conducted by the American Association of University Women Educational Foundation, questionnaire responses of 1,632 students from grades eight to eleven offered some startling information:

     - 85 percent of girls and 76 percent of boys reported having experienced sexual harassment.
     - 65 percent of girls reported being touched, grabbed, or pinched in a sexual way.
     - 13 percent of girls or 9 percent of boys reported being forced to do something sexual other than kissing.
     - 25 percent of girls stayed home from school or cut classes to avoid sexual harassment.
     - 86 percent of girls targeted reported being sexually harassed by their peers.
     - 25 percent of girls targeted reported being sexually harassed by school staff.

10   One-third of the kids surveyed reported experiencing sexual bullying in sixth grade or earlier. Boys and girls reported experiencing sexual harassment in the hallway (73 percent), in the classroom (65 percent), on the school grounds (48 percent), and in the cafeteria (34 percent). The study pointed to serious education consequences as well as significant threats to the physical and emotional well-being of targeted kids. Girls who mature early and boys who mature late are at a high risk for being targeted for sexual bullying. Kids of different sexual orientation from the majority are likely to be bullied. In the article "Young, Gay, and Bullied (Young People Now), researcher I. Rivers wrote about his 1996 study, in which he interviewed 140 gay and lesbian young people. He found that 80 percent of those responding had experienced taunting about their sexual orientation, and over half had been physically assaulted or ridiculed by peers or teachers. (pages 34, 35)

        . . . .

11   Days after the shooting at Columbine High School in Littleton, Colorado, a group of Nashville, Tennessee, students created a Web site: www.iwillpledge. nashville.com. They invited other students throughout the world to sign the following pledge:

12   As part of my community and my school, I WILL:

        • pledge to be a part of the solution.

        • eliminate taunting from my own behavior.

        • encourage others to do the same.

        • do my part to make my community a safe place by being more sensitiveto

        • others.

        • set the example of a caring individual.

        • eliminate profanity toward others from my language.

        • not let my words or actions hurt others . . .
          . . . and if others won't become a part of the solution, I WILL.

13   These kids were willing to take a leadership role, knowing that if they took a stand, others might follow. They also recognized that even if no one else followed in their footsteps, they would do what they knew was right.

14   *Cowardice asks the question: is it safe?*
        Expediency asks the question: is it politic?
        Vanity asks the question: is it popular?
        But conscience asks the question: is it right? And there comes a time when one must take a position that is neither safe, nor politic, nor popular—but one must take it because it's right.
        —Martin Luther King Jr. (pages 174, 175)

Understanding Bullying

By Tara L. Kuther
Our Children

1   Each day hundreds of thousands of children dread going to school and facing the taunts, jeers, and humiliation wrought by bullies. When we think of bullying, the easily identifiable physical and verbal harassment comes to mind, including teasing, taunting, threatening, and hitting. Relational bullying is more difficult for adults to observe and identify. Children who bully through relational means socially isolate their victims by intentionally excluding them or spreading rumors about them. Bullying, then, refers to physical or psychological intimidation that occurs repeatedly, is intended to inflict injury or discomfort on the victim, and creates an ongoing pattern of harassment and abuse.

2   The bullying relationship is characterized by an imbalance of power, such that the victim of bullying finds it hard to defend him- or herself and begins to feel powerless against the bully. The child who bullies typically is bigger, older, stronger, or more popular than the victim of bullying, and his or her intent is to exert power over the victim. For example, girls who bully through exclusion and other forms of relational aggression tend to have more social power than their victims. The bully is aware that his or her behavior causes distress, the bully enjoys the victim's reaction, and the bullying continues and escalates. Bullies hurt others in order to feel strong and powerful at a given moment.

3   It's very difficult for most parents to determine whether their children engage in bullying behaviors because most bullying occurs out of parents' sight. See factors parents and teachers can watch for to identify instances of bullying.

4   Some adults and children rationalize bullying because victims are overly sensitive, cry easily, or act in ways that set them apart from other children. Even if the victim does show these characteristics, adults and children must know bullying is not a healthy coping response—it signals that a child needs to learn how to manage his or her emotions, release anger and frustration in more healthy ways, and learn more constructive strategies for getting along with others. Your role, as parent or teacher, is to help children establish more mature and healthy ways of relating with others, thereby ensuring that they will grow into caring and adaptive adults.

Who is likely to be victimized?

5   There are at least two types of victims: passive victims and reactive victims. The stereotypical image of the bullied child is the passive victim: He or she avoids confrontation, is physically slight, quiet, does not tease others, and does not defend him- or herself from the bully. The passive victim turns inward when bullied—crying and withdrawing rather than fighting back.

6   Reactive victims are much less common than passive victims. The reactive victim provokes attacks by being aggressive, disruptive, argumentative, and antagonizing towards bullies and other children, and retaliates when he or she is bullied. Sometimes reactive victims are referred to as bully/ victims because they straddle the fence of being a bully and/or victim. They are difficult to identify because they seem to be targets for bullies, but they often taunt bullies and other children. Not only do reactive victims fight back when bullied, but they sometimes channel their rage and anger into bullying others, especially those younger and weaker than themselves. In this way, some victims of bullies transform into bullies themselves, perpetuating the abuse and singling out new victims.

What are the effects of bullying?

7   Bullying is not a normal part of growing up. Victims of bullying suffer psychological and sometimes physical scars that last a lifetime. Victims report greater fear and anxiety, feel less accepted, suffer from more health problems, and score lower on measures of academic achievement and self-esteem than students who are not bullied. Victims often turn their anger inward, which may lead to depression, anxiety, and even suicide. The experience of bullying is also linked with violence, as the fatal school shootings in Littleton, Colorado, and Jonesborough, Arkansas, have illustrated.

8   However, it's not just victims who are hurt by bullying. Bullies fail to learn how to cope, manage their emotions, and communicate effectively—skills vital to success in the adult world. Without intervention, bullies suffer stunted emotional growth and fail to develop empathy. Since bullies are accustomed to achieving their immediate goals by pushing others around, they don't learn how to have genuine relationships with other people. Instead, they externalize and blame others for their problems, never taking responsibility, nor learning how to care for another's needs. Bullies who don't learn other ways of getting what they want develop into adult bullies who are more likely to experience criminal troubles, be abusive toward their spouses, and have more aggressive children, perhaps continuing the cycle of bullying into the next generation.

Ending bullying: What works

9   The most effective way of addressing bullying is through comprehensive schoolwide programs. Schoolwide programs, developed collaboratively between school administration and personnel, students, parents, and community members, seek to change the school's culture to emphasize respect and eliminate bullying. So what has been shown to work in preventing and ending bullying?

- Increased awareness, understanding, and knowledge about bullying on the part of school staff, parents, and students
- Involvement of the wider community, including parents and service providers
- Integration of bullying-related content into the curriculum in ways that are appropriate to each grade
- Increased supervision and monitoring of students to observe and intervene in bullying situations

- Involvement of students
- Encouragement of students to seek help when victimized or witnessing victimization
- A plan to deal with instances of bullying
- Class and school rules and policies regarding bullying and appropriate social behavior
- Promotion of personal and social competencies (e.g., assertiveness, anger management, self-confidence, and emotional management skills)
- A schoolwide community of respect in which every student is valued
- Collaboration between parents, educators, service providers, and students to reinforce messages and skills across settings (e.g., home, school, community)
- Serious commitment to implementing the program on the part of administrators and school staff

How to know if your child is the victim of bullying

10   Children who are bullied often tell no one about their misery out of shame, fear of retaliation, and feelings of hopelessness. Be aware of the following signs of victimization:

- Subtle changes in behavior (withdrawn, anxious, preoccupied, demonstrates loss of interest in school and in favorite activities)
- Comes home from school with bruises and scratches, torn or dirtied clothing, or with missing or damaged books and property
- Loss of appetite
- Excessive trips to the school nurse
- Inability to sleep, bad dreams, crying in sleep
- Repeatedly loses clothing, money, or other valuables
- Appears afraid or reluctant to go to school in the morning
- Repeated headaches or stomachaches—particularly in the morning
- Chooses a roundabout or strange route to and from school
- Feels lonely
- Sensitive or withdrawn when asked about his or her day
- Big appetite after school (perhaps because lunch or lunch money was taken)
- Reluctant to take the school bus

11   Most children will not display every warning sign. The most important thing to look for is a change in a child's behavior. When determining what action to take, consider the specific warning signs the child shows: How serious are they? How frequently do they occur?

Identifying bullying

12 Concrete behaviors

- Name calling
- Rumor spreading
- Making up stories to get other children in trouble
- Telling other children not to be friends with a target child
- Hitting, kicking, tripping, or pushing another child
- Teasing other children and making remarks about their culture, religion, ethnicity, weight, physical appearance, disabilities, or medical conditions
- Intimidating others
- Taking other children's possessions or demanding money from them
- Damaging other children's property
- Bossiness
- Hiding other children's books, bags, or other property
- Picking on other children, even when they're upset
- Making threats to other children
- Manipulating others, getting them to do things that they may not want to do

13 Attitudinal signs

- Hot-tempered and quick to anger
- Impulsive—acts without thinking or considering the consequences of his or her behavior
- Low tolerance for frustration
- Difficulty conforming to rules
- Needs to dominate and subdue others
- Brags about his or her superiority over other students
- Aggressive toward adults
- Good at talking themselves out of situations
- Little empathy—has difficulty understanding others' perspectives and feelings
- Engages in antisocial behavior (e.g., stealing, vandalism, substance use)
- Enjoys putting down others
- Treats animals cruelly
- Disrespects authority
- Enjoys fighting
- Refuses to admit fear

Eliminate Bullying in Your Classroom

By Eleanor T. Migliore
Intervention in School and Clinic

Eliminate Bullying in Your Classroom

1 Significant negative effects have been documented on the physical and emotional health of both bullies and their victims (Weinhold, 2000). Bullying has been defined as behavior that is "intentional and causes physical and psychological harm to the recipient" (Smith & Thompson, 1991). Schools can do a great deal to create climates in which bullying is significantly reduced and where students feel safe and supported (Peterson & Skiba, 2001). It is important that as educators we are knowledgeable about interventions that can make a difference for students.

1. Lead a class discussion on bullying. Make certain that students understand what bullying is and why it is harmful. Have them write about their experiences and feelings, and include role-plays to clearly demonstrate what constitutes bullying. You could have older students research the effects on both victims and those who bully so they can understand the extent of the problem.

2. Write a specific no-bullying policy into your classroom rules. Although bullying is a form of aggression that may be covered by other rules, it is important that students see the unique characteristics of bullying so they can help prevent it. Consequences could also be included with the policy if this is a standard procedure with the other class rules.

3. Teach social skills routinely through specific lessons and in conjunction with other activities throughout the day. Many excellent programs, for all age levels, can be obtained through educational publishing companies. Lessons, which can be especially helpful, focus on making friends, being appropriately assertive, and learning to take turns. Although "teachable moments" are certainly important, formal lessons on these topics should also be planned and regularly scheduled into the school day.

4. Teach students how to avoid being a victim and what to do if they are victimized. Specific strategies can be useful if a student finds him- or herself in a possible victim situation. An effective approach can be to use assertive statements such as, "I don't like the way you are talking to me. You sound mean. Stop doing it." Seeking help from nearby friends or adults can also be a good strategic. Some students are able to use humor or "own" the belittling comment ("You're right, this shirt is pretty ugly. I was too lazy to iron another one this morning") to deescalate a tense situation. Avoiding a bully may be the best choice at times. Finally, using positive self-talk to maintain self-esteem during a bullying incident may be the only appropriate choice (Garrity, Jens, Porter, Sager, & Short-Camilli, 1996).

5. Support students who speak out about bullying or who seek extra adult help. All adults in the school should be encouraged to praise students who come to them with bullying concerns. The student should not be made to feel cowardly but rather that this is the duty of a student in this school. Stress that this information could be helpful to prevent other students from being subjected to bullying.

6. Use extra effort to include all students in class activities. If a class project is being planned, give everyone a role. Be on the lookout for students who are getting left out of situations or groups, and try to bring them in with specific assignments or jobs.

7. Reinforce responsible, positive behaviors whenever possible. Public praise is always a powerful tool. In addition, choose a student each week who was "caught caring" and reward him or her with age-appropriate privileges or reinforcers (Garrity et al., 1996). Make it clear that this is how to achieve status in your class, and convey this message in as many ways as possible.

8. Use a confidential "message box" for student suggestions or comments on classroom concerns. Some students may be hesitant about bringing up subtle forms of bullying in person, but a written, confidential communication method may make this easier for them. Also, make yourself available so students can talk with you privately about their concerns.

9. Always model respectful behavior toward students. Never use intimidation or sarcasm. Your behavior as an educator is extremely important and conveys a powerful message to students. Even when students are disrespectful or rude, it is imperative that your demeanor be calm and in control. As you set limits in this manner, students observe an assertive way to behave that does not imitate the person attempting to bully.

10. Make sure that situations that have the potential of becoming aggressive are closely supervised. For example, outdoor recess periods or before and after lunch free time can be opportunities for bullying students to find victims. It may be best to schedule similar age groups for free time together to avoid having older students mixed with much younger students. It also may be advisable to plan some structured activities during these nonacademic times. Make sure all areas are well patrolled so there are no isolated spots for bullying to occur (Stephenson & Smith, 1997).

11. Intervene immediately with an approach that matches the incident if bullying occurs. If the bullying involves degrading language or slurs, the adult may only need to use a firm, low-key intervention such as saying, "Those words offend me. We don't talk like that here." This may be enough to break a pattern of escalation. If a more physically aggressive incident is observed or reported, a multifaceted approach to intervening may be required. Involve student, school, and family in this case, and use appropriate consequences as well as preventive measures for the future (Wessler, 2001).

12. Insist that the bully make amends if the incident involves a specific targeted victim. Exactly how this is accomplished will depend on the situation. The victim should agree to this action, and the apology should be supervised to make certain that it is carried out in the right manner. Some ways that a bully might make amends could be a public apology, a private face-to-face apology, an apology in writing, or performance of a special favor for the victim (Pearce, 1997).

13. Arrange your class schedule to minimize chaos. A clearly organized schedule and activity stations that are separated and thoughtfully arranged make student interactions more positive. Also, make certain that there are adequate materials for all students in order to minimize potential conflicts (Stephenson & Smith, 1997).

14. Provide many ways to gain recognition in your classroom. Nonacademic as well as academic achievements should be praised. Effort should especially be rewarded. Students should get the message that there are many ways to succeed and that it is possible for them to attain recognition for their particular strengths.

15. Have a clear process to report bullying. These procedures should be discussed with the class and be publicly displayed. It should be understood that reporting is the expectation and to not do so would be breaking a rule. Be alert to students placing a stigma on reporters, and address this immediately.

16. Enlist students in no-bullying activities. Making posters for display around the school or making presentations at assemblies or PTA meetings could be projects for the whole class. Emphasizing the role of bystanders could be a theme for these public information activities because many students may think they have no part in these projects if they are not bullies or have not been victimized personally.

17. Encourage administrators and faculty members to write a no-bullying policy into the school handbook. This will make the school's attitude toward bullying official and be an important first step in establishing an environment that does not condone intimidation at any level (Froschl & Gropper, 1999).

18. Plan an in-service meeting for all staff members to address bullying. All school personnel need to know what bullying really means and how the misuse of power can affect the atmosphere of an entire school. Include bus drivers, cafeteria staff, and assistants because they may often witness bullying but not know the most effective response.

19. Involve parents in your no-bullying efforts. As a classroom teacher, include your no-bullying policy procedures with the information you send home at the beginning of the year addressing general rules and homework. Include information in your parent-teacher conferences, and encourage parents to talk with their children about this issue. Respond quickly and positively to any parent concerns about individual incidents.

20. Use the PTA to publicize the school's no-bullying policy. If parents become part of the team trying to prevent bullying, your efforts will be far more successful (Peterson & Skiba, 2001). Inviting mental health professionals to speak with the PTA about the importance of this issue may make it more relevant. Also, having speakers address how to get students to talk about being intimidated may open up important channels of communication between parents and children.

Persons interested in submitting material for 20 Ways To... should contact Robin H. Lock, College of Education, Box 41071, Texas Tech University, Lubbock, TX 76409-1701.

Eleanor T. Migliore, PhD, is associate professor of education at Trinity University San Antonio, Texas. She is also the program director for the School Psychology Program. Her research interests include counseling with students and collaboration among professionals in the educational setting.

References

Froschl, M., & Gropper, N. (1999). Fostering friendships, curbing bullying. *Educational Leadership,* 56, 72–75.

Garrity, C., Jens, K. Porter, W., Sager, N., & Short-Camilli, C. (1996). *Bully-proofing your school: A comprehensive approach for elementary schools.* Longmont, CO: Sopris West.

Pearce, J. (1997). What can be done about the bully? In M. Elliott (Ed.), *Bullying: A practical guide to coping for schools* (pp. 70–88). Washington, DC: Pitman Publishing.

Peterson, R. L., & Skiba, R. (2001). *Creating school climates that prevent school violence.* The Clearinghouse, 74, 155–163.

Smith, P. K., & Thompson, D. (1991). *Practiced approaches to bullying.* London: David Fulton.

Stephenson, P., & Smith, D. (1997). Why some schools don't have bullies. In M. Elliott (Ed.), *Bullying: A practical guide to coping for schools* (pp. 167–180). Washington, DC: Pitman Publishing.

Weinhold, B. K. (2000). Bullying and school violence: The tip of the iceberg. *The Teacher Educator,* 35, 28–33.

Wessler, S. L. (2000). Sticks and stones. *Educational Leadership,* 58, 28–33.

(In the United Kingdom, they are wearing blue wristbands to "beat bullying.") http://www.dysart.org./

Bullying Behaviors Among US Youth: Prevalence and Association With Psychosocial Adjustment

Tonja R. Nansel, PhD, Mary Overpeck, DrPH, Ramani S. Pilla, PhD, W. June Ruan, MA, Bruce **Simons-Morton, EdD, MPH**, and **Peter Scheidt, MD, MPH**
National Institute of Child Health and Human Development, Bethesda, Md. Dr Overpeck is now with the Maternal and Child Health Bureau, Health Resources and Services Administration, Rockville, Md; Dr Pilla is now with the University of Illinois at Chicago

Abstract

Context—Although violence among US youth is a current major concern, bullying is infrequently addressed and no national data on the prevalence of bullying are available.

Objectives—To measure the prevalence of bullying behaviors among US youth and to determine the association of bullying and being bullied with indicators of psychosocial adjustment, including problem behavior, school adjustment, social/emotional adjustment, and parenting.

Design, Setting, and Participants—Analysis of data from a representative sample of 15686 students in grades 6 through 10 in public and private schools throughout the United States who completed the World Health Organization's Health Behaviour in School-aged Children survey during the spring of 1998.

Main Outcome Measure—Self-report of involvement in bullying and being bullied by others.

Results—A total of 29.9% of the sample reported moderate or frequent involvement in bullying, as a bully (13.0%), one who was bullied (10.6%), or both (6.3%). Males were more likely than females to be both perpetrators and targets of bullying. The frequency of bullying was higher among 6th-through 8th-grade students than among 9th- and 10th-grade students. Perpetrating and experiencing bullying were associated with poorer psychosocial adjustment (*P*<.001); however, different patterns of association occurred among bullies, those bullied, and those who both bullied others and were bullied themselves.

Conclusions—The prevalence of bullying among US youth is substantial. Given the concurrent behavioral and emotional difficulties associated with bullying, as well as the potential long-term negative outcomes for these youth, the issue of bullying merits serious attention, both for future research and preventive intervention.

Corresponding Author and Reprints: Tonja R. Nansel, PhD, Division of Epidemiology, Statistics, and Prevention Research, National Institute of Child Health and Human Development, 6100 Executive Blvd, Room 7B05, MSC 7510, Bethesda, MD 20892-7510 (e-mail: nanselt@mail.nih.gov).

Author Contributions: *Study concept and design:* Nansel, Overpeck, Pilla, Simons-Morton, Scheidt.

Acquisition of data: Overpeck, Scheidt.

Analysis and interpretation of data: Nansel, Overpeck, Pilla, Ruan, Simons-Morton, Scheidt.

Drafting of the manuscript: Nansel, Overpeck, Pilla.

Critical revision of the manuscript for important intellectual content: Nansel, Overpeck, Pilla, Ruan, Simons-Morton, Scheidt.

Statistical expertise: Nansel, Overpeck, Pilla, Ruan, Simons-Morton.

Study supervision: Overpeck, Simons-Morton.

Obtained funding: Overpeck, Simons-Morton, Scheidt.

Administrative, technical, or material support: Nansel, Overpeck, Pilla, Simons-Morton, Scheidt.

BULLYING AMONG SCHOOL-AGED youth is increasingly being recognized as an important problem affecting well-being and social functioning. While a certain amount of conflict and harassment is typical of youth peer relations, bullying presents a potentially more serious threat to healthy youth development. The definition of bullying is widely agreed on in literature on bullying.[1–4] Bullying is a specific type of aggression in which (1) the behavior is intended to harm or disturb, (2) the behavior occurs repeatedly over time, and (3) there is an imbalance of power, with a more powerful person or group attacking a less powerful one. This asymmetry of power may be physical or psychological, and the aggressive behavior may be verbal (eg, name-calling, threats), physical (eg, hitting), or psychological (eg, rumors, shunning/exclusion).

The majority of research on bullying has been conducted in Europe and Australia. Considerable variability among countries in the prevalence of bullying has been reported. In an international survey of adolescent health-related behaviors, the percentage of students who reported being bullied at least once during the current term ranged from a low of 15% to 20% in some countries to a high of 70% in others.[5,6] Of particular concern is frequent bullying, typically defined as bullying that occurs once a week or more. The prevalence of frequent bullying reported internationally ranges from a low of 1.9% among 1 Irish sample to a high of 19% in a Malta study.[1,7–12]

Bullying takes many forms, and findings about the types of bullying that occur are fairly similar across countries. A British study involving 23 schools found that direct verbal aggression was the most common form of bullying, occurring with similar frequency in both sexes.[13] Direct physical aggression was more common among boys, while indirect forms were more common among girls. Similarly, in a study of several middle schools in Rome, the most common types of bullying reported by boys were threats, physical harm, rejection, and name-calling.[14] The most common forms for girls were name-calling, teasing, rumors, rejection, and taking of personal belongings.

Research examining characteristics of youth involved in bullying has consistently found that both bullies and those bullied demonstrate poorer psychosocial functioning than their noninvolved peers. Youth who bully others tend to demonstrate higher levels of conduct problems and dislike of school, whereas youth who are bullied generally show higher levels of insecurity, anxiety, depression, loneliness, unhappiness, physical and mental symptoms, and low self-esteem.[1–4,8,15–25] Males who are bullied also tend to be physically weaker than males in general.[2] The few studies that have examined the characteristics of youth who both bully and are bullied found that these individuals exhibit the poorest psychosocial functioning overall.[15,17,19,26]

The current research provides a foundation for an understanding of the bullying problem. However, it is insufficient to guide intervention and policy development. Moreover, little is known specifically about bullying among US youth.[6] In one county-wide middle school survey, 24.1% of youth reported bullying others at least once in the past semester[26]; it is not known whether this is characteristic of the rest of the nation.

The purpose of this study was to report the prevalence of bullying in a nationally representative sample of US youth in grades 6 through 10, along with information on differences in the prevalence of bullying by sex, grade, and race. In addition, the relationships among bullying, being bullied, and psychosocial adjustment are explored for 3 distinct groups: bullies only, those bullied only, and those who both bully and are bullied.

METHODS

Study Population

The National Institute of Child Health and Human Development supported a nationally representative survey of US youth in grades 6 through 10 during spring of 1998. The survey, entitled the Health Behaviour of School-aged Children (HBSC), was part of a collaborative, cross-national research project involving 30 countries and coordinated by the World Health Organization.[27] The US survey was approved by the National Institute of Child Health and Human Development Institutional Review Board and was carried out by Macro International Inc (Calverton, Md). Both parental and student consent were solicited.

The US sampling universe consisted of all public, Catholic, and other private school students in grades 6 through 10, or their equivalent, excluding schools with enrollment of fewer than 14 students. The sample design used a stratified 2-stage cluster of classes. The sample selection was stratified by racial/ethnic status to provide an oversample of black and Hispanic students. The sample was also stratified by geographic region and counties' metropolitan statistical area status (largest urban areas/not largest urban areas) with probability proportional to total enrollment in eligible grades of the primary sampling units. Sample size was determined on the criteria of making estimates for all US students in grades 6 through 10 with a precision of 3% at a 95% confidence level, and for minority students with a precision of 5% at a 95% confidence level.

An 83% participation rate was achieved. The school-based sample design, using 1 class period for completion of the questionnaire, precluded ability to compare respondent characteristics with those of nonparticipants. Responding students in sampled classes were excluded if they were out of the target range for grade or if age was outside of the 99th percentile for grade (n=440 students), or if either grade or age were unknown (n=39 students), yielding an analytic sample of 15686 students.

Measures

Measures were obtained from a self-report questionnaire containing 102 questions about health behavior and relevant demographic variables. Items were based on both theoretical hypotheses related to the social context of adolescents and measurements that had been validated in other studies or previous WHO-HBSC surveys.[27] Measures were pretested.

Bullying—Questions about bullying were preceded with the following explanation.[10,28] *Here are some questions about bullying. We say a student is BEING BULLIED when another student, or a group of students, say or do nasty and unpleasant things to him or her. It is also bullying when a student is teased repeatedly in a way he or she doesn't like. But it is NOT BULLYING when two students of about the same strength quarrel or fight.*

Participation in bullying was assessed by 2 parallel questions that asked respondents to report the frequency with which they bullied others in school and away from school during the current term. Similarly, being bullied was assessed by 2 parallel questions asking respondents to report the frequency with which they were bullied in school and away from school during the current term. Because the analytic focus of the current study was the relationship of bullying behaviors to overall psychosocial adjustment, frequencies of bullying behaviors in and out of school were combined for all analyses. Response categories were "I haven't ...," "once or twice," "sometimes," "about once a week," and "several times a week." An analysis of the response distribution revealed fewer subjects in the fourth category than the fifth, a deviation from the expected skewed pattern. Hence, the latter 2 response options were collapsed. Additional questions asked respondents to report the frequency with which they were bullied in each of 5 ways—belittled about religion/race, belittled about looks/speech, hit/slapped/pushed, subject of rumors or lies, and subject of sexual comments/gestures.

Psychosocial Adjustment—Measures of psychosocial adjustment included questions about problem behaviors, social/emotional well-being, and parental influences. Alcohol use was measured by 3 items assessing frequency of alcohol consumption. The frequency of smoking, fighting, and truancy were assessed by 1 item each. Academic achievement was assessed by an item querying perceived school performance. Three items (α=.70) queried the frequency of feeling lonely, feeling left out, and being alone because others at school did not want to spend time with the person. One item assessed ease of making friends. Three items (α=.72) were used to assess relationship with classmates: "enjoy being together," "are kind and helpful," and "accept me." School climate was measured by 7 items (α=.82) related to the respondent's perception of the school and teachers. Three items measured parental involvement in school (α=.82), and 1 item assessed respondents' perceptions about their parents' attitudes toward teen drinking.

Statistical Methods

Statistical sample weights were developed to adjust the minority oversampling and to obtain student totals by grade comparable to population grade estimates from the US National Center for Education Statistics. Weighted data analyses were conducted using SUDAAN software.[29] Descriptive statistics were conducted using SUDAAN to obtain percentage distributions and confidence intervals (CIs) based on the weighted data, with SEs adjusted for the sample design. All CIs are shown at the 95% level.

To examine the relationship between psychosocial adjustment and bullying/being bullied, students were classified as noninvolved, bullies only, those bullied only, or both bully and bullied coincidentally, and a separate model was fit for each outcome. Students who were neither bullies nor bullied served as the reference group. Each outcome had 4 ordinal levels based on frequency of the behavior—never, once or twice, sometimes, and once a week or more. The proportional odds model[30] was used to examine the relationship between a range of psychosocial adjustment constructs and each of the outcomes. Inherent in this model is the proportional odds assumption, which states that the cumulative odds ratio for any 2 values of the covariate is constant across response categories. Its interpretation is that the odds of being in category $\leq\kappa$ is $\exp[\beta'(x_1-x_2)]$ times higher at the covariate vector $x=x_1$ than at $x=x_2$, where the parameter vector β contains the regression coefficients for the covariate x. A cumulative logit function was used to estimate the model parameters via the generalized estimating equations.[31] The dependence of responses within clusters was specified using an exchangable working correlation structure. To account for the dependence between outcomes in estimating the variances, robust variance estimates were used for the estimated parameters. The MULTILOG procedure of SUDAAN was used to fit the proportional odds model with exchangable correlation structure. Each model was first fit using the full sample, and then refit using 4 sub-samples stratified by sex and education level (middle school vs high school).

RESULTS

Prevalence of Bullying

Overall, 10.6% of the sample reported bullying others "sometimes" (moderate bullying) and 8.8% admitted to bullying others once a week or more (frequent bullying), providing a national estimate of 2027254 youth involved in moderate bullying and 1681030 youth in frequent bullying (Table 1). Experiencing bullying was reported with similar frequency, with 8.5% bullied "sometimes" and 8.4% bullied once a week or more, for a national estimate of 1634095 students bullied with moderate frequency and 1611809 bullied frequently (Table 2). A sizable number of students reported both bullying others and being bullied themselves. Of the total sample, 29.9% (an estimated 5736417 youth) reported some type of involvement in moderate or frequent bullying, as a bully (13.0%), a target of bullying (10.6%), or both (6.3%).

Demographic variation in the frequency of bullying was observed. Males both bullied others and were bullied significantly more often than females. Bullying occurred most frequently in 6th through 8th grade. Hispanic youth reported marginally higher involvement in moderate and frequent bullying of others, whereas black youth reported being bullied with significantly less frequency overall. No significant differences in the frequency of being bullied were observed among youth from urban, suburban, town, and rural areas ($x_9^2 = 11.72$, $P=.24$). However, small differences were observed in the frequency of bullying others ($x_9^2 = 19.13$, $P=.03$): 2% to 3% fewer suburban youth reported participation in moderate bullying, and 3% to 5% more rural youth reported ever bullying than youth from town, suburban, and urban areas (data not shown).

Table 3 presents the frequency with which those bullied reported being bullied in each of 5 specific ways. Being bullied through belittling one's looks or speech was common for both sexes. Males reported being bullied by being hit, slapped, or pushed more frequently than did females. Females more frequently reported being bullied through rumors or sexual comments. Being bullied through negative statements about one's religion or race occurred with the lowest frequency for both sexes.

Results of the analyses of the relationship among indicators of psychosocial adjustment and bullying/being bullied using the proportional odds model are presented in Table 4. The overall model for each of the outcomes was significant ($P<.001$). All main effects were significant in at least 1 of the models. Table 4 also shows the estimated odds ratios for each psychosocial adjustment construct in the model (adjusting for all other constructs in the model), indicating the odds of having a greater frequency of the outcome variable compared with the reference group.

Bullies, those bullied, and individuals reporting both bullying and being bullied all demonstrated poorer psychosocial adjustment than noninvolved youth; however, differences in the pattern of maladjustment among the groups were observed. Fighting was positively associated with all 3 outcomes. Alcohol use was positively associated with bullying and negatively associated with being bullied. Smoking and poorer academic achievement were associated with both bullying and coincident bullying/being bullied; poorer perceived school climate was related only to bullying. Poorer relationships with classmates and increased loneliness, on the other hand, were associated with both being bullied and coincident bullying/being bullied. Ability to make friends was negatively related to being bullied and positively related to bullying. A permissive parental attitude toward teen drinking was associated only with coincident bullying/being bullied, while increased parental involvement in school was related to both being bullied and coincident bullying/being bullied.

Results from the analyses of the 4 sex/age subgroups (data not shown) yielded findings similar to the model based on the full sample. No notable differences among groups were observed for fighting, academic achievement, perceived school climate, and relationship with classmates. However, differences by sex and age were observed for several variables. While smoking was positively associated with bullying and coincident bullying/being bullied among all groups, the magnitude of the relationship was greater for middle school youth than high school youth. Middle school males also showed a positive relationship between loneliness and bullying; this was not the case for any of the other groups. Among high school youth, bullying/being bullied was positively related to alcohol consumption; this relationship was not observed among middle school youth. High school females, on the other hand, did not demonstrate a significant relationship between poorer friendship-making and being bullied, whereas the other groups did. In addition, permissive parental attitude toward teen drinking was associated with bullying/being bullied for all groups except high school females. Finally, greater parental involvement in school was related to being bullied and bullying/being bullied for males (both middle and high school) but not females. It was related to bullying for high school males only.

COMMENT

This study indicates that bullying is a serious problem for US youth. Consistent with previous studies,[1,7,8,11,12] bullying was reported as more prevalent among males than females and occurred with greater frequency among middle school–aged youth than high school–aged youth. For males, both physical and verbal bullying were common, while for females, verbal bullying (both taunting and sexual comments) and rumors were more common. However, verbal bullying through derogatory statements about one's religion or race occurred infrequently for both sexes. This finding may reflect stronger social norms among adolescents against such behavior. That is, it may be more socially acceptable for a youth to taunt peers about their appearance than to make derogatory racial statements.

Both bullying and being bullied were associated with poorer psychosocial adjustment; however, there were notable differences among those bullied, bullies, and those reporting both behaviors. Those bullied demonstrated poorer social and emotional adjustment, reporting greater difficulty making friends, poorer relationships with classmates, and greater loneliness. Youth who are socially isolated and lack social skills may be more likely targets for being bullied. This is consonant with the finding by Hoover and colleagues[32,33] that the most frequent reason cited by youth for persons being bullied is that they "didn't fit in." At the same time, youth who are bullied may well be avoided by other youth, for fear of being bullied themselves or losing social status among their peers. Considering the high degree of relationship observed, it is likely that both processes occur. Being bullied was also associated with greater parental involvement in school, which may reflect parents' awareness of their child's difficulties. Conversely, parental involvement may be related to a lower level of independence among these youth, potentially making them more vulnerable to being bullied. Interestingly, being bullied was associated with less frequency of alcohol use and had a nonlinear relationship with smoking. This is not altogether surprising, given Farrington's[34,35] finding that socially inept youth were less likely to be involved in delinquency than other youth.

Persons who bullied others were more likely to be involved in other problem behaviors such as drinking alcohol and smoking. They showed poorer school adjustment, both in terms of academic achievement and perceived school climate. Yet they reported greater ease of making friends, indicating that bullies are not socially isolated. Considering their greater involvement in other problem behaviors, it is likely that these youth have friends who endorse bullying and other problem behaviors, and who may be involved in bullying as well.

Those youth who reported both bullying and being bullied demonstrated poorer adjustment across both social/emotional dimensions and problem behaviors. Considering the combination of social isolation, lack of success in school, and involvement in problem behaviors, youth who both bully others and are bullied may represent an especially high-risk group. It is not known whether these youth were first bullied and then imitated the bullying behavior they experienced or whether they were bullies who then received retaliation. Current understanding tends to support the former explanation. Olweus[2] describes a small subset of bullied youth he terms "provocative victims," individuals who demonstrate both anxious and aggressive behavior patterns and who are known for starting fights and engaging in disruptive behavior. Pellegrini and colleagues[36,37] further discuss the "aggressive victim," defined as youth who respond to bullying with reactive aggression. These youth do not tend to use aggression in a proactive or instrumental manner, but rather are aggressive in retaliatory circumstances.

The patterns of relationships between bullying/being bullied and psychosocial adjustment observed in this study were similar across age and sex groups, providing support for the stability of the findings. The differences that emerged may be useful for those conducting research or developing interventions targeting specific populations. For example, the stronger relationship between bullying and smoking observed among middle school youth may reflect an association of bullying with deviance; as smoking becomes more normative in the older youth, it is less associated with bullying. The lack of a relationship between being bullied and poorer friendship-making among high school females could indicate that by this age, females are more apt to find a peer group in which they "fit," even though the peer group may consist of youth of similar social status.[38]

Several limitations of the study should be noted. The HBSC is a broadly focused survey regarding the health behaviors of middle– and high school–aged youth. As such, more in-depth information, such as might be obtained from an intervention study addressing bullying, are not available. This study includes middle– and high school–aged youth but does not address elementary school youth. The data are cross-sectional, and as such, the direction of relationships among the variables cannot be determined. Another limitation is the reliance on self-report for measurement of bullying. While self-report is a common and accepted method of measuring bullying, individual perceptions of bullying nevertheless may vary. To minimize subjectivity, students were provided with a detailed definition of bullying along with examples.

While research on the long-term consequences of bullying is minimal, the studies that have been conducted show negative effects into adulthood. Olweus[39] found former bullies to have a 4-fold increase in criminal behavior at the age of 24 years, with 60% of former bullies having at least 1 conviction and 35% to 40% having 3 or more convictions. Their earlier pattern of achieving desired goals through bullying likely inhibited the learning of more socially acceptable ways of negotiating with others. Conversely, individuals formerly bullied were found to have higher levels of depression and poorer self-esteem at the age of 23 years, despite the fact that, as adults, they were no more harassed or socially isolated than comparison adults.[40] Those who have been bullied may view such treatment as evidence that they are inadequate and worthless and may internalize these perceptions. No study has assessed the long-term outcomes for those who both bully others and are bullied. Given their initial poorer adjustment status, it is possible that they fare worse than either bullies or those bullied.

While this study provides important data on the prevalence and psychosocial correlates of bullying among US youth, further research is needed. Of particular importance would be prospective studies addressing factors that lead to bullying, as well as studies on the long-term consequences of bullying and being bullied. Longitudinal studies also would be valuable in better understanding the nature of those who bully and are bullied.

The prevalence of bullying observed in this study suggests the importance of preventive intervention research targeting bullying behaviors. Effective prevention will require a solid understanding of the social and environmental factors that facilitate and inhibit bullying and peer aggression. This knowledge could then be used to create school and social environments that promote healthy peer interactions and intolerance of bullying. School-based interventions have demonstrated positive outcomes in Norway and England,[40–43] with reductions in bullying of 30% to 50%. These interventions focused on changes within the school and classroom climate to increase awareness about bullying, increase teacher and parent involvement and supervision, form clear rules and strong social norms against bullying, and provide support and protection for individuals bullied. This type of approach has not been tested in the United States.

References

1. Boulton MJ, Underwood K. Bully/victim problems among middle school children. Br J Educ Psychol 1992;62:73–87. [PubMed: 1558813]

2. Olweus, D. Aggression in the Schools: Bullies and Whipping Boys. Washington, DC: Hemisphere Publishing Corp; 1978.

3. Salmivalli C, Kaukiainen A, Kaistaniemi L, Lagerspetz KM. Self-evaluated self-esteem, peer-evaluated self-esteem, and defensive egotism as predictors of adolescents' participation in bullying situations. Pers Soc Psychol Bull 1999;25:1268–1278.

4. Slee PT. Bullying in the playground: the impact of inter-personal violence on Australian children's perceptions of their play environment. Child Environ 1995;12:320–327.

5. King, A.; Wold, B.; Tudor-Smith, C.; Harel, Y. The Health of Youth: A Cross-National Survey. Canada: WHO Library Cataloguing; 1994. WHO Regional Publications, European Series No. 69

6. US Department of Education. 1999 Annual Report on School Safety. Washington, DC: US Dept of Education; 1999. p. 1-66.

7. Borg MG. The extent and nature of bullying among primary and secondary schoolchildren. Educ Res 1999;41:137–153.

8. Kaltiala-Heino R, Rimpela M, Marttunen M, Rimpela A, Rantanen P. Bullying, depression, and suicidal ideation in Finnish adolescents: school survey. BMJ 1999;319:348–351. [PubMed: 10435954]

9. Menesini E, Eslea M, Smith PK, et al. Cross-national comparison of children's attitudes towards bully/victim problems in school. Aggressive Behav 1997;23:245–257.

10. Olweus, D. Bullying at School: What We Know and What We Can Do. Oxford, England: Blackwell; 1993.

11. O'Moore AM, Smith KM. Bullying behaviour in Irish schools: a nationwide study. Ir J Psychol 1997;18:141–169.

12. Whitney I, Smith PK. A survey of the nature and extent of bullying in junior/middle and secondary schools. Educ Res 1993;34:3–25.

13. Rivers I, Smith PK. Types of bullying behaviour and their correlates. Aggressive Behav 1994;20:359–368.

14. Baldry AC. Bullying among Italian middle school students. Sch Psychol Int 1998;19:361–374.

15. Austin S, Joseph S. Assessment of bully/victim problems in 8 to 11 year-olds. Br J Educ Psychol 1996;66:447–456. [PubMed: 9008423]

16. Bijttebier P, Vertommen H. Coping with peer arguments in school-age children with bully/victim problems. Br J Educ Psychol 1998;68:387–394. [PubMed: 9788212]

17. Forero R, McLellan L, Rissel C, Bauman A. Bullying behaviour and psychosocial health among school students in New South Wales, Australia: cross sectional survey. BMJ 1999;319:344–348. [PubMed: 10435953]

18. Byrne BJ. Bullies and victims in a school setting with reference to some Dublin schools. Ir J Psychol 1994;15:574–586.

19. Kumpulainen K, Rasanen E, Henttonen I, et al. Bullying and psychiatric symptoms among elementary school-age children. Child Abuse Negl 1998;22:705–717. [PubMed: 9693848]

20. Rigby K. Peer victimisation at school and the health of secondary school students. Br J Educ Psychol 1999;68:95–104.

21. Slee PT, Rigby K. The relationship of Eysenck's personality factors and self-esteem to bully-victim behaviour in Australian schoolboys. Pers Individual Differences 1993;14:371–373.

22. Salmivalli C, Lappalainen M, Lagerspetz KM. Stability and change of behavior in connection with bullying in schools. Aggressive Behav 1998;24:205–218.

23. Salmon G, James A, Smith DM. Bullying in schools: self reported anxiety, depression and self esteem in secondary school children. BMJ 1998;317:924–925. [PubMed: 9756812]

24. Slee PT, Rigby K. Australian school children's self appraisal of interpersonal relations: the bullying experience. Child Psychiatry Hum Dev 1993;23:273–282. [PubMed: 8325135]

25. Williams K, Chambers M, Logan S, Robinson D. Association of common health symptoms with bullying in primary school children. BMJ 1996;313:17–19. [PubMed: 8664762]

26. Haynie DL, Nansel TR, Eitel P, et al. Bullies, victims, and bully/victims: distinct groups of youth at-risk. J Early Adolescence 2001;21:29–50.

27. Health Behaviour in School-aged Children: research protocol for the 1997–98 survey. Available at: http://www.ruhbc.ed.ac.uk/hbsc/protdesc.html. Accessibility verified March 26, 2001

28. Olweus, D. The Nature of School Bullying: A Cross-National Perspective. London, England: Routledge; 1999.

29. Shah, BV.; Barnwell, GG.; Bieler, GS. SUDAAN User's Manual, Release 7.5. Research Triangle Park, NC: Research Triangle Institute; 1997.

30. McCullah P. Regression models for ordinal data. J R Stat Soc 1980;42:109–142.

31. Zeger SL, Liang KY. Longitudinal data analysis for discrete and continuous outcomes. Biometrics 1996;42:121–130.

32. Hoover JH, Oliver R, Hazler RJ. Bullying: perceptions of adolescent victims in the Midwestern USA. Sch Psychol Int 1992;13:5–16.

33. Hoover JH, Oliver RL, Thomson KA. Perceived victimization by school bullies: new research and future direction. J Hum Educ Dev 1993;32:76–84.

34. Farrington DP. The development of offending and antisocial behaviour from childhood: key findings from the Cambridge Study in Delinquent Development [The Twelfth Jack Tizard Memorial Lecture]. J Child Psychol Psychiatry 1995;36:929–964. [PubMed: 7593403]

35. Farrington DP. Childhood aggression and adult violence: early precursors and later-life outcomes. Child Aggression Adult Violence 1996:5–29.

36. Pellegrini AD. Bullies and victims in school: a review and call for research. J Appl Dev Psychol 1998;19:165–176.

37. Pellegrini AD, Bartini M, Brooks F. School bullies, victims, and aggressive victims: factors relating to group affiliation and victimization in early adolescence. J Educ Psychol 1999;91:216–224.

38. Huttunen A, Salmivalli C, Lagerspetz KM. Friendship networks and bullying in schools. Ann N Y Acad Sci 1996;794:355–359.

39. Olweus, D. Bullying among schoolchildren: intervention and prevention. In: Peters, RD.; McMahon, RJ.; Quinsey, VL., editors. Aggression and Violence Throughout the Life Span. London, England: Sage Publications; 1992. p. 100-125.

40. Olweus, D. Bullying at school: long-term outcomes for the victims and an effective school-based intervention program. In: Huesmann, LR., editor. Aggressive Behavior: Current Perspectives. New York, NY: Plenum Press; 1994. p. 97-130.

41. Olweus, D. Bully/victim problems among school children: basic facts and effects of a school based intervention program. In: Pepler, D.; Rubin, KH., editors. The Development and Treatment of Childhood Aggression. Mahwah, NJ: Lawrence Erlbaum Associates Inc; 1991. p. 411-448.

42. Smith PK. Bullying in schools: the UK experience and the Sheffield Anti-Bullying Project. Ir J Psychol 1997;18:191–201.

43. Sharp S, Smith PK. Bullying in UK schools: the DES Sheffield Bullying Project. Early Child Dev Care 1991;77:47–55.

Table 1

Weighted Percentage of Students Reporting Bullying Others During the Current Term[*]

Sample	Reported Bullying, % (95% CI)			
	None	Once or Twice	Sometimes	Weekly
Total	55.7 (53.6–57.8)	25.0 (23.9–26.1)	10.6 (9.5–11.6)	8.8 (7.9–9.6)
By sex Males	47.1 (44.8–49.4)	27.0 (25.5–28.5)	13.0 (11.9–14.1)	12.9 (11.5–14.3)
Females	63.2 (60.5–65.8)	23.2 (21.8–24.6)	8.5 (7.0–9.9)	5.2 (4.4–6.0)
By grade 6th	54.3 (50.0–58.7)	26.9 (23.8–29.9)	8.4 (6.7–10.2)	10.4 (8.2–12.6)
7th	53.5 (49.8–57.2)	26.9 (24.1–29.8)	9.8 (8.0–11.5)	9.8 (8.0–11.5)
8th	50.5 (47.3–53.7)	25.4 (22.9–28.0)	14.3 (11.8–16.8)	9.8 (8.2–11.4)
9th	56.4 (53.2–59.5)	25.0 (22.9–27.1)	11.6 (9.1–14.2)	7.0 (6.0–8.0)
10th	64.0 (60.7–67.4)	20.4 (18.3–22.5)	8.6 (7.3–9.9)	6.9 (5.8–8.1)
By race White	54.8 (52.2–57.4)	26.2 (24.7–27.7)	10.5 (9.0–12.0)	8.5 (7.4–9.5)
Black	59.8 (56.2–63.5)	21.7 (19.0–24.4)	10.2 (8.1–12.2)	8.3 (6.5–10.0)
Hispanic	53.2 (50.5–55.9)	24.4 (21.9–26.9)	12.0 (10.4–13.5)	10.4 (8.4–12.4)

[*] CI indicates confidence interval.

Table 2
Weighted Percentage of Students Reporting Being Bullied During the Current Term[*]

Sample	Reported Being Bullied, % (95% CI)			
	None	**Once or Twice**	**Sometimes**	**Weekly**
Total	58.9 (57.1–60.8)	24.2 (23.0–25.3)	8.5 (7.4–9.6)	8.4 (7.6–9.2)
By sex				
Males	53.3 (50.7–55.9)	26.1 (24.5–27.7)	9.9 (8.3–11.5)	10.8 (9.5–12.0)
Females	63.8 (61.8–65.9)	22.5 (21.0–23.9)	7.3 (6.4–8.3)	6.4 (5.3–7.4)
By grade				
6th	49.6 (45.7–53.4)	26.2 (23.3–29.1)	10.9 (9.0–12.9)	13.3 (11.3–15.3)
7th	51.5 (48.2–54.8)	28.6 (26.2–31.0)	9.4 (7.8–11.0)	10.5 (8.4–12.6)
8th	58.7 (54.9–62.5)	25.0 (22.7–27.3)	8.7 (5.9–11.4)	7.6 (6.4–8.9)
9th	63.4 (61.2–65.6)	22.1 (20.4–23.8)	8.8 (7.3–10.3)	5.7 (4.3–7.2)
10th	71.9 (69.6–74.1)	18.8 (17.1–20.4)	4.6 (3.4–5.8)	4.8 (3.8–5.8)
By race				
White	56.3 (54.2–58.4)	26.2 (24.8–27.6)	8.7 (7.2–10.1)	8.8 (7.9–9.7)
Black	70.1 (66.6–73.6)	15.8 (13.4–18.3)	7.4 (5.9–8.9)	6.7 (4.7–8.7)
Hispanic	59.4 (55.9–62.9)	24.5 (21.8–27.2)	8.0 (6.9–9.2)	8.1 (6.7–9.5)

[*] CI indicates confidence interval.

Table 3

Weighted Percentage of Those Bullied Reporting 5 Specific Types of Bullying*

	Reported Being Bullied, % (95% CI)					
	Total of Those Bullied		Males Bullied		Females Bullied	
	Ever	Frequent	Ever	Frequent	Ever	Frequent
Belittled about religion or race	25.8 (23.1–28.5)	8.08 (6.9–9.3)	27.7 (24.5–30.8)	8.8 (7.1–10.6)	23.7 (20.8–26.7)	7.2 (5.7–8.8)
Belittled about looks or speech	61.6 (60.0–63.3)	20.1 (18.5–21.7)	58.4 (55.9–60.9)	19.8 (17.8–21.7)	65.3 (62.9–67.6)	20.5 (18.3–22.7)
Hit, slapped, or pushed	55.6 (53.0–58.2)	14.6 (13.0–16.2)	66.1 (62.5–69.7)	17.8 (15.4–20.1)	43.9 (41.5–46.3)	11.1 (9.0–13.2)
Subjects of rumors	59.9 (57.9–61.8)	17.0 (15.2–18.8)	55.0 (52.0–57.9)	16.7 (14.1–19.4)	65.3 (62.8–67.8)	17.3 (14.8–19.8)
Subjects of sexual comments or gestures	52.0 (49.7–54.3)	18.9 (17.5–20.3)	47.3 (44.4–50.2)	17.5 (15.6–19.5)	57.2 (54.1–60.3)	20.5 (18.0–22.9)

*"Ever" includes all those reporting the behavior "once or twice" or more. "Frequent" includes those reporting the behavior "once a week" or "several times a week." CI indicates confidence interval.

Table 4

Results of Fitting the Proportional Odds Model to the HBSC Data[*]

Covariate	Outcome, OR (95% CI)		
	Being Bullied	Bullying	Bullying/Being Bullied
Alcohol use	$P = .03$	$P < .001$	$P = .76$
Never	1.00	1.00	1.00
Rarely	0.98 (0.85–1.14)	1.44 (1.24–1.67)	1.09 (0.89–1.34)
Every month	0.67 (0.50–0.90)	2.11 (1.68–2.64)	1.09 (0.83–1.44)
Every week	0.76 (0.58–0.99)	1.89 (1.47–2.44)	1.12 (0.84–1.50)
Every day	0.56 (0.34–0.93)	1.42 (0.98–2.08)	0.97 (0.63–1.50
Smoking	$P = .03$	$P < .001$	$P < .001$
Never	1.00	1.00	1.00
<Once a week	1.36 (0.97–1.90)	1.66 (1.32–2.08)	1.59 (1.27–1.98)
Every week	0.94 (0.68–1.29)	1.79 (1.36–2.36)	2.11 (1.41–3.16)
Every day	0.70 (0.49–1.00)	1.67 (1.24–2.24)	1.68 (1.22–2.31)
Fighting	$P < .001$	$P < .001$	$P < .001$
None	1.00	1.00	1.00
Once	2.16 (1.85–2.52)	2.87 (2.42–3.39)	3.17 (2.59–3.89)
2 Times	2.34 (1.75–3.13)	3.31 (2.64–4.16)	4.39 (3.20–6.03)
3 Times	2.47 (1.72–3.55)	4.59 (3.41–6.19)	5.36 (3.76–7.64)
≥4 Times	2.39 (1.82–3.14)	5.20 (4.16–6.49)	3.58 (2.46–5.21)
Academic achievement	$P = .97$	$P < .001$	$P = .048$
Very good	1.00	1.00	1.00
Good	0.99 (0.83–1.19)	1.19 (0.99–1.42)	1.15 (0.91–1.44)
Average	0.96 (0.80–1.16)	1.46 (1.22–1.74)	1.19 (0.97–1.46)
Below average	0.97 (0.68–1.38)	1.82 (1.33–2.47)	1.70 (1.16–2.49)
Perceived school climate[†]	$P = .85$	$P < .001$	$P = .65$
1 (least positive)	1.00	1.00	1.00
2	0.99 (0.90–1.09)	0.83 (0.73–0.93)	0.97 (0.86–1.09)
3	0.98 (0.80–1.19)	0.68 (0.54–0.87)	0.94 (0.74–1.19)
4	0.97 (0.72–1.31)	0.57 (0.40–0.81)	0.91 (0.64–1.31)
5 (most positive)	0.96 (0.65–1.43)	0.47 (0.29–0.75)	0.89 (0.55–1.43)
Relationship with classmates[†]	$P < .001$	$P = .64$	$P < .001$
1 (least positive)	1.00	1.00	1.00
2	0.69 (0.63–0.76)	0.98 (0.90–1.07)	0.79 (0.71–0.87)
3	0.48 (0.39–0.58)	0.96 (0.82–1.13)	0.62 (0.51–0.75)
4	0.33 (0.24–0.44)	0.94 (0.74–1.19)	0.49 (0.36–0.66)
5 (most positive)	0.23 (0.15–0.34)	0.92 (0.67–1.27)	0.38 (0.26–0.57)
Friendship making	$P < .001$	$P < .001$	$P = .73$
Very easy	1.00	1.00	1.00
Easy	1.05 (0.91–1.20)	0.80 (0.72–0.89)	1.01 (0.85–1.20)
Difficult	1.46 (1.13–1.87)	0.74 (0.59–0.93)	0.88 (0.66–1.17)
Very difficult	1.92 (1.42–2.59)	0.67 (0.43–1.05)	1.15 (0.70–1.89)
Loneliness[†]	$P < .001$	$P = .62$	$P < .001$
1 (least lonely)	1.00	1.00	1.00
2	2.41 (2.17–2.69)	1.02 (0.94–1.12)	1.90 (1.67–2.16)
3	5.81 (4.77–7.09)	1.04 (0.85–1.27)	3.60 (2.84–4.56)
4	14.01 (10.41–18.86)	1.06 (0.79–1.43)	6.82 (4.78–9.74)
5 (most likely)	33.78 (22.74–50.20)	1.08 (0.73–1.61)	12.94 (8.04–20.81)
Parental attitude toward teen drinking	$P = .29$	$P = .55$	$P < .001$
Shouldn't drink	1.00	1.00	1.00
Don't like but allow	1.19 (0.98–1.45)	1.05 (0.89–1.25)	1.33 (1.07–1.64)
Okay to drink/not get drunk	1.13 (0.86–1.49)	1.16 (0.86–1.57)	1.43 (1.06–1.94)
Okay to get drunk	1.12 (0.82–1.53)	1.19 (0.90–1.58)	2.10 (1.53–2.88)
Parental involvement in school[†]	$P = .01$	$P = .53$	$P = .003$
1 (least involved)	1.00	1.00	1.00
2	1.12 (1.02–1.22)	1.02 (0.96–1.08)	1.12 (1.04–1.21)
3	1.25 (1.06–1.46)	1.04 (0.92–1.17)	1.25 (1.06–1.46)
4	1.39 (1.10–1.76)	1.06 (0.89–1.27)	1.39 (1.10–1.76)
5 (most involved)	1.55 (1.13–2.13)	1.08 (0.85–1.37)	1.55 (1.13–2.13)
Wald χ^2_{27}[‡]	337.30	4878.42	2678.37

[*] HBSC indicates Health Behaviour of School-aged Children survey; OR, odds ratio; CI, confidence interval. P values represent the significance of the category overall.

[†] Odds ratios for continuous variables were calculated for each level for illustrative purposes. In each case, the OR provided at the level "2" represents the increase in odds attributable to an increase in 1 unit of the covariate.

[‡] $P < .001$ for outcome overall.

Bully-Proof Your School

Recognized as more than just a problem between kids, schools are called upon to put forth a team effort to end bullies' longtime reign of terror.

By Collen Newquist
Education World

1   In *Arthur's April Fool*, Marc Brown's lovable aardvark gets the best of a school bully by playing a joke on him. Lucky for Arthur, the book ends there.

2   As most children know, and many adults remember, struggles with reallife bullies rarely are resolved so easily. The enormity of those struggles are now recognized, and bullying in schools, once shrugged off with a kidswill- be-kids attitude, has come to be regarded as a serious problem around the world.

3   The facts about bullying show that 10 to 15 percent of children are bullied regularly, and bullying most often takes place in school, frequently right in the classroom. The facts show, too, that bullying is an equalopportunity torment— the size of a school, its setting (rural, urban or suburban) and racial composition seem to have no bearing on its occurrence.

4   Bullying takes a heavy toll on the victims. As many as 7 percent of eighth grade students in the United States stay home at least once a month because of bullies. Chronic fear can be the source of all-too-real stomachaches and headaches and other stress-related illnesses. According to Norway's Dan Olweus, a leading authority on the subject, being bullied also leads to depression and low self-esteem, problems that can carry into adulthood.

5   The effects of such behavior are grim for the offender, too. One study by Olweus shows that 60 percent of kids characterized as bullies in sixth through ninth grades had at least one criminal conviction by age 24.

6   Rather than help resolve the issue, schools have contributed to the problem. Teachers and principals underestimate the amount of bullying in schools and, when they do witness it, often are reluctant to get involved, says Nan Stein, a researcher at Wellesley College, in "Beating the Bullies" (*Teacher* magazine, August/September 1997). "Kids say that when they tell the adults about the bullying, adults don't take them seriously, or they make them feel responsible for going back and working it out." In the same article, researcher Charol Shakeshaft of Hofstra University said she found that "kids believe that teachers thought it was OK to behave that way because teachers didn't intervene."

7   Until recent years, the problem of bullying has been addressed primarily through efforts to raise the self-esteem of victims, many of whom are more passive and physically weaker than their tormentors. While this helps, it's not nearly enough. Olweus and other researchers emphatically agree that preventing and eliminating bullying in schools requires a clearly stated, zerotolerance attitude toward bullying and a wholehearted team effort involving teachers, administrators and support staff, as well as students and parents.

8   The approach advocated by Olweus, detailed in his book *Bullying at School: What We Know and What We Can Do,* includes first distributing a questionnaire on bullying to students and teachers to foster awareness, justify intervention efforts and establish a benchmark for later comparison. He also recommends:

- Conducting a parental awareness campaign through newsletters, parent-teacher conferences and PTA meetings, and publicizing the results of the questionnaire;

- Intervening individually with bullies and victims, implementing cooperative learning activities, and stepping up adult supervision at recess and lunch (opportune times for bully behavior);

- Working with students in role-playing exercises and related assignments that teach alternative methods of interaction, and developing strong antibullying rules, such as "we won't bully other kids" and "we'll include other kids who are easily left out." Such messages repeated on a regular basis can have a lasting positive effect.

9   In his article "What Schools Can Do About Bullying," Ken Rigby of the University of South Australia says teachers can have a significant impact on the problem by specifically:

- Expressing disapproval of bullying whenever it occurs, not only in the classroom but also on the school playground;

- Listening sympathetically to students who need support when they are victimized, and then initiating or taking action according to procedures approved by the school;

- Encouraging cooperative learning in the classroom and not setting a bad example with their own behavior (Assess yourself honestly: Do you use sarcasm or mean-spirited humor?);

- Talking with groups of students about bullying, and mobilizing student support for action to reduce bullying--for example, by including victimized students in their activities. "Most students are in fact against bullying," Rigby says, "and, given the chance, can provide not only active support for the school policy but also make positive proposals and undertake constructive actions to counter bullying."

10   Anti-bullying campaigns make a difference. Schools in Norway and in South Carolina that adopted Olweus' program reported incidents of bullying dropped by 50 percent. For anybody who's ever felt the sting of a schoolmate's punch or caustic words, that's very good news.

Related Resources

Sources from *Teacher* magazine:

* *Bully-Proofing Your School,* by Carla Garrity, Kathryn Jens, William Porter, Nancy Sager, and Cam Short-Camilli, 1996; $29.95. Contact: Sopris West, 1140 Boston Ave., Longmont, CO; 80501; (303) 651-2829.

* *Bullying at School: What We Know and What We Can Do,* by Dan Olweus, 1993; $19.95. Contact: Blackwell Publishers, P.O. Box 20, Williston, VT 05495; (800) 216-2522.

* *The Bullying Prevention Handbook: A Guide for Principals, Teachers, and Counselors,* by John Hoover and Ronald Oliver, 1996; $21.95. Contact: National Education Service, 1252 Loesch Rd., Bloomington, IN 47402; (812) 336-7700 or (800) 733-6786.

* *Bullyproof: A Teacher's Guide on Teasing and Bullying for Use With Fourth and Fifth Grade Students,* by Nan Stein, Lisa Sjostrom, and Emily Gaberman, 1996; $19.95, plus $5 shipping and handling. Contact: Centers for Women, Publications, Wellesley College, 106 Central St., Wellesley, MA 02181; (617) 283-2532.

From the National PTA:

* *Safe at School: Awareness and Action for Parents of Kids K–12,* by Carol Silverman; Saunders Free Spirit Publishing Inc. 400 First Ave. N., Suite 616 Minneapolis,MN 55401-1730 (612) 338-2068. The tips in this book help parents deal with bullying, gangs, sexual harassment, and other school safety issues.

* *Set Straight on Bullies,* by Stuart Greenbaum with Brenda Turner and Ronald D. Stephens; National School Safety Center 4165 Thousand Oaks Blvd., Suite 290 Westlake Village, CA 91362 (805) 373-9977. The problem of bullying is examined in this book. It offers prevention and intervention strategies for parents, teachers, and students.

* *Why is Everybody Always Picking on Me? A Guide to Handle Bullies,* by Terrence Webster- Doyle; Atrium Society Publications P.O. Box 816 Middlebury, VT 05753 (800) 966-1998 or (802) 388-0922. This book helps children and teens to develop the confidence needed to resolve conflicts without fighting and to cope with bullies.

Related Sites

Dr. Ken Rigby's Bullying Pages
Includes information on resources concerned with bullying in schools and questionnaires (for sale) for use in schools, plus the article "What Schools Can Do About Bullying."

* Teaching Children Not to Be—or Be Victims of—Bullies
From the National Association for the Education of Young Children (NAEYC).

* Safeguarding Your Children at School: Helping Children Deal with a School Bully
From the National PTA.

* Dealing with Bullies
From the Safe Child Organization.

* Prevent Bullying: A Parents Guide from Kidscape

Credits

Module 1: What's Next? Thinking About Life After High School

Graff, Gerald. "Hidden Intellectualism." *They Say/I Say: The Moves That Matter in Academic Writing.* Eds. Gerald Graff and Cathy Birkenstein. 2nd ed. New York: W. W. Norton, 2010. 198-205. Print.

Hansen, Rick. "FAQ Guide for College or Work." 2012. Print.

Hansen, Rick. "Web Site Resources." 2012. Print.

Pérez, Angel B. "Want to Get into College? Learn to Fail." *Education Week* 31.19 (2012): 23. Print.

Rodriguez, Joe. "10 Rules for Going to College When Nobody Really Expected You To." *Mercury News.com.* San Jose Mercury News, 4 June 2012. Web. 1 Aug. 2012. <http://www.mercurynews.com/ci_20778835/10-rules-college-nobody-expected-blue-collar>.

Schlack, Lawrence B. "Not Going to College is a Viable Option." *Education.com,* n.d. Web. 1 Aug. 2012. <http://www.education.com/reference/article/Ref_Going_College_Not/>.

"The 10 Most Common Excuses for Not Going to College and Why They're All Wrong!" *everycircle.com,* n.d. Web. 1 Aug. 2012. <https://everycircle.com/ec/articles/tenexcuses.htm>.

University of North Texas. "Why Go to College?" *How 2 Choose.* University of North Texas, 23 Mar. 2010. Web. 18 Aug. 2012. <http://www.unt.edu/pais/howtochoose/why.htm>.

Module 2: Rhetoric of the Op-Ed Page

Braithwaite, Victoria. "Hooked on a Myth." *Los Angeles Times* 8 Oct. 2006: M5. Print.

Edlund, John R. "Letters to the Editor in Response to 'A Change of Heart About Animals.'" 2003. Print.

Edlund, John R. "Three Ways to Persuade." 2011. Print.

Rifkin, Jeremy. "A Change of Heart About Animals." Editorial. *Los Angeles Times* 1 Sept. 2003: B15. Print.

Yong, Ed. "Of Primates and Personhood: Will According Rights and 'Dignity' to Nonhuman Organisms Halt Research?" *Seed.* Seed Magazine, 12 Dec. 2008. Web. 24 Jul. 2012.

Module 3: Racial Profiling

Herbert, Bob. "Jim Crow Policing." *New York Times* 2 Feb. 2010, late ed.: A27. Print.

Module 4: Value of Life

A Human Life Value Calculator. Web.

Feinberg, Kenneth. "What Is the Value of a Human Life?" *This I Believe.* National Public Radio, 25 May 2008. Web. 20 Nov. 2012. <http://www.npr.org/templates/story/story.php?storyId=90760725>.

Jobs, Steve. Commencement Address. Stanford University Commencement Weekend. Stanford, CA. 12 June 2005. Address. <http://news.stanford.edu/news/2005/june15/jobs-061505.html>.

Jones, Chris. "Roger Ebert: The Essential Man." *Esquire* 16 Feb. 2010. Web.

Ripley, Amanda. "What Is a Life Worth?" *Time* 11 Feb. 2002. 22-27. Print.

Shakespeare, William. *Hamlet.* Act III, Sc. i: Hamlet's "To be, or not to be" soliloquy.

Module 5: Good Food/Bad Food

Bittman, Mark. "Bad Food? Tax It, and Subsidize Vegetables." *New York Times* 23 July 2011, late ed.: Sunday Review 1. Print.

Brody, Jane E. "Attacking the Obesity Epidemic by First Figuring Out Its Cause." *New York Times* 12 Sept. 2011: D7(L). Print.

Waters, Alice and Katrina Heron. "No Lunch Left Behind." *New York Times* 19 Feb. 2009: A31. Print.

Module 8: Juvenile Justice

Anderson, Scott. "Greg Ousley Is Sorry for Killing His Parents. Is That Enough?" *New York Times Magazine.* 19 July 2012. Web. 11 June 2012. <http://www.nytimes.com/2012/07/22/magazine/greg-ousley-is-sorry-for-killing-his-parents-is-that-enough.html?pagewanted=all&_r=0>.

Garinger, Gail. "Juveniles Don't Deserve Life Sentences." *New York Times* 15 Mar. 2012, New York ed.: A35. Print.

Jenkins, Jennifer Bishop. "On Punishment and Teen Killers." *Juvenile Justice Information Exchange.* 2 Aug. 2011.Web.11 June 2012. < http://jjie.org/jennifer-bishop-jenkins-on-punishment-teen-killers/19184>.

Lundstrom, Marjie. "Kids Are Kids—Until They Commit Crimes." *Sacramento Bee* 1 Mar. 2001: A3. Print.

Thompson, Paul. "Startling Finds on Teenage Brains." *Sacramento Bee* 25 May 2001: B7. Print.

Module 9: Language, Gender, and Culture

Brooks, David. "Honor Code." *New York Times* 6 July 2012, New York ed.: A23. Print.

Butler, Judith. "phylosophe." *You Tube.* 23 Feb. 2007. Web. 8 Sept. 2012. <http://www.youtube.com/watch?v=DLnv322X4tY>.

Lorde, Audre. "Transformation of Silence into Language and Action." *The Cancer Journals.* San Francisco: Spinsters/Aunt Lute, 1980. 18-23. Print.

Tannen, Deborah. "His Politeness Is Her Powerlessness." *You Just Don't Understand: Women and Men in Conversation.* New York: HarperCollins, 1990. 203-5. Print.

Young, Vershawn Ashanti. "Prelude:The Barbershop." Preface. *Your Average Nigga: Performing Race, Literacy, and Masculinity.* By Young. Detroit: Wayne State UP, 2007. xi-xvi. Print.

Module 10: 1984

Maass, Peter and Megha Rajagopalan. "That's No Phone. That's My Tracker." *New York Times* 13 July 2012. Web. <http://www.nytimes.com/2012/07/15/sunday-review/thats-not-my-phone-its-my-tracker.html?_r=1&ref=technology>.

Winton, Richard. "Long Beach Police to Use 400 Cameras Citywide to Fight Crime." *Los Angeles Times* 15 Aug. 2012. Web. < http://www.latimes.com/news/local/la-me-long-beach-cameras-20120815,0,783037.story >.

Module 12: Bullying: A Research Project

Agatson, Patricia W., Robin Kowalski, and Susan Limber. "Students' Perspectives on Cyber Bullying." *Journal of Adolescent Health* 41 (2007): S59-S60. Web. 27 Jan. 2013. <http://ac.els-cdn.com/S1054139X07003680/1-s2.0-S1054139X07003680-main.pdf?_tid=1f4d3e52-69a1-11e2-8158-00000aacb360&acdnat=1359415331_4ceec0b1e89140ba0dfd9a728a58cfe3>.

Banks, Ron. "Bullying in Schools. ERIC Digest" *ERIC Digests* ED407154, Apr. 1997. ERIC Clearinghouse on Elementary and Early Childhood Education. Web. 15 August 2003. <http://www.ericdigests.org/1997-4/bullying.htm>.

Brown, Mark. "Life After Bullying." *PTA,* 20 Feb. 2005. Web. 10 Apr. 2005. <http://www.pta.org/archive_article_details_1117638232140.html>.

Coloroso, Barbara. *The Bully, the Bullied, and the Bystander.* New York: Harper/Quill, 2004. Print.

Duncan, Arne. *Elementary and Secondary Education: Key Policy Letters from the Education Secretary and Deputy Secretary.* US Department of Education, 14 June 2011. Web. 3 Sept. 2012. <http://www2.ed.gov/policy/elsec/guid/secletter/110607.html>.

Kan-Rice, Pamela. "School Bullies Are Often Also Victims; Feeling Safe Reduces Youth Bullying." *University of California Agriculture and Natural Resources News and Information Outreach,* 2 Sept. 2003. Web. 8 July 2004 <http://news.ucanr.org/newsstorymain.cfm?story=502>.

Kowalski, Kathiann. "How to Handle a Bully." *Current Health* 2 25.6 (1999): 13-16. Web. 15 Aug. 2004. <http://bgeagles.tripod.com/webquest/handle.htm>.

Olweus, Dan. "A Profile of Bullying at School." *Educational Leadership* 60.6 (2003): 12-17. Print.

Additional Readings:

Kuther, Tara L. "Understanding Bullying." *Our Children* 29.2 (2004): 12-13. Print.

Migliore, Eleanor T. "Eliminate Bullying in Your Classroom." *Intervention in School and Clinic* 38.3 (2003): 172-77. Print.

Nansel, Tonja R., Mary Overpeck, Ramani S. Pilla, W. June Ruan, Bruce Simons-Morton, and Peter Scheidt. "Bullying Behaviors Among U.S. Youth: Prevalence and Association with Psychosocial Adjustment." *NIH Public Access,* 25 Apr. 2001. Web. 21 June 2008. <http://www.pubmedcentral.gov/articlerender.fcgi?artid=2435211>.

Newquist, Colleen. "Bully-Proof Your School." *Education World,* 8 Sept. 1997. Web. 21 Jan. 2005. <http://www.education-world.com/a_issues/issues/issues007.shtml>.